PHENOMENOLOGICAL THEORIES OF HIGH ENERGY SCATTERING

Frontiers In Physics

DAVID PINES, Editor

PHENOMENOLOGICAL THEORIES OF HIGH ENERGY SCATTERING

AN EXPERIMENTAL EVALUATION

VERNON D. BARGER

DAVID B. CLINE

University of Wisconsin

W. A. Benjamin, Inc.

New York

1969

PHENOMENOLOGICAL THEORIES OF HIGH ENERGY SCATTERING
An Experimental Evaluation

Standard Book Numbers: 8053–0470–3 (Cloth)
　　　　　　　　　　　　8053–0471–1 (Paper)
Library of Congress Catalog Card Number 75–76545
Manufactured in the United States of America
12345 R 432109

*The manuscript was put into production on December 24, 1968;
this volume was published on September 1, 1969*

W. A. BENJAMIN, INC.
NEW YORK, NEW YORK 10016

Preface

Although fundamental particle physics is a relatively new subject, a vast amount of experimental data has accumulated over the last decade. Over the same period several theories have been put forward that rely heavily on phenomenological input. The purpose of this book is twofold: to present the important features of a large body of existing strong-interaction scattering data and to describe present theoretical interpretations of this data. An intrinsic goal is to emphasize the overall agreement of a peripheral picture of scattering dynamics as related to the discrete particle spectra.

The diverse nature of the subject matter necessarily limits the extent to which any one subject can be covered. However, it is hoped that the representative trends discussed here are sufficiently basic to survive the coming decade of the monster accelerators.

In this book we rely heavily on the available experimental data to deduce empirical regularities. We also examine current theoretical interpretations and extrapolate predictions to ultra-high energies. Thus we hope this book provides a convenient source for both trends in present experimental data and extrapolations to unexplored energy regions. Numerous secondary sources are listed at the end of the book instead of a running list of references. We expect that the overall picture as given here is intelligible to newcomers to the field but not tedious for experts.

We have drawn liberally from the existing literature in compiling the material for this book. In particular, the figures carrying a reference are adaptations or reproductions from figures in published articles. We gratefully acknowledge the assistance of Mr. K. Maas in preparing the artwork and Miss C. Zahn in typing the manuscript.

Vernon D. Barger
David B. Cline

Madison, Wisconsin
April 1969

Contents

Chapter 1

Particle Classification

1.1 QUANTUM NUMBERS

An enormous number of particle states have been discovered in recent years. Certain empirical regularities of the quantum numbers and masses of these states suggest the usefulness of two complementary classification schemes. The first of these focuses on internal additive quantum numbers (charge, isotopic spin, hypercharge) for particles with the same spin and parity. The broadest classification of this sort involves representations of the SU(3) symmetry group. The second level of classification involves angular momentum rotational bands (Regge recurrences) of particles with the same parity and internal quantum numbers. All established particles appear to fit into a classification based on the combination of these two

Table 1.1

Range of (Y, Q, I) quantum numbers of the established fundamental particles.

Quantum Numbers of Known Baryons

Y	Q	I	Example
+ 1	2, 1, 0, −1,	1/2, 3/2	N, N^*_{33}
0	± 1, 0	0, 1	Λ, Σ
− 1	−1, 0	1/2	Ξ
− 2	− 1	0	Ω^-

Quantum Numbers of Known Mesons

Y	Q	I	Example
+ 1	+1, 0	1/2	K
0	± 1, 0	0, 1	η, π
− 1	− 1	1/2	$\overline{K}$

1

schemes. More ambitious schemes have been proposed that require a connection between spin-parity and SU(3) classifications, examples of which are SU(6) and the quark model. In this chapter we limit our considerations to some tentative classifications of the presently observed particles in terms of the simple SU(3) and Regge recurrence ideas. We anticipate that the elements of the classification presented here will survive experimental test, although many of the detailed particle assignments may change as more experimental data become available.

Each strongly interacting particle carries a set of quantum numbers that are conserved by the strong interactions. We adopt the following notation for these quantum numbers: baryon number (B); charge (Q); hypercharge (Y); isotopic spin (I); spin (J); parity (P); charge conjugation (C) for neutral mesons; G parity (G), for $Y = 0$ mesons. The quantum numbers of the strongly interacting particles satisfy the empirical Gell-Mann–Nishijima rule: $Q = I_3 + Y/2$. The (Y, Q, I) quantum numbers of the observed mesons and baryons extend only over a surprisingly restrictive range, as illustrated in Table 1.1. The antibaryons $(B = -1)$ have Y and Q values of opposite sign from the baryon quantum numbers listed in the table.

1.2 SU(3) SYMMETRY

Only certain patterns of the possible (Y, Q, I) values appear to be realized in the particle spectra. This restricted class of quantum numbers can be accommodated by the singlet (1), octet (8), and decuplet (10) representations of the SU(3) symmetry group. The quantum numbers of the discrete states that fill out these multiplets are shown in Figure 1.1. A growing mass of evidence indicates that for a given B, J^P the fundamental particles appear to fill out such representations. Higher SU(3) representations such as 10, 27, 35, and so forth, require the existence of at least some particles with (Y, Q, I) outside the observed range in Table 1.1.

According to Table 1.1 and Figure 1.1, the baryons should be classified as either 1, 8, or 10 multiplets, whereas the mesons should fall into 1 and 8 multiplets. If SU(3) were an exact symmetry of nature, then we should expect all particles in a given SU(3) multiplet to be degenerate in mass. Although this idealized picture of degenerate masses is not exactly realized, the success of the classification alone is adequate evidence for an underlying SU(3) symmetry. Applications to particle scattering to be considered in Chapters 4 and 5 provide further justification for the meaningfulness of this internal symmetry. Typical baryon and meson levels illustrating SU(3) classification schemes are shown in Figures 1.2 and 1.3. The order of the magnitude of the symmetry breaking in the masses of the baryons is $\Delta m/m \sim 0.2$. Deviations of this order of magnitude are nominally expected from exact SU(3). When applying SU(3) predictions to decay rates or scattering amplitudes, such departures from exact symmetry are difficult to estimate reliably.

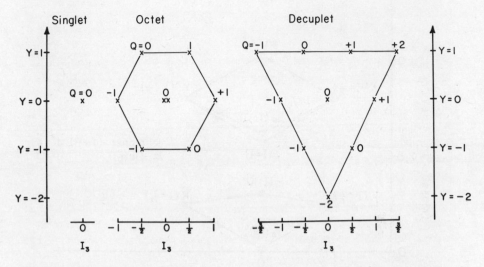

Figure 1.1. (Y, Q, I) quantum numbers of singlet, octet, and decuplet SU(3) multiplets.

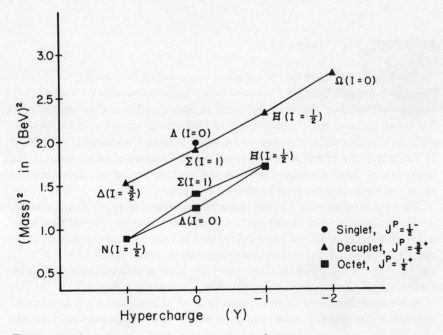

Figure 1.2. Baryons in 1, 8, and 10 SU(3) representations.

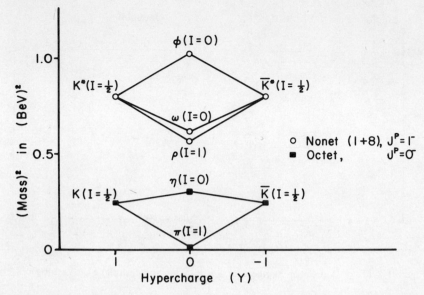

Figure 1.3. Octet of pseudoscalar mesons (π, η, K, $\bar{K}$) and nonet of vector mesons (ρ, ω, ϕ, K^*, $\bar{K}^*$).

1.3 REGGE RECURRENCES

The Regge recurrence idea is complementary to SU(3) classification in connecting states differing by $\Delta J = 2$ but with other quantum numbers the same. The concept of the Regge trajectory has come to play a central role in both the classification of particles and the description of high energy scattering data. We begin with the limited viewpoint of presenting some tentative assignments of particles to Regge trajectories and return later to the ramifications of this concept in scattering theory. The foundations of Regge theory have been thoroughly discussed in various books and need not be elaborated here.

The rotational rule $\Delta J = 2$ arises from the existence of an additional quantum number in Regge theory known as the signature (τ). For baryons the signature quantum number is defined as $\tau = (-)^{J-1/2}$. Thus the rotational sequence of particles $J = 1/2, 5/2, 9/2, \ldots$ is denoted by $\tau = +1$ and the sequence $J = 3/2, 7/2, 11/2, \ldots$ by $\tau = -1$. Similarly, for mesons signature is defined as $\tau = (-)^{J}$ with corresponding particle sequences $J = 0, 2, 4, \ldots$ and $J = 1, 3, 5, \ldots$.

A convenient representation for classification of particles on a Regge trajectory is a plot of spin (J) versus (mass)^2 as proposed by Chew and Frautschi. The

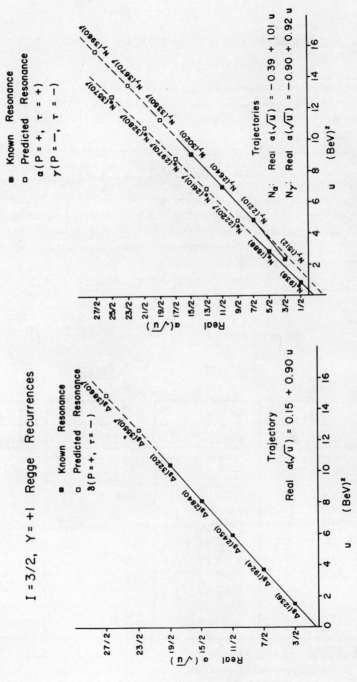

Figure 1.4. Particle recurrences on Δ_δ, N_α and N_γ baryon Regge trajectories: from V. Barger and D. Cline, *Phys. Rev. Letters* **16**, 913 (1968).

trajectory α interpolates between the particle recurrences such that

$$\text{Re } \alpha(M_R{}^2) = J_R$$

The functional dependence of $\alpha(t)$ on the variable t is a priori unknown and must be empirically deduced. The trajectory is presumed to be an analytic function of t for mesons and $\sqrt{u}$ for baryons, where t and u are Mandelstam variables representing (energy)^2.

A proposed Regge classification for the prominent baryons is shown in Figure 1.4. The baryons that have been assigned to these trajectories are enumerated in Table 1.2. It should be noted that only the lowest few members of each trajectory have experimentally established spin assignments. This scheme is speculative in the sense that not all the quantum numbers are known; nevertheless, there is little doubt that the elements of this classification will endure.

The striking feature of the trajectories is the indication for approximate straight lines in u, that is, (mass)^2 :

$$\text{Re } \alpha(\sqrt{u}) \simeq a + bu$$

Table 1.2

Baryons assigned to the Δ_δ, N_α, and N_γ Regge trajectories.

DOMINANT Y = +1 RESONANCES

(J - L = I - 1)

Δ_δ		N_γ		N_α		Δ_β	
Mass	J^P	Mass	J^P	Mass	J^P	Mass	J^P
1236	$\frac{3}{2}^+$	1525	$\frac{3}{2}^-$	938	$\frac{1}{2}^+$	1670	$\frac{1}{2}^-$
1920	$\frac{7}{2}^+$	2190	$\frac{7}{2}^-$	1688	$\frac{5}{2}^+$		
2420	$\frac{11}{2}^+$	2650	$\frac{11}{2}^-$	2210	$\frac{9}{2}^+$		
2850	$\frac{15}{2}^+$	3030	$\frac{15}{2}^-$				
3230	$\frac{19}{2}^+$	3340	$\frac{19}{2}^-$				

NOTATION : $\tau = (-)^{J - \frac{1}{2}}$ $N_\gamma\,(I = \frac{1}{2},\ \tau = -\,)$

⊓ means established $N_\alpha\,(I = \frac{1}{2},\ \tau = +\,)$

$\Delta_\delta(I = \frac{3}{2},\ \tau = -\,)$ $\Delta_\beta\,(I = \frac{1}{2},\ \tau = +\,)$

In the mass region where baryon resonances are presently observable (up to $M \simeq 3.5$ BeV), the trajectories show no sign of turning over. Inasmuch as the turnover of a trajectory would signal the termination of the sequence of particle recurrences, the observed behavior leaves open the possibility of an infinite string of particles on a trajectory. Unfortunately the experimental detection of particles appears to increase significantly in difficulty with increasing mass.

The experimental identification of high mass meson resonances is considerably more difficult because of the absence of meson targets. The bulk of the $Y = 1$ baryon states have been observed in *formation* experiments $\pi N \to N^* \to \pi N$. The analogous reactions for meson resonances, for example, $\pi \rho \to \rho^* \to \pi \rho$, are not feasible. The meson resonances discovered thus far have been identified in *production* experiments of the type $\pi + N \to N +$ mesons. The existence and quantum numbers of resonances are generally more difficult to establish in production experiments than in formation experiments. For this reason present information on the meson particle spectrum is somewhat more limited than for the baryon spectrum. Nevertheless, there are indications that a large number of high mass meson states exist and hints that their spins increase with the masses. In analogy with the $Y = +1$ baryon system, it is possible to make some speculative assignments of the mesons to Regge trajectories.

The known $I = 1$ mesons are tentatively assigned as recurrences on straight-line trajectories

$$\mathrm{Re}\, \alpha(t) = a + bt$$

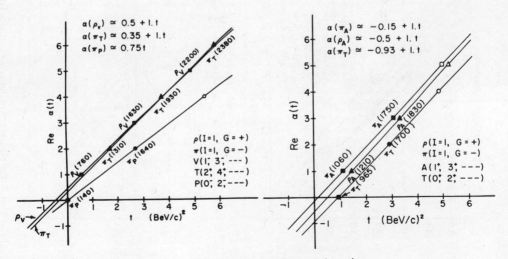

Figure 1.5. Tentative assignments of $I = 1$ mesons to Regge trajectories.

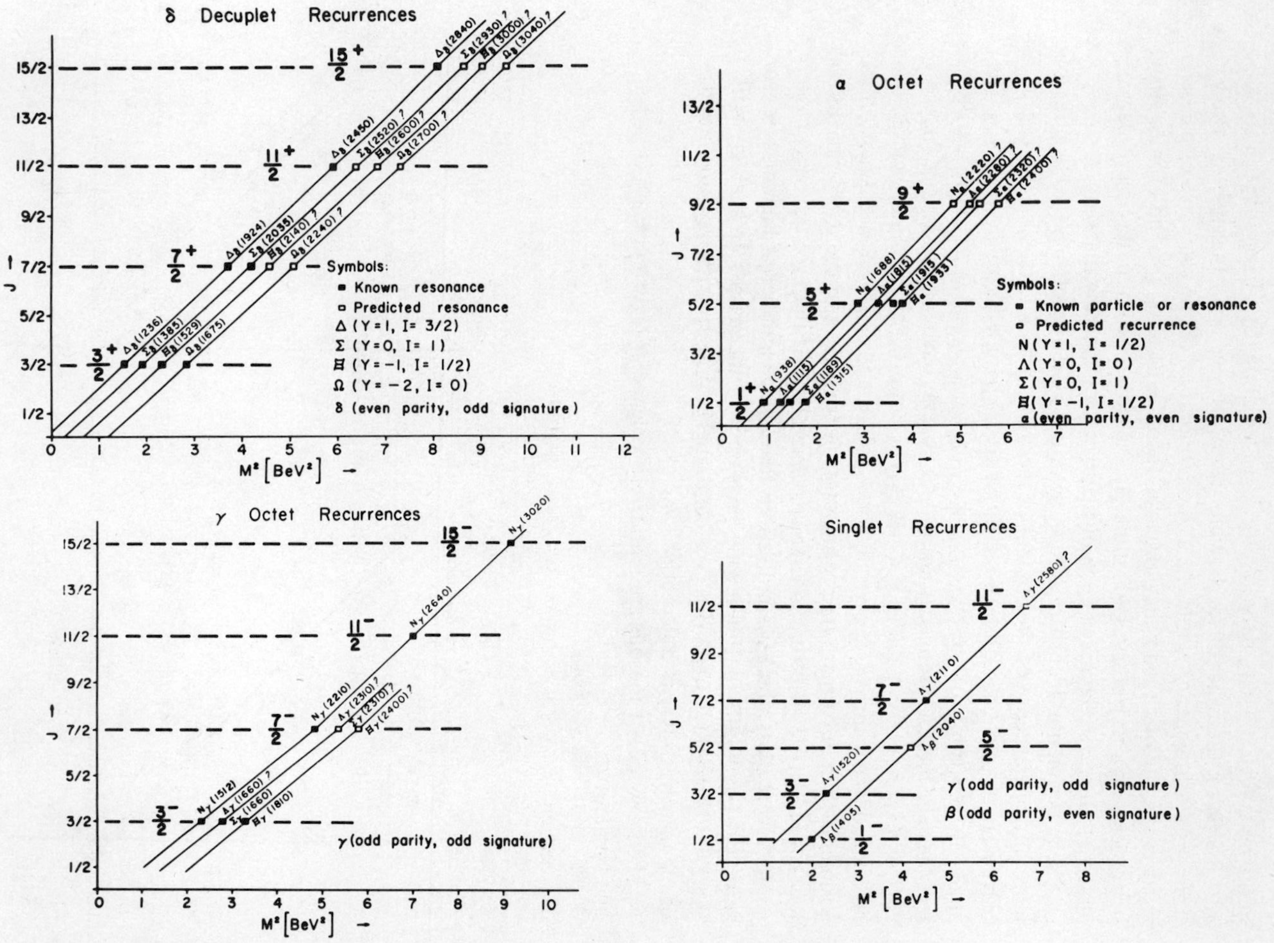

Figure 1.6. Regge recurrence patterns for 1, 8, and 10 SU(3) multiplets of baryons: from V. Barger and Cline, *Phys. Rev.* 155, 1792 (1967).

8

in Figure 1.5. There is an interesting possibility that certain of these trajectories are nearly degenerate. For example, the ρ_V trajectory with spins $1^-, 3^-, 5^-, \ldots$ appears to coincide with the π_T trajectory with spins $2^+, 4^+, 6^+, \ldots$. This phenomenon is termed "exchange degeneracy" and will be discussed in more detail in Chapter 4. On the π_T trajectory the 0^+ state is absent. An extrapolation from the other particles on the trajectory would place the 0^+ particle at negative t and hence negative M^2. Such a state is called a "ghost state," which clearly cannot be realized as a physical particle.

The slopes of the established meson and baryon trajectories are approximately $\simeq 1 \; (\text{BeV})^{-2}$. The origin of this universal slope is intriguing in that it may imply a profound relation between the baryon and meson systems.

1.4 SU(3) AND REGGE CLASSIFICATIONS

With the application of both the SU(3) and Regge classification schemes, the particle spectrum can be understood in a cohesive way. The recurrence patterns of the leading singlet, octet, and decuplet baryon trajectories are shown in Figure 1.6. We expect similar SU(3) Regge patterns for the meson system, but our present knowledge of $Y = \pm 1$ mesons is very limited and does not warrant further speculation.

The usual SU(3) symmetry breaking interactions for particle masses leads to the following mass formulas:

octet baryons:

$$\tfrac{1}{2}M_N + \tfrac{1}{2}M_\Xi = \tfrac{3}{4}M_\Lambda + \tfrac{1}{4}M_\Sigma$$

decuplet baryons:

$$M_\Delta - M_\Sigma = M_\Sigma - M_\Xi = M_\Xi - M_\Omega$$

octet mesons:

$$M_K{}^2 = \tfrac{3}{4}M_\eta{}^2 + \tfrac{1}{4}M_\pi{}^2$$

Such mass formulas are frequently used in assigning particles to SU(3) multiplets. It has been a theoretical question of some debate as to what function of mass should appear in these mass formulas. If straight-line, parallel SU(3) trajectories describe the high mass states, as suggested in Figure 1.6, then presumably the appropriate mass formulas for the baryons should also be written as a function of (mass)^2.

Chapter 2

General Features of Scattering Data

2.1 PERIPHERAL EXCHANGES: POLE DOMINANCE

The S-matrix approach to hadron interactions presently gives the only viable technique for describing a broad class of scattering data. The philosophy behind S-matrix theory relies heavily on phenomenological input. In contrast to quantum electrodynamics in which the fine structure constant and the electron mass appear as basic constants, no fundamental constants are presumed to enter into the S-matrix description of strong interactions. A self-consistent picture of hadron physics is expected to ultimately emerge in which all hadron coupling constants and masses are intimately interrelated.

The phenomenological aspects of S-matrix theory are frequently based on dominance of nearby singularities. Pion-nucleon scattering provides a suitable illustration of the pole dominance approximation. The basic principles of analyticity and crossing symmetry specify that the three processes

$$\pi^- p \to \pi^- p \tag{I}$$

$$\pi^+ p \to \pi^+ p \tag{II}$$

$$\bar{p} p \to \pi^+ \pi^- \tag{III}$$

are described by continuations of the *same* analytic functions of the Mandelstam variables s, t, u:

$$s = -(q_1 + p_1)^2$$

$$t = -(q_1 - q_2)^2$$

$$u = -(p_2 - q_1)^2$$

Here q_1, p_1 denote the momenta of the initial π^- and p, respectively, and q_2, p_2 the corresponding outgoing momenta in channel (I) above. Only two of the s, t, u variables are independent. The constraint equation is

$$s + t + u = 2M_N{}^2 + 2M_\pi{}^2$$

10

Mandelstam Diagram

A convenient representation of the physical regions of the processes I, II, and III is shown in Figure 2.1. The shaded areas denote the range of the s, t, u variables for the physical regions of the three processes:

process I:
$$s \geqslant (M + \mu)^2$$
$$t \leqslant 0$$

process II:
$$u \geqslant (M + \mu)^2$$
$$t \leqslant 0$$

process III:
$$t \geqslant 4M^2$$
$$s \leqslant 0$$
$$u \leqslant 0$$

In channel I, s is the square of the center of mass (c.m.) energy and t is the invariant momentum transfer between the initial and final protons. In terms of the c.m. momentum k, scattering angle θ_s, and laboratory energy E_{Lab}, the kinematics are

$$s = M^2 + \mu^2 + 2ME_{\text{Lab}}$$
$$t = -2k^2(1 - \cos \theta_s)$$

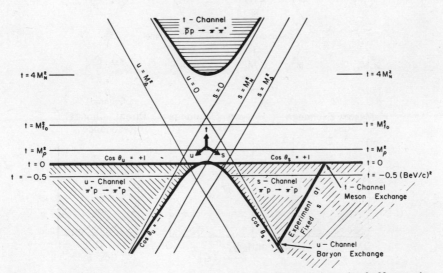

Figure 2.1. Mandelstam diagram of physical regions for the three channels of πN scattering.

For the physical region of channel II, u becomes the square of the corresponding c.m. energy, and similarly for t in channel III.

The dominant singularities in S-matrix calculations are thought to be poles owing to the presence of stable or resonance particles. The singularity structure of the S matrix was originally inferred from quantum theory. The lowest-order Feynman diagrams give the πN scattering amplitude the structure $g_\rho h_\rho/(t - m_\rho^2)$ from the ρ-meson singularity. On the other hand, the nucleon singularity takes the form

$$\frac{g_N^2}{s - M_N^2} \quad \text{and} \quad \frac{g_N^2}{u - M_N^2}$$

For unstable particles the actual pole positions are at complex values of s, t, or u. Because of such pole structures, the amplitude will be enhanced in physical regions near to singularities.

In Figure 2.1 the positions of some example singularities are plotted for real values of s, t, and u on the Mandelstam diagram. In the s- and u-channels the poles are associated with baryons [e.g., $N_\alpha(938, J^P = 1/2^+, I = 1/2)$ and $\Delta_\delta(1236,$

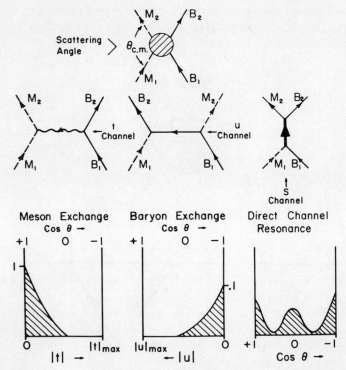

Figure 2.2. Pictorial illustration of meson exchange, baryon exchange, and direct channel resonances. Qualitative predictions for scattering via these mechanisms are illustrated.

$J^P = 3/2^+, I = 3/2)$], whereas in the t-channel meson poles appear [e.g., $\rho(750, J^P = 1^-, I = 1)$ and $f_0 (1250, J^P = 2^+, I = 0)$]. Although the real part of the complex position of a pole may lie outside the physical region for a particular channel, it can still have a considerable influence on the scattering in that channel. As an approximate rule of thumb we expect the poles nearest to the physical region of a given channel to exert maximal influence on the scattering amplitude.

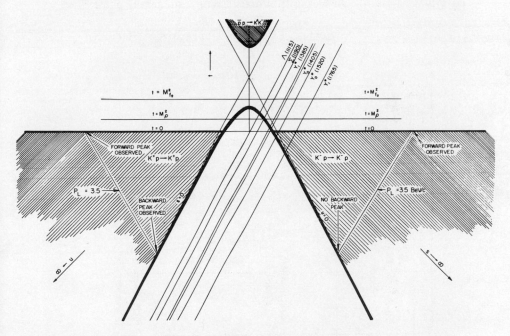

Figure 2.3. Illustration of effects of nearby poles on angular distributions of KN and $\bar{K}N$ scattering.

A pictorial diagram of the s-, t-, and u-channel singularities in meson–baryon scattering is given in Figure 2.2. In this Figure the particle exchanges (i.e., poles) in the t- and u-channels are represented by horizontal lines. The vertical line represents an s-channel singularity owing to the presence of a stable or resonant particle. The singularity structure of these poles leads to qualitative predictions of structure in the scattering differential cross sections. For example, as illustrated in Figure 2.2, meson exchange singularities give a forward-peaked angular distribution whereas baryon exchange leads to backward peaking. Isolated direct channel poles lead to symmetric and rather complex scattering angular distributions.

As an illustration of this idea consider the physical region of the s-channel process $\pi^- p \to \pi^- p$ in Figure 2.1. Suppose that an experiment is done at fixed high energy (constant s). For small t ($\cos \theta_s \approx +1$) the nearest singularities are due to the ρ and f^0 meson poles that give rise to a forward peak. For small u ($\cos \theta_s \simeq -1$), and hence large $|t|$, the Δ_δ is the nearest singularity and gives rise to a backward peak.

The corresponding diagram in Figure 2.3 for $K^- p$ and $K^+ p$ elastic scattering directly illustrates the angular distributions arising from nearby poles. Since

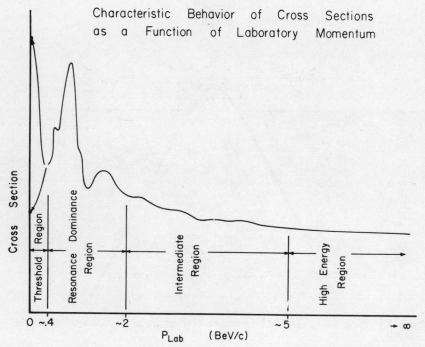

Figure 2.4. Representative energy dependence of a cross section from low to high energies.

there are no known u-channel poles (i.e., no baryons with $Y = +2$), the $K^- p$ elastic scattering distribution should not show a backward peak.

This introduction gives an indication of the experimental method by which we can phenomenologically locate and study the singularity structure of the S matrix. Mapping out the singularity pattern requires considerable experimental data on a wide variety of reactions. Even then only the simplest types of singularities, that is, poles, can be readily studied. In the remainder of this chapter we survey the gross features of fundamental particle reactions that give an idea of the poles that dominate scattering behavior.

Energy Dependence of Cross Sections

Peaks in angular distributions in differential cross sections provide important clues to the existence of particle poles. The energy dependence of cross sections provides equally valuable information about the singularities of the S matrix.

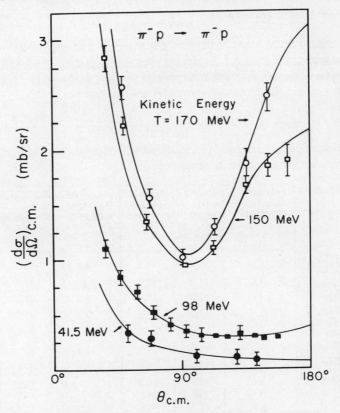

Figure 2.5. Angular distribution for $\pi^- p$ elastic scattering in the region of the $\Delta_\delta(1236, J^P = 3/2^+)$ resonance: from S. W. Barnes *et al.*, *Phys. Rev.* 117, 238 (1960).

Representative energy-dependent behavior of a cross section is shown in Figure 2.4. Several characteristic momentum regions of the cross section are distinguished in this figure. Near threshold a limited number of partial waves are important because of the long wavelength of the incident particles. In the momentum range up to 2 BeV/c cross sections frequently show strong fluctuations indicative of s-channel resonance states. The positions of the prominent resonances are correlated with the peaks in the cross section. Moving up to the intermediate momentum region, 2 to 5 BeV/c, the effects of t- or u-channel poles become increasingly important and the direct-channel effects are superimposed as minor oscillations. Finally at high energy, greater than or equal to 5 BeV/c, the presence of t- or u-channel singularities are observed. These produce a cross section that varies smoothly with momentum.

Resonance Angular Distribution

The angular distribution of the reaction $\pi^- p \to \pi^- p$ for momenta in the resonance region is shown in Figure 2.5. In this case the direct channel resonance $\Delta_\delta(1236, 3/2^+)$ is the dominant singularity for kinetic energies in the range 150–250 MeV. At lower energies the threshold behavior begins to occur.

Table 2.1

Association of peaks in angular distributions with the existence of particles with appropriate exchange quantum numbers.

REACTION	t-CHANNEL QUANTUM NUMBERS Q_t, I_t, Y_t			MESONS WITH THESE QUANTUM NUMBERS	FORWARD PEAK?	u-CHANNEL QUANTUM NUMBERS Q_u, I_u, Y_u			BARYONS WITH THESE QUANTUM NUMBERS	BACKWARD PEAK?
$\pi^+ p \to \{{}^{\pi^+}_{\rho^0}\}p$	0	0,1	0	YES	YES	0	½,3/2	1	YES	YES
$\pi^- p \to \{{}^{\pi^-}_{\rho^-}\}p$	0	0,1	0	YES	YES	2	3/2	1	YES	YES
$\pi^- p \to \{{}^{\pi^0}_{\rho^0}\}n$	1	1	0	YES	YES	1	½,3/2	1	YES	YES
$K^+ p \to \{{}^{K^+}_{K^{*+}}\}p$	0	0,1	0	YES	YES	0	0,1	0	YES	YES
$K^- p \to \{{}^{K^-}_{K^{*-}}\}p$	0	0,1	0	YES	YES	2	1	2	NO	NO
$K^+ n \to \{{}^{K^0}_{K^{*0}}\}p$	-1	1	0	YES	YES	0	0,1	0	YES	YES
$K^- p \to \{{}^{\bar{K}^0}_{\bar{K}^{*0}}\}n$	1	1	0	YES	YES	1	0,1	2	NO	NO
$\pi^- p \to K^0 \Lambda$	1	½	1	YES	YES	1	1	0	YES	YES
$\pi^- p \to K^+ \Sigma^-$	2	3/2	1	NO	NO	0	0,1	0	YES	YES
$\pi^+ p \to K^+ \Sigma^+$	0	½,3/2	1	YES	YES	0	0,1	0	YES	YES
$K^- p \to K^+ \Xi^-$	2	1	2	NO	NO	0	0,1	0	YES	YES
$K^- p \to K^0 \Xi^0$	1	0,1	2	NO	NO	1	1	0	YES	YES
$K^- p \to (K^+K^0)\Omega^-$	2	½	3	NOT KNOWN	?	0	½	-1	YES	?
$\pi^- p \to \pi^+ N^{*-}$	2	2	0	NO	NO	0	½,3/2	1	YES	YES
$\pi^+ p \to \pi^0 N^{*++}$	-1	1,2	0	YES	YES	1	½,3/2	1	YES	YES
$\{K^- p \to \{{}^{\pi^+}_{\rho^0}\}\Sigma^-$	2	½	1	NO	NO	0	½,3/2	1	YES	YES
$\{K^- p \to \{{}^{\pi^-}_{\rho^-}\}\Sigma^+$	0	½,3/2	1	YES	YES	2	½	1	YES	YES
$\bar{p}p \to \bar{\Lambda}\Lambda$	1	½	+1	YES	YES	1	½	1	B=2	NO
$\bar{p}p \to \bar{\Lambda}\Sigma^0 \text{ or } \bar{\Sigma}^0\Lambda$	1	½	+1	YES	YES	1	½	1	B=2	NO
$\bar{p}p \to \bar{\Sigma}^-\Sigma^-$	2	3/2	+1	NO	NO	0	½,3/2	1	B=2	NO
$\bar{p}p \to \bar{\Sigma}^+\Sigma^+$	0	½,3/2	+1	YES	YES	2	3/2	1	B=2	NO

Direct channel resonances are known to play a dominant role in $\pi^-p, \pi^+p,$ $K^-p, K^-n,$ and perhaps $\bar{p}p, \bar{p}n$ elastic and inelastic processes below 2 BeV/c. On the other hand, no resonances are definitely established with the $K^+p, K^+n, pp,$ or pn quantum numbers, and these channels do not display the characteristic resonant fluctuations at low energy.

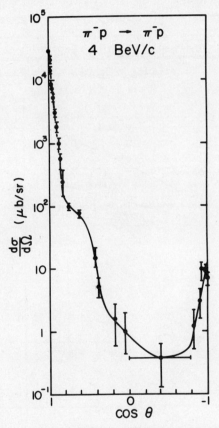

Figure 2.6. Forward and backward peaks in π^-p elastic scattering at 4 BeV/c.

Association of Particles with Poles

The S-matrix framework leads us to expect a one-to-one correspondence between particles and prominent singularities. The presence of singularities with particular quantum numbers is inferred from the qualitative trends of differential cross sections as discussed above. Specifically the absence of peaks that would result from the exchange of a certain set of quantum numbers (Q, I, Y) should reflect the absence of physical particles in nature with those quantum numbers. A remarkable verification of this association of observed particles with t- or u-channel peaks has been accomplished in the last several years through the study of a great variety of two-body processes. Table 2.1 summarizes this association for a fraction of the experimentally studied processes. The t- and u-channel quantum numbers are defined in the same way as in Figure 2.2. The association of particles with exchanges can be readily made by comparison of Tables 1.1 and 2.1.

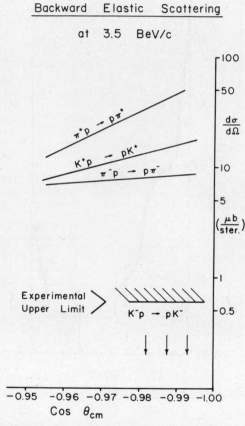

Figure 2.7. Comparison of data on elastic scattering differential cross sections for cos $\theta \simeq -1$: from V. Barger, *Rev. Mod. Phys.* **40**, 129 (1968).

Elastic Scattering Angular Distributions

In order to document this association we now show data from a general class of reactions. Elastic scattering usually has the largest cross section of the two-body processes. Figure 2.6 shows the $\pi^- p$ elastic-scattering differential cross section for p_L = 4 BeV/c. Striking forward and backward peaks are evident, as would be expected from Table 2.1, since the appropriate exchange quantum numbers have been realized as particles. The magnitude of the forward peak is of

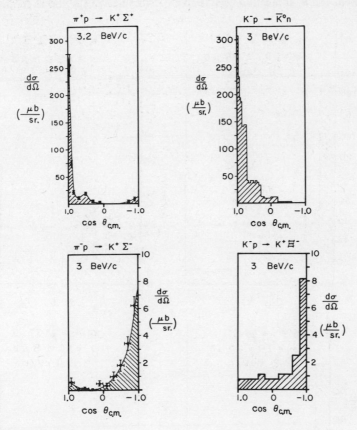

Figure 2.8. Differential cross section data at 3 BeV/c for the inelastic reactions $\pi^+ p \to K^+ \Sigma^+$, $K^- p \to \bar{K}^0 n$, $\pi^- p \to \Sigma^- K^+$, and $K^- p \to K^+ \Xi^-$: from V. Barger, *Rev. Mod. Phys.* **40**, 129 (1968).

the order of about 10^4 μb/sr, whereas the backward peak is of the order ~ 10 μb/sr. A sizeable difference in the magnitude of meson and baryon exchange peaks is a characteristic that is maintained for all processes.

Elastic $\pi^\pm p$, $K^\pm p$ reactions all show forward peaks of comparable magnitude for momenta above 2 or 3 BeV/c. The situation for the backward peaks in these reactions is quite different as evidenced in Figure 2.7. Here the lines represent the measured values of the backward differential cross sections at 3.5 BeV/c. The π^+p, π^-p, and K^+p cross sections are comparable size. No backward peak has ever been observed above 3 BeV/c for K^-p elastic scattering. This observation is in accordance with Table 2.1 since no baryons with the u-channel quantum numbers of the K^-p reaction have been experimentally established.

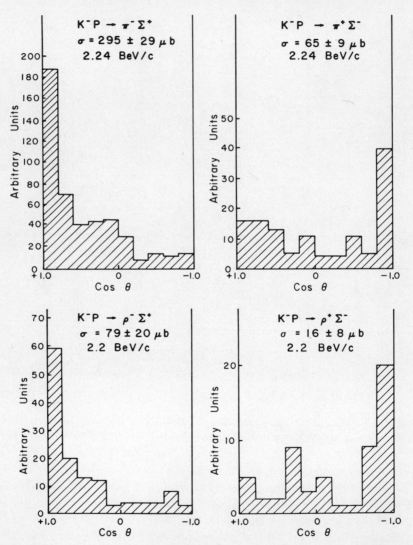

Figure 2.9. Comparison of data on the reactions $\bar{K}p \to \pi\Sigma$ and $\bar{K}p \to \rho\Sigma$ at 2.2 BeV/c: from G. W. London *et al.*, *Phys. Rev.* **143**, 1034 (1966).

Inelastic Scattering Angular Distributions

Turning next to inelastic processes, Figure 2.8 shows typical data for pseudo-scalar meson–nucleon scattering at 3 BeV/c. The reaction $\pi^+ p \rightarrow K^+ \Sigma^+$ is representative of inelastic processes involving *both* meson and baryon exchanges. The

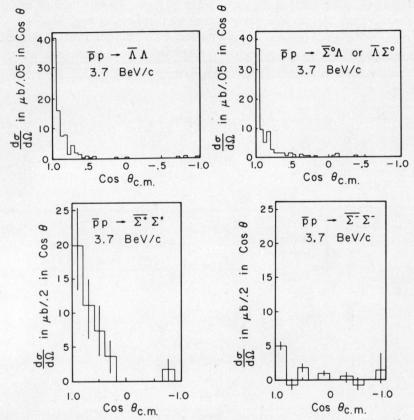

Figure 2.10. Data on some baryon–baryon and baryon–antibaryon inelastic reactions: from C. Baltay *et al., Phys. Rev.* **140**, B1027 (1965).

data show a forward peak of about 250 μb/sr and a backward peak of about 10 μb/sr. Note that the forward cross section is considerably smaller than that of elastic scattering; the backward cross section is comparable to that of elastic scattering. This observation is true for most other inelastic processes as well.

In the reaction $K^- p \rightarrow \bar{K}^0 n$ a sharp forward peak is present but no events are observed near $\cos \theta = -1$, as expected. The distinct features of a baryon exchange peak are more clearly illustrated by the data on the reactions $\pi^- p \rightarrow \Sigma^- K^+$

and $K^-p \to K^+ \Xi^-$. Neither of these reactions has allowed meson exchanges, and the cross sections are notably small for $\cos \theta \sim +1$. In particular, the forward cross sections are more than two orders of magnitude down from the forward cross section for $\pi^+p \to K^+\Sigma^+$. The considerable suppression of these forward cross sections, which have no nearby meson singularities, set the level to be expected from other kinds of singularities. For example, the simultaneous exchange of two or more particles can mediate reactions that have no nearby poles. The singularity structure of these multiple exchange mechanisms is that of cuts rather than simple poles. It is exceedingly fortunate that the pole-dominance approximation is empirically valid to about two orders of magnitude or more in the cross sections.

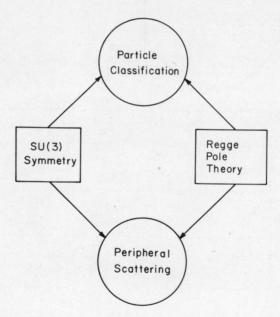

Figure 2.11. Schematic illustration of unification of classification and scattering phenomena within the framework of Regge pole and SU(3) symmetry theories.

To exphasize that the above conclusions are dependent *only* on the t- or u-channel quantum numbers we show in Figure 2.9 a comparison of the reactions $\bar{K}p \to \pi\Sigma$ and $\bar{K}p \to \rho\Sigma$. The reactions $K^-p \to \pi^-\Sigma^+$ and $K^-p \to \rho^-\Sigma^+$ have allowed t- and u-channel exchanges, whereas $K^-p \to \pi^+\Sigma^-$ and $K^-p \to \rho^+\Sigma^-$ allow only u-channel exchanges. The qualitative features of the data are independent of whether the final state has a π or ρ meson. These data are at relatively low

momentum (approximately 2.2 BeV/c) and may show some background from
s-channel resonances.

As a final example, Figure 2.10 illustrates similar behavior for reactions with
only baryons and antibaryons in the initial and final states. The u-channel for
these reactions requires $B = 2$ for exchanges. Since no backward peaks are observed, there are either no $B = 2$ particles with the appropriate quantum numbers
or the singularities of possible $B = 2$ particles are very far from the physical region
in these reactions. The forward peaks in the reactions $pp \rightarrow \bar{\Lambda}\Lambda$, $\bar{p}p \rightarrow \bar{\Lambda}\Sigma^0$, and
$\bar{p}p \rightarrow \bar{\Sigma}^+\Sigma^+$ all result from exchanges of known mesons. The smallness of the
forward cross section for $\bar{p}p \rightarrow \bar{\Sigma}^-\Sigma^-$ is apparently attributable to the absence of
mesons with appropriate quantum numbers.

Overall Picture

In Chapter 1 we discussed the classification of particles according to the complementary SU(3) symmetry and Regge pole theoretical models. In the rest of the
book we attempt to show that the same theories also account for the salient
features of much of the scattering data. The Regge pole theory is useful in the
description of the scattering amplitude in terms of particle pole singularities.
SU(3) symmetry provides an interrelationship between the residues of particle
poles associated with the same SU(3) multiplets. The overall unification of classification and scattering phenomena is schematically illustrated in Figure 2.11.
We note as a specific example of this unification that the absence of a baryon
exchange peak in the above mentioned reaction $K^-p \rightarrow \bar{K}^0n$ is related to the non-
occurrence of baryons in $\bar{10}$ or 27 SU(3) multiplets.

2.2 DETAILED CHARACTERISTICS OF CROSS SECTIONS

Beyond the peripheral nature of differential cross sections, a number of empirical aspects have been observed in scattering data. In this section we simply list
these features and later return to possible theoretical interpretations.

Total Cross Sections

To begin with, because of the relative ease of measurement, the most precise
data available at high energy are those of total cross sections. Figure 2.12 shows
the total cross sections and integrated elastic differential cross sections for $\pi^\pm p$
scattering from threshold to about 7 BeV/c. These cross sections resemble the

behavior illustrated in Figure 2.4. The resonant structure region extends up to about 3 BeV/c. Small resonance fluctuations on top of a large background have been uncovered in the region 3–5 BeV/c. The total cross sections for $K^\pm p$ and $K^\pm n$ scattering from low to intermediate energies are shown in Figure 2.13.

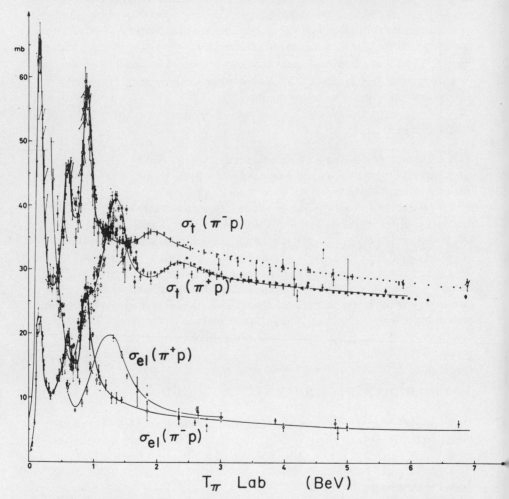

Figure 2.12. Total and integrated elastic cross sections for $\pi^\pm p$ scattering from threshold to 7 BeV/c: from data compilations by M. Focacci and G. Giacomelli in CERN Report NP 66-18.

Here $\sigma_t(K^-p)$ and $\sigma_t(K^-n)$ both show strong resonance effects, but $\sigma_t(K^+p)$ and $\sigma_t(K^+n)$ are relatively smooth and considerably smaller.

The high energy data on total cross sections are shown in Figure 2.14. The

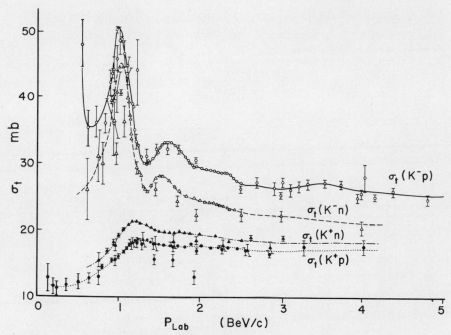

Figure 2.13. Total cross sections for $K^{\pm}p$ and $K^{\pm}n$ scattering: from data compilations by Y. Sumi in *Prog. of Theor. Phys. Suppl.* **41** (1968).

first thing to note is that all the total cross sections fall smoothly or remain constant with increasing momentum. It is a remarkable fact that all of the total cross sections approach asymptotic values from above. The second important feature is that antiparticle total cross sections are always greater than the corresponding particle total cross sections at high energies; that is,

$$\sigma_t(\bar{p}p) > \sigma_t(pp) \qquad\qquad \sigma_t(K^- n) > \sigma_t(K^+ n)$$

$$\sigma_t(\bar{p}n) > \sigma_t(pn) \qquad\qquad \sigma_t(\pi^- p) > \sigma_t(\pi^+ p)$$

$$\sigma_t(K^- p) > \sigma_t(K^+ p)$$

It is interesting to note that the channels with the larger total cross sections at high energy are also the channels that have resonances at low energy. The pp, pn, K^+p, and K^+n channels have no known resonances, whereas the $\bar{p}p$, $\bar{p}n$, K^-p, and K^-n channels have resonance structure. Another important empirical regularity is the equality and approximate constancy of

$$\sigma_t(K^+ p) \simeq \sigma_t(K^+ n)$$

$$\sigma_t(pp) \simeq \sigma_t(pn)$$

The constancy of $\sigma_t(K^+p)$ and $\sigma_t(K^+n)$ persists down to momenta of 2 BeV/c. Finally we note a decreasing isotopic spin dependence at high energies for all, channels. In particular, we see that

$$\frac{\sigma_t(\pi^-p) - \sigma_t(\pi^+p)}{\sigma_t(\pi^-p) + \sigma_t(\pi^+p)} \sim 5\%$$

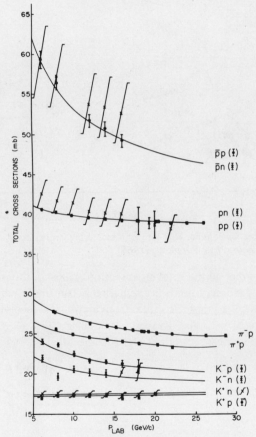

Figure 2.14. High energy data on total cross sections: from V. Barger *et al.*, *Nucl. Phys.* **B5**, 411 (1968).

Total cross section data are of considerable theoretical interest because of their simple relationship to the imaginary part of the forward scattering amplitude. Conservation of probability leads directly to the optical theorem

$$\sigma_t(s) = \frac{4\pi}{k} \operatorname{Im} f_{el}(s, t = 0)$$

where f is normalized such that

$$\frac{d\sigma}{d\Omega}(s, t = 0)_{el} = |f_{el}(s, t = 0)|^2$$

By means of the optical theorem, theoretical models for the elastic scattering amplitude can frequently be compared with total cross section data.

Crossover Phenomenon

A common experimental feature of high energy $\pi^\pm p$, $K^\pm p$, $\bar{p}p$ and pp elastic scattering is the change in sign of the cross section differences

$$\frac{d\sigma}{dt}(\bar{A}B) - \frac{d\sigma}{dt}(AB)$$

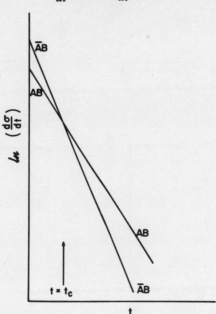

Figure 2.15. Diagrammatic illustration of the crossover phenomenon.

at momentum transfers $t = t_c \simeq -0.15$ (BeV/c)^2, as schematically illustrated in Figure 2.15. This change in sign is commonly called the "crossover phenomenon." Figure 2.16 shows experimental data relating to the crossovers for $K^\pm p$, $\bar{p}p$, pp, and $\pi^\pm p$. This feature of the forward elastic peaks can be crudely understood from an optical model viewpoint. In the simplest version of the optical model, in which the scattering is described by black sphere absorption, the total cross section is $2\pi R^2$, where R is the radius of interaction. With complete absorption

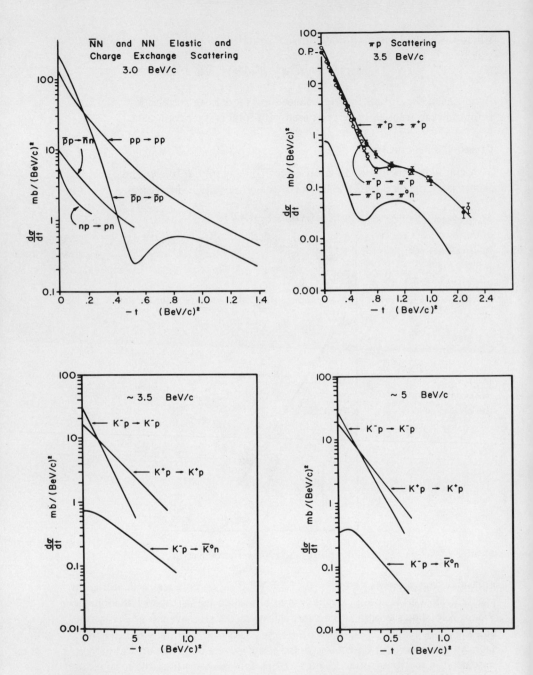

Figure 2.16. Comparison of elastic and charge exchange differential cross sections.

the forward amplitude is pure imaginary and the differential cross section for small t is

$$\frac{d\sigma}{dt} = \frac{\pi R^4}{4} \exp\left(\frac{tR^2}{4}\right)$$

$$= \frac{\sigma_t^2}{16\pi} \exp\left(\frac{t\sigma_t}{8\pi}\right)$$

In comparing $\pi^- p$ and $\pi^+ p$ scattering we conclude that at $t = 0$,

$$(d\sigma/dt)\,(\pi^- p) > (d\sigma/dt)\,(\pi^+ p) \text{ since } \sigma_t(\pi^- p) > \sigma_t(\pi^+ p)$$

Moreover, the slope of the diffraction peak for $\pi^- p$ will be greater than for $\pi^+ p$, and hence the forward peaks must cross. Although this simple model provides a qualitative explanation for the crossover, it does not adequately describe other important features of the data. For example, the real amplitudes are found experimentally to be nonnegligible at present energies. Also the total cross sections decrease with energy, thus requiring an energy-dependent radius of interaction.

Charge Exchange Processes

Among the simplest inelastic processes are the charge exchange reactions. The isospin invariance of hadron interactions relates charge exchange amplitudes to the elastic amplitudes. For example,

$$A(\pi^- p \rightarrow \pi^0 n) = \frac{1}{\sqrt{2}} [A(\pi^+ p) - A(\pi^- p)]$$

$$A(K^- p \rightarrow \bar{K}^0 n) = [A(K^- p) - A(K^- n)]$$

$$A(K^+ n \rightarrow K^0 p) = [A(K^+ p) - A(K^+ n)]$$

$$A(\bar{p}p \rightarrow \bar{n}n) = [A(\bar{p}p) - A(\bar{p}n)]$$

$$A(pn \rightarrow np) = [A(pp) - A(pn)]$$

Since the $\pi^- p$ and $\pi^+ p$ amplitudes are of comparable size at high energy, the charge exchange amplitude is expected to be small near the forward direction. The charge exchange data at 3.5 BeV/c are compared with the elastic cross sections in Figure 2.16. The smallness of charge exchange amplitudes relative to elastic amplitudes also can be qualitatively related to t-channel meson exchanges. The elastic amplitudes allow both $I = 0$ and $I = 1$ exchanges, whereas charge exchange allows only $I = 1$ t-channel singularities.

The structure and energy dependence of the differential cross sections of the reactions $\pi^- p \to \pi^0 n$, $\pi^- p \to \eta n$, $K^- p \to \bar{K}^0 n$, $K^+ n \to K^0 p$ are shown in Figure 2.17. These so-called charge exchange processes are among the simplest reactions to describe theoretically in terms of t-channel exchanges and occupy a central role in Chapter 4. The principal characteristics of the angular distributions are

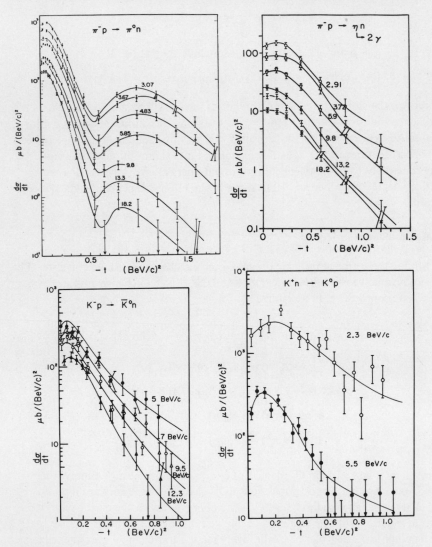

Figure 2.17. Structure and energy dependence of differential cross sections of charge exchange reactions.

strong forward peaking with a turnover or flattering around $t \simeq -0.1 \ (\text{BeV}/c)^2$, followed in the $\pi^- p \to \pi^0 n$ case by a pronounced dip near $t \simeq -0.5 \ (\text{BeV}/c)^2$. All these cross sections fall with energy. The energy dependence is approximately

$$\frac{d\sigma}{dt} \sim C(t)(E_{\text{Lab}})^{-1-2|t|}$$

Shrinkage

If we roughly parametrize the differential cross section as

$$\frac{d\sigma}{dt} = \left(\frac{d\sigma}{dt}\right)_{t=0} e^{-b|t|}$$

then the width of the charge exchange peaks is energy dependent:

$$b \simeq b_0 + 2 \ln E_{\text{Lab}}$$

In general, an increase of b with energy is called "shrinkage" and a decrease "antishrinkage." Accurate experimental data are required to separate shrinkage from the energy dependence of $(d\sigma/dt)_{t=0}$.

The values of b range from $b \simeq 5$ to $15 \ (\text{BeV})^{-2}$ at present energies (below 20 BeV) for a wide class of elastic and inelastic reactions. Notable exceptions are some π-exchange mediated reactions where $b \simeq 50$.

Elastic differential cross sections have shrinkage patterns that are not as rapidly changing as in inelastic reactions. The shrinkage behavior can be categorized as: $\pi^\pm p$, little or no shrinkage; pp, shrinks; $\bar{p}p$, antishrinks (i.e., expanding peak); $K^+ p$, shrinks; $K^- p$, little or no shrinkage. Most inelastic processes have not been studied well enough to determine shrinkage or antishrinkage.

Minima in Angular Distributions

Certain of the elastic differential cross sections show pronounced structure as a function of t. A dramatic example is $\bar{p}p$ elastic scattering as illustrated in Figure 2.16. There is some indication that dips of this variety remain at fixed t as s varies. Minima have also been observed in $\bar{p}n$ and $\pi^\pm p$ elastic channels. The $K^- p$ elastic differential cross section shows a hint of a dip. On the other hand, pp and $K^+ p$ show no similar structure. Perhaps it is significant that these dips at high energy occur in elastic channels that also have direct channel resonances at low energy.

Similar minima have been observed in a variety of inelastic reactions. The $\pi^- p \to \pi^0 n$ data in Figure 2.17 provide an example of such structure. In reactions that have dips, the first dip usually occurs near $t \simeq -0.5 \ (\text{BeV}/c)^2$. Preliminary evidence exists for the occurrence of at least a second dip in some reactions. The

existence of such minima has far-reaching theoretical implications, as discussed
in later chapters.

I-Spin Independence

All existing data on high energy elastic scattering differential cross sections
suggest isospin independence. For example, recent evidence indicates that the

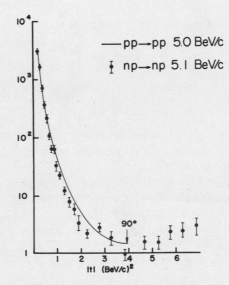

Figure 2.18. Comparison of *pn* and *pp* elastic scattering differential cross sections: from M.
Perl, CERN Report 68-7.

approximate equality

$$\frac{d\sigma^{\text{elastic}}}{dt}(pn) \approx \frac{d\sigma^{\text{elastic}}}{dt}(pp)$$

holds at least out to $| t | \simeq 4 \, (\text{BeV/c})^2$, as shown in Figure 2.18. Likewise experi-
ments indicate that $\sigma_t(pn) \approx \sigma_t(pp)$. Similar empirical equalities for differential
and total cross sections apply to $(\pi^+ p, \pi^- p)$ data at high energy. These approximate
equalities imply approximate isotopic spin independence for elastic scattering
amplitudes at energies above about 2 BeV. In terms of meson exchange models
these experimental results imply that $I = 0$ meson exchange amplitudes dominate
over $I = 1$ meson exchanges. Although the Pomeranchuk theorem requires isospin

independence at infinite energies, it is surprising to find these approximate equalities at such low energies. The Pomeranchuk theorem likewise requires $\bar{p}p$ and pp cross sections to coincide at infinite energies, but this relation is not so closely realized at present energies (see, e.g., Figures 2.14 and 2.16).

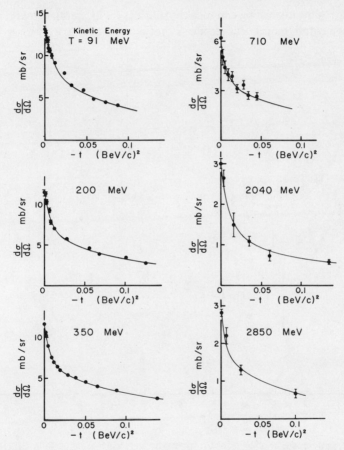

Figure 2.19. Data on the $np \rightarrow pn$ charge exchange process: from R. Wilson, *Ann. Phys.* (N.Y.) **32**, 201 (1965).

Low to High Energy Behavior

In reactions that do not have direct channel resonances, the high energy characteristics are also apparent at low energy. A striking example is provided by the $np \rightarrow pn$ charge exchange process. Figure 2.19 shows a comparison of the differential cross sections from about 450 MeV/C up to 3.7 BeV/c. This reaction presumably proceeds by one-pion exchange; the width of the angular distribution is roughly $(1/m_\pi^2)$.

High Momentum Transfer Scattering

There are some interesting empirical regularities in differential cross sections at large momentum transfer for reactions that have no baryon exchanges. The

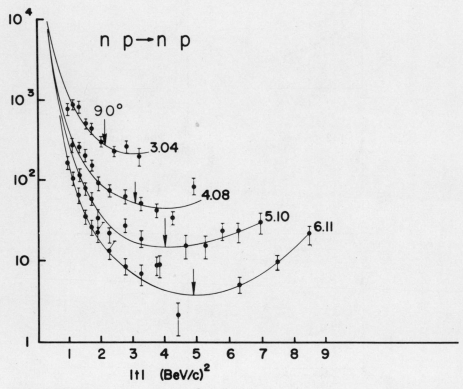

Figure 2.20. Differential cross sections for *np* elastic scattering: from M. Perl, CERN Report 68-7.

np elastic process is an example of this sort. Data for this process are shown in Figure 2.20. Near $t = 0$ the strong diffraction peak is evident. For $t \simeq t_{max}$ (i.e., $\cos\theta \simeq -1$) we have the charge exchange process $np \rightarrow pn$ discussed above (note that the sharp charge exchange peak at $\cos\theta \simeq -1$ is not shown in the figure). For $\theta \simeq 90°$ the nature of the scattering mechanism has not been established. It is amusing that the *np* angular distribution is approximately symmetric around $90°$.

Furthermore at 90° the ratio

$$\frac{[(d\sigma/dt)(np)]}{[(d\sigma/dt)(pp)]}$$

is unity, thus implying isospin independence. For comparison Figure 2.21 shows the $\bar{p}p$ high momentum transfer scattering data. The difference between the np and $\bar{p}p$ elastic processes at high momentum transfers is striking.

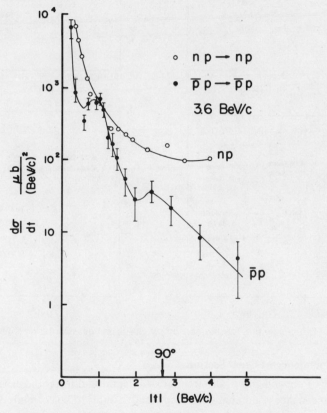

Figure 2.21. High momentum transfer data on np and pp elastic scattering: from M. Perl, CERN Report 68-7.

High momentum transfer data for pp elastic and quasielastic collisions are shown in Figure 2.22. This data is suggestive of a universal behavior at large $|t|$ for production of the $I = 1/2\,p$, $N_\alpha(1688)$, $N_\gamma(1512)$ particles. The $I = 3/2\,\Delta_\delta$ (1236) does not follow the same pattern, thus indicating an isospin dependence of the production mechanism.

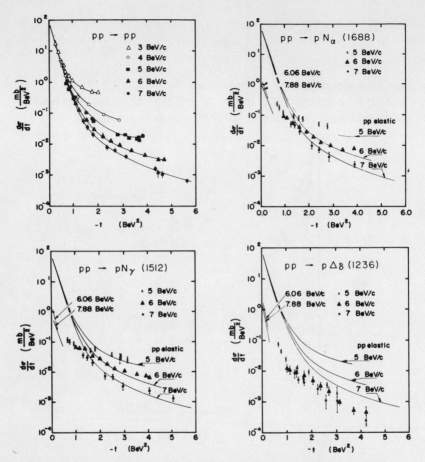

Figure 2.22. High momentum transfer data on pp elastic and quasielastic reactions.

Energy Dependence of Cross Sections

The energy dependence of differential or integrated differential cross sections above the resonance region has been empirically found to be correlated with the quantum numbers of allowed exchanges. This information has been effectively presented in a compilation of data by Morrison who fitted the energy dependence of integrated cross sections to the form $\sigma = K(p_{Lab})^{-n}$. Figure 2.23 summarizes the n values for a large variety of reactions. The values of n cluster into four groups corresponding to different t- or u-channel exchange quantum numbers. Diffraction-like processes have the least energy dependence ($n \sim 0$ to 0.5). Nonstrange meson exchange (e.g., ρ, ω, and π quantum numbers) leads to $n \sim 1.5$, whereas strange meson exchange (e.g., K, K^*) falls off slightly faster ($n \sim 2.0$). Finally baryon exchange reactions fall precipitously with energy ($n \sim 3.8$). Obviously these gross features must be accomodated in any sensible theoretical model of scattering dynamics. In the Regge model this separation in energy dependence is naturally explained in terms of the hierarchy of trajectories inferred from the discrete particle spectrum.

Diffraction-like processes occupy a special role in most theoretical models. These are processes that can proceed via $I = 0$, $G = +$ mesonic exchanges. The characteristics of diffraction scattering are (1) a very strong forward peak, (2)

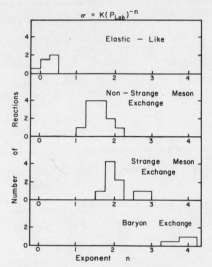

Figure 2.23. Momentum dependence $(p_{Lab})^{-n}$ for integrated cross sections: from D. Morrison, CERN Report 66-20.

predominantly imaginary forward amplitude, (3) near energy independence of the cross section, and (4) isospin independence. Although the elastic processes at small $|t|$ present prime examples of diffraction behavior, there are also examples of this behavior in inelastic processes. Among the best studied of these processes are quasielastic $I = 1/2$, N^* productions in πp or pp collisions. Figure 2.24 shows energy dependence and angular distributions for the processes

$$pp \rightarrow pN_\alpha(1450, J^P = \tfrac{1}{2}^+)$$

$$pp \rightarrow pN_\alpha(1688, J^P = \tfrac{5}{2}^+)$$

$$pp \rightarrow p\Delta_\delta(1236, J^P = \tfrac{3}{2}^+)$$

The $I = 1/2$ isobars are produced with cross sections that are fairly constant with energy. On the other hand, the cross section for the $I = 3/2$ isobar falls rapidly with energy. In the latter case the quantum numbers of the *t*-channel meson exchange cannot be $I = 0$ as needed for diffraction scattering.

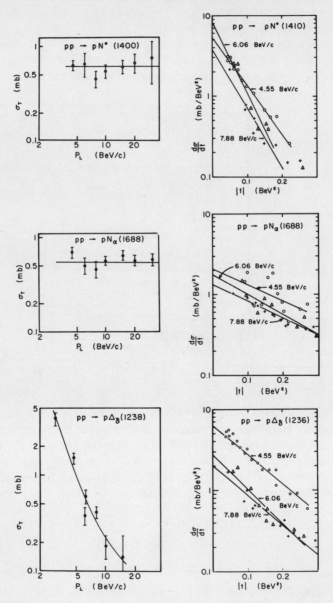

Figure 2.24. Characteristics of cross sections for $pp \rightarrow pN^*$ reactions.

A striking illustration of the different energy dependence of meson- and baryon-exchange-mediated inelastic processes is shown in Figure 2.25 for reactions

$$\left.\begin{array}{l} \pi^- p \to \Lambda K \\ \quad \to \Sigma^0 K^0 \end{array}\right\} \quad \text{strange meson exchange}$$

$$\pi^- p \to \Sigma^- K^+ \quad \text{strange baryon exchange}$$

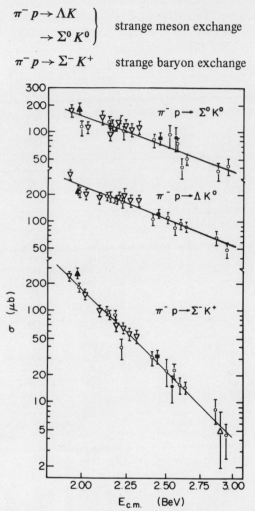

Figure 2.25. Energy dependence of integrated cross sections for $\pi^- p \to \Lambda K$, ΣK reactions: from O. Dahl *et al.*, *Phys. Rev.* **163,** 1430 (1967).

Summary

A reasonable expectation is that the experimental data collected over the past few years have already established many of the trends that will persist at higher

incident energies. The most remarkable fact that has emerged is the intimate
correlation between peripheral scattering and the discrete particle spectra. Even
with primitive theoretical models it has been possible to qualitatively understand
many aspects of the existing scattering data discussed in this chapter. In later
chapters we present the essential features of theoretical models along with attempts
to quantitatively describe high energy scattering.

Chapter 3

Basic Regge Pole Theory

3.1 ORIGIN OF REGGE POLES

The central theme of Regge pole theory is the connection between particle classification and high energy scattering. In Chapter 1 we reviewed the evidence for strings of particle recurrences on Regge trajectories. We begin this chapter with a discussion of the Van Hove–Durand model which clearly shows how a Regge pole exchange amplitude could arise in a Feynman-type field theory from single exchanges of particles on a trajectory.

We consider the simplest case of an s-channel scattering process $(A + B \to A + B)$ involving spinless particles of equal mass. The Feynman amplitude for the exchange of a single meson of spin J and mass M_J in the t-channel $(\bar{A} + A \to \bar{B} + B)$ is given by

$$F(s,t) = \frac{g_J{}^2 [-(s/s_0)]^J}{M_J{}^2 - t} \qquad s \to \infty$$

in the high energy limit of the s-channel. Here $g_J{}^2$ is essentially the product of coupling constants and s_0 is an energy scale factor. Now suppose that the exchanged particle is a member of a Regge trajectory having an infinite series of particle recurrences with spins $J = 1, 3, 5, \ldots$. The scattering amplitude due to a summation of the single exchanges of all the mesons on the trajectory is given by

$$F(s,t) = \sum_{J=0}^{\infty} \frac{g_J{}^2}{M_J{}^2 - t} \left[\frac{(-1)^J - 1}{2} \right] \left(\frac{s}{s_0} \right)^J$$

If we assume that all coupling constants are equal and the mass M_J increases linearly with J, $M_J{}^2 = \mu^2(J - a)$, as suggested by the empirical classifications of the observed particles in Chapter 1, then the series sum can be expressed in closed form. The resulting asymptotic s-channel scattering amplitude is

$$F(s,t) = -\frac{g^2 \pi}{2\mu^2} \frac{[1 - e^{-i\pi\alpha}]}{\sin \pi\alpha} \left(\frac{s}{s_0} \right)^\alpha$$

This is just the familiar form for the exchange of a Regge pole with odd signature. In this model the trajectory is given by $\alpha(t) = a + t/\mu^2$. The conditions on which the above derivation was based can be considerably relaxed. For example the "particles" which are exchanged need not even appear as resonances if the functional form for $M_J{}^2$ becomes negative for large J.

The physical interpretation of Regge pole exchange is apparent in the above derivation. The crossed-channel Regge pole represents the collective amplitude due to single exchanges of all particles that lie on the trajectory. Furthermore the trajectory $\alpha(t)$ determined for $t > 0$ from assignments of resonances as Regge recurrences is a smooth continuation of the trajectory for $t \leqslant 0$ that describes scattering due to Regge pole exchange. This observation is a direct consequence of Regge pole theory that can be subject to experimental test.

Rather than further elaborate at this point on the characteristic features of Regge pole scattering amplitude, we shall proceed directly to more realistic cases involving external particles with spin and unequal masses. The treatment in this chapter is designed to encompass the general problems that are encountered in Regge pole theory, but the emphasis is placed particularly on aspects of the theory that are relevant to interpretations of experiments. The formalism that we develop here will form the backbone of the phenomenological descriptions in later chapters of the experimental data.

3.2 MESON REGGE POLES

Kinematics

We begin with the relatively simple s-channel reaction $\pi N \to \pi N$. As usual we take s and t to be the invariant squares of energy and momentum transfer for the s-channel. Let p_s and θ_s refer to the c.m. momenta and angles in the s-channel, then

$$s = [(p_s{}^2 + M^2)^{1/2} + (p_s{}^2 + \mu^2)^{1/2}]^2$$

$$t = -2p_s{}^2(1 - \cos\theta_s)$$

$$s + t + u = 2M^2 + 2\mu^2$$

The meson Regge poles occur in the t-channel which represents the crossed process $\bar{\pi}\pi \to \bar{N}N$. In the t-channel physical region we have

$$t = 4(k_t{}^2 + \mu^2) = 4(p_t{}^2 + M^2)$$

$$s = -2k_t p_t \cos\theta_t + 2\mu^2 - 2(k_t{}^2 + \mu^2)^{1/2}(p_t{}^2 + M^2)^{1/2}$$

where the momenta and angle are t-channel c.m. quantities. In our later discussion we will make considerable use of the expression for $\cos\theta_t$ in terms of s, t, and u:

$$z_t = \cos\theta_t = -\frac{(s-u)}{4k_t p_t} = -\frac{(s - M^2 - \mu^2 + t/2)}{2[(t/4) - \mu^2]^{1/2}[(t/4) - M^2]^{1/2}}$$

In particular we note that the high energy, small t physical region of the s-channel corresponds to $-\cos\theta_t \gg 1$. This fact makes life simple for calculations of s-channel scattering with Regge poles in the t-channel.

Kinematic Singularities and Threshold Restriction

The familiar decomposition for $\bar{\pi}\pi \to N\bar{N}$ in terms of invariant amplitudes $A(s, t, u)$ and $B(s, t, u)$ is

$$\bar{u}_\lambda(p')\left[-A + i\gamma\cdot\left(\frac{q-\bar{q}}{2}\right)B\right]v_{\bar{\lambda}}(\bar{p})$$

where the bars denote momenta or helicities of antiparticles. The t-channel helicity amplitudes are obtained by evaluating this expression in the corresponding c.m. frame. Straightforward manipulation leads to the result

$$f_{++}(t,s) = (t-4M^2)^{-1/2}\left[(4M^2-t)A + M(s-u)B\right]$$

$$f_{+-}(t,s) = \frac{2\sqrt{t}\,p_t\,k_t\sin\theta_t}{(t-4M^2)^{1/2}}B$$

In addition to the dynamical singularities of A and B implied by the Mandelstam representation, the amplitudes $f_{\bar{\lambda}\lambda}$ possess kinematic singularities. In the process of Reggeizing it is important to work with kinematic singularity-free helicity amplitudes $\tilde{f}_{\bar{\lambda}\lambda}$. In our example these modified amplitudes are

$$\tilde{f}_{++}(t,s) = (4M^2-t)A + M(s-u)B$$

$$\tilde{f}_{+-}(t,s) = B$$

At the normal threshold $t = 4M^2$ both helicity amplitudes become proportional to the B amplitude and their ratio is given by

$$(\tilde{f}_{++}/\tilde{f}_{+-})_{t=4M^2} = M(s-u)$$

This threshold restriction must later be imposed on our Regge pole helicity amplitudes.

Cross Sections

The differential cross section for the s-channel process is

$$\frac{d\sigma}{dt} = \frac{1}{64\pi s p_s^2}\left[|g_{++}|^2 + |g_{+-}|^2\right]$$

where g_{++} and g_{+-} are s-channel helicity amplitudes. The orthogonality of the crossing matrix for helicity amplitudes leads to the alternative expression:

$$\frac{d\sigma}{dt} = \frac{1}{64\pi s p_s^2}[|f_{++}|^2 + |f_{+-}|^2]$$

where $f_{\bar{\lambda}\lambda}$ are t-channel amplitudes continued in the variables s and t to the s-channel physical region. The s-channel polarization in the direction

$$\hat{n} = (\mathbf{p}_i \times \mathbf{p}_f)/ |\mathbf{p}_i \times \mathbf{p}_f|$$

is given by

$$P(s,t) = -\frac{\sin\theta_s}{16\pi\sqrt{s}} \frac{Im(\hat{f}_{++}\hat{f}_{+-}^*)}{(4M^2 - t)}\left(\frac{d\sigma}{dt}\right)^{-1}$$

Finally, from the optical theorem for elastic amplitudes, the total cross section can be expressed as

$$\sigma_t(s) = \frac{1}{4M^2 p_{\text{Lab}}} Im\,\bar{f}_{++}(s, t=0)$$

Sommerfeld–Watson Transformation

The partial wave expansions of the kinematic singularity-free t-channel amplitudes are

$$\bar{f}_{++}(t,s) = \sum_J (2J+1)\hat{f}_{++}(J,t)P_J(z_t)$$

$$\bar{f}_{+-}(t,s) = -\sum_J (2J+1)\bar{f}_{+-}(J,t)\frac{P_J'(z_t)}{[J(J+1)]^{1/2}}$$

In order to make an analytic continuation of

$$\bar{f}_{++}(J,t) \qquad \text{and} \qquad \frac{\bar{f}_{+-}(J,t)}{[J(J+1)]^{1/2}}$$

into the complex J plane, we must treat separately even and odd J amplitudes. Physically, this separation is required by the possible existence of exchange forces which make the dynamics of even and odd J differ. The separation is accomplished by the replacement

$$P_J(\cos\theta_t) = [P_J(\cos\theta_t) + \tau P_J(-\cos\theta_t)]/2$$

where $\tau = (-)^J$ is the signature quantum number. Henceforth the $\tau = +1$ and $\tau = -1$ terms are handled independently. The sums over J can be expressed as integrals around a contour C_1 that encloses the integer points on the positive real axis. Thus, for example

$$\bar{f}_{++} = \frac{i}{4} \int_{C_1} dJ(2J+1)\frac{\bar{f}_{++}(J,t)}{\sin \pi J}[P_J(-\cos\theta_t) + \tau P_J(\cos\theta_t)]$$

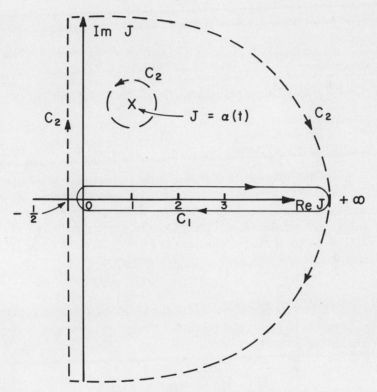

Figure 3.1. Contours C_1 and C_2 in the complex J plane used in the derivation of the Regge pole representation for the scattering amplitude.

We now make the dynamical postulate that the partial wave amplitudes $f_{++}(J, t)$ are meromorphic functions of J. The positions $J = \alpha_i(t)$ of these (Regge) poles in the complex angular momentum plane move with t. In order to isolate the Regge pole contributions to f_{++} we can continuously distort contour C_1 into C_2 as shown in Figure 3.1 with no change in the integral. The integral around the infinite semicircle gives no contribution. The background integral

$$\frac{i}{4} \int\limits_{-1/2-i\infty}^{-1/2+i\infty} dJ(2J+1)\frac{\bar{f}_{++}(J,t)}{\sin \pi J}[P_J(-z_t) + \tau P_J(z_t)]$$

can be neglected for t values of interest or pushed further into the left half J plane. We are then left with only Regge pole contributions to f_{++}. Representing a single pole by the form

$$\bar{f}_{++}(J,t) = \frac{\beta_{++}(t)}{J - \alpha(t)}$$

we obtain from the Cauchy formula on the contours surrounding the poles the desired result that

$$\bar{f}_{++}(t,s) = -\pi \sum_{\substack{\text{Regge} \\ \text{poles}}} (\alpha + \tfrac{1}{2})\beta_{++}\frac{1 + \tau e^{-i\pi\alpha}}{\sin \pi\alpha}P_\alpha(-z_t)$$

Extrapolation to Particle Poles

Before proceeding to calculate scattering in the s-channel due to a t-channel Regge pole, we shall briefly demonstrate the connection of the above Regge amplitude with the Feynman graph for a t-channel meson exchange with fixed spin J. For definiteness consider a $\tau = -1$ pole. The first physical realization of this trajectory as a particle of mass M will occur at $t = M^2$ with $J = \text{Re } \alpha(M^2) = 1$. In this vicinity the denominator, $\sin \pi\alpha$, can be expanded as

$$\sin \pi\alpha(t) \approx -\pi\alpha'_R(M^2)(t - M^2) - i\pi\alpha_I(M^2)$$

where R and I subscripts denote real and imaginary parts, respectively, of the trajectory function. In the above expansion we have assumed that α_I is small. The amplitude $\bar{f}_{++}$ becomes

$$\bar{f}_{++}(t,s) \approx \frac{3[\beta_{++}(M^2)/\alpha'_R(M^2)]P_1(z_t)}{M^2 - t - i\alpha_I(M^2)/\alpha'_R(M^2)}$$

The result is cast in the form of a Breit–Wigner resonance amplitude for an unstable particle with full width

$$\Gamma = \alpha_I(M^2)/[M\alpha'_R(M^2)]$$

In the case of a stable particle the Regge amplitude extrapolates to the S-matrix energy pole at $\alpha(M^2) = J$ (i.e., to the renormalized Born approximation of quantum field theory) and β will be proportional to the product of the coupling constants of the Feynman amplitude. The $\tau = -1$ Regge amplitude also reduces to a Breit–Wigner form at Re $\alpha(t) = 3, 5, \ldots$ corresponding to the spins of higher mass particle recurrences.

Regge Exchange Amplitudes

In order to calculate s-channel scattering due to the t-channel Regge poles, the Regge amplitudes must be continued to the region $t \leqslant 0, s \geqslant (M + \mu)^2$. The Regge pole approximation to the complete amplitude is nominally expected to be valid only for $s \gg M^2$ and $s \gg |t|$. For this kinematic region, considerable simplification occurs in the Regge formula. As noted previously, the cosine of the t-channel scattering angle then satisfies $-z_t \gg 1$. In this limit we can use the asymptotic expansion of the Legendre function,

$$P_\alpha(-z_t) \to \frac{\Gamma(\alpha + 1/2)}{\Gamma(\alpha + 1)} \frac{(-2z_t)^\alpha}{\Gamma(1/2)}$$

for $\alpha > -1/2$. For $\alpha < -1/2$ the background integral must first be pushed to the left of $J = -1/2$ and in our Regge pole amplitude the function

$$\frac{P_\alpha(-z_t)}{\sin \pi \alpha}$$

is replaced by

$$\frac{-Q_{-\alpha-1}(-z_t)}{\pi \cos \pi \alpha}$$

The form of the asymptotic expansion remains the same as above however. Of course in pushing the background to the left we realistically expect to pick up additional contributions in the Regge pole summation from lower lying trajectories.

Using the asymptotic formula for the high energy limit in the s-channel, the t-channel helicity amplitude becomes

$$\tilde{f}_{++} \sim \frac{\Gamma(\alpha + 3/2)}{\Gamma(\alpha + 1)} \beta_{++} \frac{1 + \tau e^{-i\pi\alpha}}{\sin \pi \alpha} \left(\frac{s - u}{2p_t k_t}\right)^\alpha$$

A threshold barrier factor $(p_t k_t / s_0)^\alpha$ is to be extracted from β_{++} to construct a reduced residue γ_{++} with suitable analytic properties. In addition the residue β_{++} of the leading trajectory must have zeros at $\alpha = -3/2, -7/2, \ldots$ to cancel the unphysical poles from $\Gamma(\alpha + 3/2)$. Thus we write

$$\beta_{++} = \frac{1}{\Gamma(\alpha + 3/2)} \left(\frac{p_t k_t}{s_0}\right)^\alpha \gamma_{++}$$

where s_0 is an energy scale factor. This leads to the final form of the asymptotic Regge amplitude for the nonflip helicity amplitude $\tilde{f}_{++} = \gamma_{++} R(s, t)$, with $R(s, t)$ the standard Regge amplitude for scattering with spinless particles:

$$R(s, t) = \frac{1}{\Gamma(\alpha + 1)} \frac{1 + \tau e^{-i\pi\alpha}}{\sin \pi\alpha} \left(\frac{s - u}{2s_0}\right)^\alpha$$

An analogous derivation for $\tilde{f}_{+-}$ produces the result

$$\tilde{f}_{+-} = \alpha\gamma_{+-} \frac{R(s, t)}{(-4Mp_t k_t \cos \theta_t)}$$

The additional factor of α can be traced back to the occurrence of P_J' in the partial wave expansion of $\tilde{f}_{+-}$. Using these results, the final forms of the t-channel helicity amplitudes in the Regge pole approximation are

$$f_{++} = \frac{\gamma_{++}(t)}{(t - 4M^2)^{1/2}} R(s, t)$$

$$f_{+-} = \frac{\alpha(t)\gamma_{+-}(t)}{(t - 4M^2)^{1/2}} \frac{\sqrt{t}\sin \theta_t}{(-2M \cos \theta_t)} R(s, t)$$

The reduced residues $\gamma_{\bar{\lambda}\lambda}(t)$ appearing above are free of any kinematic singularities. Both trajectory and reduced residues develop imaginary parts above the t-channel threshold $t = 4\mu_\pi^2$. In practice we assume that they are real for $t \ll 4\mu_\pi^2$ and satisfy dispersion relations with only a right-hand cut.

The helicity nonflip and flip amplitudes from a single Regge pole have the same phase and energy dependence. This is a fact of considerable import in the description of high energy scattering data. Substituting the helicity amplitudes in the formula for the differential cross section we obtain for the $-z_t \gg 1$ limit:

$$\frac{d\sigma}{dt} = \frac{|R(s, t)|^2}{64\pi s p_s^2} \frac{1}{4M^2 - t}\left[\gamma_{++}(t)^2 - \frac{t}{4M^2}\alpha^2 \gamma_{+-}(t)^2\right]$$

In writing this result the reality of $\alpha(t)$ and $\gamma_{\bar{\lambda}\lambda}(t)$ for $t \leqslant 0$ has been used.

Threshold Condition

The residues are arbitrary functions except to the extent that the threshold restriction

$$(\tilde{f}_{++}/\tilde{f}_{+-})_{t=4M^2} = M(s - u)$$

is satisfied. The resulting constraint on the residues is

$$\left[\frac{\alpha(t)\gamma_{+-}(t)}{\gamma_{++}(t)}\right]_{t=4M^2} = 1$$

When this threshold relation is taken into account, the spurious $(4M^2 - t)^{-1}$ pole-like factor in the differential cross section expression above is cancelled provided that the variables (s, t) lie in the physical region of the s-channel. To see this, we write for arbitrary t

$$\gamma_{+-}(t) = \gamma(t)$$

$$\gamma_{++}(t) = \alpha(t)\,\gamma_{+-}(t) + \lambda(t)\left(1 - \frac{t}{4M^2}\right)$$

where $\lambda(t)$ is finite at $t = 4M^2$. Then upon substitution we obtain

$$\frac{d\sigma}{dt} = \frac{|R(s,t)|^2}{64\pi s p_s^2}\frac{1}{4M^2}\left[\lambda^2\left(1 - \frac{t}{4M^2}\right) + \alpha(2\lambda + \alpha\gamma)\gamma\right]$$

The differential cross section in this form has the proper behavior in t.

Energy Dependence

The energy dependence of the Regge amplitude

$$R(s,t) \sim \left(\frac{s-u}{2s_0}\right)^{\alpha(t)}$$

can be cast in several forms:

$$\left(\frac{s-u}{2s_0}\right)^{\alpha} = \left(\frac{s - M^2 - \mu^2 + t/2}{s_0}\right)^{\alpha} = \left(\frac{E_{\text{Lab}} + t/4M}{E_0}\right)^{\alpha}$$

In the last form we have introduced $E_0 = (s_0/2M)$. For high energy and small t the approximate forms

$$\left(\frac{E_{\text{Lab}}}{E_0}\right)^{\alpha}, \quad \left(\frac{s}{s_0}\right)^{\alpha}$$

are commonly used in the literature.

If $\alpha_1(t)$ and $\alpha_2(t)$ are the two highest trajectories for $t \leqslant 0$ then the cross sections will behave asymptotically $(s \to \infty)$ as

$$\sigma_t(s) \to C(0)\left(\frac{s}{s_0}\right)^{\alpha_1(0)-1}$$

$$\frac{d\sigma}{dt}(s,t) \to F(t)\left(\frac{s}{s_0}\right)^{2\alpha_1(t)-2}$$

$$P(s,t) \to G(t)\left(\frac{s}{s_0}\right)^{[\alpha_2(t)-\alpha_1(t)]}$$

Since a single Regge pole gives $\bar{f}_{++}$ and $\bar{f}_{+-}$ the same phase, one pole alone gives no polarization. The leading term in the polarization must therefore come from interference between two poles.

The Froissart bound on the asymptotic total cross section

$$\sigma_t(s) < C \ln^2\left(\frac{s}{s_0}\right) \qquad \text{as} \qquad s \to \infty$$

has been proved from the axioms of quantum field theory. In the Regge pole framework this bound requires $\alpha_1(0) \leqslant 1$ for the leading trajectory. If total cross sections approach constant limits asymptotically, as suggested by experiment, then $\alpha_1(0) = 1$. The signature for this pole must be $\tau = +1$, since a $\tau = -1$ Regge pole amplitude is real at $\alpha = 1$.

Shrinkage

If we parametrize the trajectory as $\alpha(t) = \alpha(0) + t\alpha'(0)$ for small $t \leqslant 0$, then the differential cross section for a process mediated by a single Regge exchange can be written

$$\frac{d\sigma}{dt} = F(t)\left(\frac{s}{s_0}\right)^{2\alpha(0)-2} \exp\left[t\, 2\alpha'(0) \ln(s/s_0)\right]$$

From assignments of particles as recurrences on trajectories as in Chapter 1, we are led to expect $\alpha'(0) \approx 1$ (BeV/c)$^{-2}$. Thus in the Regge pole exchange model it is natural to expect to find shrinkage of the forward peak with energy. The standard method of determining Regge trajectories from scattering data relies on the s dependence at fixed t:

$$\alpha(t) = 1 + \frac{1}{2} \cdot \ln\left[\frac{(d\sigma/dt)(s_2, t)}{(d\sigma/dt)(s_1, t)}\right] \bigg/ \ln[s_2/s_1]$$

For reactions mediated by single Regge pole exchange, the slopes determined by use of this formula are typically about 1 (BeV/c)$^{-2}$.

Signature Factor

The phase of a meson Regge pole amplitude is completely specified by the trajectory through its signature factor

$$\mathscr{S}_\alpha{}^\tau \equiv \frac{1 + \tau e^{-i\pi\alpha}}{\sin \pi\alpha}$$

Alternative useful forms for this factor are

$$\mathscr{S}_\alpha^+ = \frac{\exp(-i\pi\alpha/2)}{\sin(\pi\alpha/2)} = \cot\left(\frac{\pi\alpha}{2}\right) - i \qquad \text{for} \qquad \tau = +1$$

and

$$\mathscr{S}_\alpha^- = \frac{i\exp(-i\pi\alpha/2)}{\cos(\pi\alpha/2)} = \tan\left(\frac{\pi\alpha}{2}\right) + i \qquad \text{for} \qquad \tau = -1$$

As a matter of terminology, integral values of $\alpha = J_0$ at which $(-)^{J_0} = \tau$ are called "right signature points"; conversely "wrong signature points" have $(-)^{J_0} = -\tau$. The signature factor is $\infty \mp i$ at right signature points and $0 \mp i$ at wrong signature points.

Wrong Signature, Nonsense Zeros of Amplitudes

The essential α dependence of the t-channel $\pi\pi \to \bar{N}N$ amplitudes was

$$f_{++} \sim \frac{1}{\Gamma(\alpha+1)} \cdot \mathscr{S}_\alpha^\tau$$

$$f_{+-} \sim \frac{\alpha}{\Gamma(\alpha+1)} \cdot \mathscr{S}_\alpha^\tau$$

In the subsequent discussion we consider for definiteness a $\tau = -1$ Regge pole. From the above expressions we conclude that f_{++} vanishes at wrong signature points with $\alpha = -2, -4, \ldots$ and f_{+-} vanishes at wrong signature points with $\alpha = 0, -2, -4, \ldots$. To interpret the physical origin of such amplitude zeros, we note that in the t-channel the $\bar{N}N$ form a state of zero helicity in f_{++} and unit helicity in f_{+-}. At $\alpha = 0$ the exchanged trajectory acts like a spin-zero particle under three-dimensional (Euclidean) rotations and cannot support a unit of helicity; hence there is a zero in f_{+-} at $\alpha = 0$ but not in f_{++}. The point $\alpha = 0$ is therefore a *nonsense* value of angular momentum for f_{+-} and a *sense* value for f_{++}. The points $\alpha = -1, -2, -3, \ldots$ of the angular momentum are nonsense for both helicity amplitudes. For arbitrary fractional α we may think of a superposition of all integers J being present. We conclude that the dependence on α causes Regge pole helicity amplitudes to vanish at *wrong signature, nonsense* values of the trajectory $\alpha(t)$. This conclusion has a special relevance to the interpretation of dips observed experimentally in differential cross sections at fixed t values. Such an interpretation of the data will be explored in subsequent chapters.

The situation at wrong signature, nonsense values of $\alpha(t)$ is in fact more complicated than the above intuitive arguments would suggest. A scattering amplitude with a third double spectral function ρ_{su} possesses fixed poles at wrong signature, nonsense values of J, and the existence of these fixed poles modifies our previous conclusions regarding amplitude zeros. The fixed poles do not change the s^α Regge pole energy dependence of the asymptotic amplitude; their only effect is to modify the behavior of the residue of the moving pole. In the $\pi\pi \to \bar{N}N$ example the behavior $f_{+-} \sim \alpha(t)C s^{\alpha(t)}$ would be modified to

$$f_{+-} \sim [\alpha(t) \cdot C + D] s^{\alpha(t)}$$

by the presence of a fixed pole at $J = 0$. If the effect of the fixed pole is small (D small), then the former position of the fixed pole at $\alpha(t_0) = 0$ will be only slightly displaced from t_0. On the other hand if D is large, then branch cuts in the angular momentum plane are also expected and simple Regge pole behavior should no longer be observed.

To summarize, the amplitude zeros at wrong signature, nonsense points require that $\rho_{su} = 0$. Fixed poles at these points originate as first order effects in ρ_{su} and displace the positions of the amplitude zeros. The branch cuts are second order effects in ρ_{su}. The present experimental situation seems to favor a small ρ_{su} inasmuch as energy dependences are explainable in terms of Regge poles alone (branch cuts are not necessary) and the predicted dips at wrong signature, nonsense values of α seem to occur roughly at the expected t values, properly correlated with the trajectories. The problem of experimentally establishing the first order effects of ρ_{su} through differential cross section measurements is exceedingly difficult. Normally a contribution of some other lower lying trajectory can have similar effects of partially filling a dip or producing a slight shift in its position.

Ghost States

For right signature points the term $\mathscr{S}_\alpha{}^\tau/\Gamma(\alpha + 1)$ is finite except at $\alpha = 0$ for $\tau = 1$ or $\alpha = 1$ for $\tau = -1$. Suppose then that $\alpha(t) = 0$ at some $t < 0$ for a $\tau = +1$ Regge pole. A "ghost" state appears which represents a t-channel particle with $(\text{mass})^2 < 0$. In the f_{+-} amplitude the kinematic factor of $\alpha(t)$ cancels the pole. However the pole in the f_{++} amplitude leaves the unacceptable situation of an infinity in the s-channel scattering. As a minimal requirement the nonflip residue must develop a zero to kill the ghost

$$\gamma_{++}(t) \sim \alpha(t)\, C(t) \qquad \text{near} \qquad \alpha(t) = 0$$

Beyond this essential α dependence, the residues may acquire additional dynamical factors of $(\alpha - J_0)$ at the exceptional points $\alpha(t) = J_0$, $J_0 = 0, -1, -2, \ldots$. The behavior of residues at these values of α plays an important role in Regge phenomenology. We will return shortly to further considerations relevant to behavior of residues at exceptional points.

Factorization

The t-channel Regge pole amplitude reduces to a Breit-Wigner resonance amplitude in the vicinity of the mass ($t \simeq M^2$) of a particle on the trajectory. Since
the numerator of the Breit-Wigner resonance pole factors into a product of partial widths of formation and decay channels, we likewise expect the Regge residue
to factorize for $t \simeq M^2$. Factorization of Regge pole residues at arbitrary t can be
proven in potential scattering from generalization of unitarity to complex J. This
factorization property is generally assumed to apply also to relativistic theory.
Thus for a Regge pole in the t-channel $\bar{c} + b \rightarrow \bar{a} + d$, the partial wave amplitude
can be written as

$$f(J, t) = \frac{\beta_{\bar{c}b}(t)\,\beta_{\bar{a}d}(t)}{J - \alpha(t)}$$

In this form the couplings of the Regge pole to the initial and final t-channel
states appear as vertex coupling strengths of the exchange.

The factorization property has far-reaching consequences for the analysis of
experimental data. Despite its usefulness, however, it has not yet been possible
to subject this principle to direct experimental test. As a particularly simple
example of a prediction following from factorization, we consider the spin-
averaged forward scattering amplitudes for $\pi\pi$, πN, and NN elastic scattering.
Each Regge pole contributes terms like

$$f_{\pi\pi} \sim (\beta_{\pi\pi})^2 \, \mathscr{S}_\alpha{}^\tau \cdot \left(\frac{E_{\mathrm{Lab}}}{E_0}\right)^{\alpha(0)}$$

$$f_{\pi N} \sim \beta_{\pi\pi}\,\beta_{\bar{N}N} \, \mathscr{S}_\alpha{}^\tau \cdot \left(\frac{E_{\mathrm{Lab}}}{E_0}\right)^{\alpha(0)}$$

$$f_{NN} \sim (\beta_{\bar{N}N})^2 \, \mathscr{S}_\alpha{}^\tau \cdot \left(\frac{E_{\mathrm{Lab}}}{E_0}\right)^{\alpha(0)}$$

where $\beta_{\pi\pi}$ and $\beta_{\bar{N}N}$ characterize the $t = 0$, nonflip couplings at the π and N vertices. At asymptotic energies only the leading Regge pole contribution survives,
and from the optical theorem we obtain

$$\sigma_t^{\pi\pi}(\infty)\,\sigma_t^{NN}(\infty) = [\sigma_t^{\pi N}(\infty)]^2$$

In the next chapter the factorization principle will be used in applying SU(3)
symmetry to Regge residue factors.

Sense–Nonsense Residue Zeros

In the discussion of the ghost-killing mechanism we alluded to the possibility of dynamical zeros of the residues at the exceptional points $\alpha(t) = J_0$, $J_0 = 0, -1, -2, \ldots$. Since the behavior of the residues at these angular momentum values is crucial to the Regge interpretation of minima in cross sections, we shall discuss this problem in some detail for the exceptional point $\alpha = 0$. Our discussion will be limited to the leading asymptotic power s^α of the Regge amplitude.

The residue factors for the coupling of the exchanged Regge pole to $\pi\pi, \bar{N}N$ helicity nonflip, and $\bar{N}N$ helicity flip will be denoted by $\pi\pi \to f$, $(\bar{N}N)_{++} \to g$, and $(\bar{N}N)_{+-} \to h$. The t-channel helicity amplitudes for $\pi\pi \to \pi\pi$, $\pi\pi \to \bar{N}N$, and $\bar{N}N \to \bar{N}N$ have kinematical factors of $\sqrt{\alpha}$ and α that come from the rotation functions of the partial wave expansion. For example, in the helicity flip amplitude for $\pi\pi \to \bar{N}N$, the partial wave expansion involves $P_J'/[J(J+1)]^{1/2}$ which leads to a kinematical factor of $\sqrt{\alpha}$ near $\alpha = 0$:

$$f_{+-}(\pi\pi \to \bar{N}N) \sim (\alpha)^{1/2} fh s^\alpha$$

The complete kinematic α structure for the above three t-channel reactions can be read from the following matrix:

$$
\begin{array}{cc}
& \begin{array}{ccc} (\pi\pi) & \quad (\bar{N}N)_{++} & \quad (\bar{N}N)_{+-} \end{array} \\
\begin{array}{c} (\pi\pi) \\ (\bar{N}N)_{++} \\ (\bar{N}N)_{+-} \end{array} &
\left(\begin{array}{ccc}
f^2 & fg & (\alpha)^{1/2} fh \\
fg & g^2 & (\alpha)^{1/2} gh \\
(\alpha)^{1/2} fh & (\alpha)^{1/2} gh & \alpha h^2
\end{array} \right) \cdot \mathscr{S}_\alpha^\tau
\end{array}
$$

Since we are presently considering these amplitudes only near $\alpha = 0$, right signature corresponds to $\tau = +1$ and wrong signature to $\tau = -1$. The signature factor goes like $\mathscr{S}_\alpha^\tau \sim 1/\alpha$ for right signature and $\mathscr{S}_\alpha^\tau \sim 1$ for wrong signature.

At $\alpha = 0$ the f and g residue factors correspond to transitions allowed by angular momentum considerations and h corresponds to a forbidden transition. Hence f and g are sometimes called *sense* residue factors and h a *nonsense* residue factor.

The behavior of the residue factor f, g, and h must be such that all the helicity amplitudes are free from branch points or poles at $\alpha = 0$. From the matrix we can conclude that

$$gh \sim \alpha^{m/2} \qquad fh \sim \alpha^{n/2} \qquad m = 1, 3, 5, \ldots \quad n = 1, 3, 5, \ldots$$

Four possibilities for the behavior of the residues that satisfy the analyticity criteria at $\alpha = 0$ have been considered in the literature. They are as follows.

f	g	h	Mechanism name
1	1	$\sqrt{\alpha}$	sense (wrong signature only)
$\sqrt{\alpha}$	$\sqrt{\alpha}$	1	nonsense (or Gell-Mann)
$\sqrt{\alpha}$	$\sqrt{\alpha}$	α	Chew
α	α	$\sqrt{\alpha}$	no-compensation

The sense mechanism is impossible for the right signature point since the $\pi\pi \to \pi\pi$ and $\pi\pi \to (\bar{N}N)_{++}$ amplitudes would have a pole at $\alpha = 0$.

It is instructive to compare the overall α dependence near $\alpha = 0$ for the $\pi\pi \to \bar{N}N$ amplitudes obtained from the various mechanisms:

f_{++}	f_{+-}	Mechanism
$1\mathscr{S}_\alpha{}^\tau$	$\alpha\mathscr{S}_\alpha{}^\tau$	sense
$\alpha\mathscr{S}_\alpha{}^\tau$	$\alpha\mathscr{S}_\alpha{}^\tau$	nonsense
$\alpha\mathscr{S}_\alpha{}^\tau$	$\alpha^2\mathscr{S}_\alpha{}^\tau$	Chew
$\alpha^2\mathscr{S}_\alpha{}^\tau$	$\alpha^2\mathscr{S}_\alpha{}^\tau$	no-compensation

In our earlier derivation of the $\pi\pi \to \bar{N}N$ Regge pole formulas we assumed the sense mechanism for simplicity. The nonsense mechanism corresponds to our earlier discussion of ghost killing. The Chew and no-compensation mechanisms correspond just to the multiplication by a factor of α of all the terms in the choosing-sense or Gell-Mann mechanisms (i.e., the residues acquire an additional factor of α through the dynamics).

Present theory does not give us clues as to which mechanism nature chooses for the residues. Consequently the choice must be made through phenomenological analysis of data. There are indications that the ρ trajectory ($\tau = -1$) chooses the sense mechanism at $\alpha = 0$ and the f^0 trajectory ($\tau = +1$) chooses the no-compensation mechanism at $\alpha = 0$. These deductions will be discussed in later chapters.

Finally, as we mentioned earlier, the situation at wrong signature, nonsense points is even more complicated if there are fixed poles. The behavior of that part of the residue factor which comes from a fixed pole at $J = 0$ is $f \sim 1/\sqrt{\alpha}$, $g \sim 1/\sqrt{\alpha}$, $h \sim 1/\alpha$ for sense or nonsense mechanisms, and $f \sim \sqrt{\alpha}$, $g \sim \sqrt{\alpha}$,

$h \sim 1$ for Chew or no-compensation mechanisms. The fixed pole residue contribution is to be added to the normal residue.

The methods discussed in this section for determining the behavior of residues at the $\alpha = 0$ exceptional point can be applied to $\alpha(t) = J_0$ where $J_0 = 0, -1, -2, \ldots$

t Dependence of Residues

The reduced Regge residues $\gamma(\alpha(t), t)$ can, in general, depend on t both explicitly and implicitly through $\alpha(t)$. Present relativistic theory does not provide us with a calculational basis to determine the residues and we are forced to rely heavily on empirical parameterizations. Potential scattering theory results suggest that the entire dependence of the residues on t could be through $\alpha(t)$.

After the appropriate sense–nonsense factors of $(\alpha(t) - J_0)$ are extracted from the residue, we are faced with the problem of parameterizing the remainder, which we denote by $\bar{\gamma}(t)$. Since the Regge amplitude involves

$$\bar{\gamma}(t)\left(\frac{s}{s_0}\right)^{\alpha(t)}$$

it is clear that different choices of the scaling parameter s_0 should produce different variations with t or $\bar{\gamma}(t)$. In the literature two different approaches to the parameterization problem have been proposed. One is to treat $\bar{\gamma}$ as a constant or slowly varying function of t and allow s_0 as an abitrary parameter. The other approach has been to fix s_0, usually at 1 (BeV/c)^2, and allow $\bar{\gamma}(t)$ to be a rapidly varying function such as $\bar{\gamma}(t) = Ce^{Dt}$. There is very little practical difference in the two approaches since the Regge amplitude for a linear trajectory can be written as

$$[Cs_0^{-\alpha(0)}] \exp\{t[D - \alpha'(0)\ln s_0]\} s^{\alpha(t)}$$

and an appropriate choice of s_0 can therefore lead to a $D = 0$.

The flexibility in the t dependence of the residues is the greatest deficiency of present Regge pole theory. For the moment we must be content to fix empirically the unknown residue parameters from experiment. One of the most pressing unsolved theoretical problems is the development of a technique for dynamical calculations of Regge residues. Finite energy sum rules are a step in the direction of a solution for this problem. We defer the discussion of this approach to Chapter 10.

Line Reversal

The two s-channel processes

(I) $\quad a + b \rightarrow c + d$

(II) $\quad \bar{c} + b \rightarrow \bar{a} + d$

have t-channels that differ only by the interchange of initial particles

(I) $\quad \bar{c} + a \rightarrow d + \bar{b}$

(II) $\quad a + \bar{c} \rightarrow d + \bar{b}$

Line   Reversed   Reactions

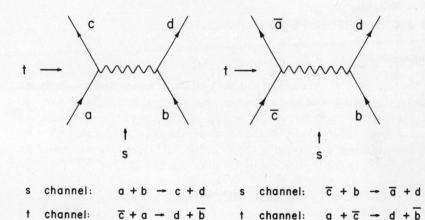

s channel: $\quad a + b \rightarrow c + d \qquad$ s channel: $\quad \bar{c} + b \rightarrow \bar{a} + d$

t channel: $\quad \bar{c} + a \rightarrow d + \bar{b} \qquad$ t channel: $\quad a + \bar{c} \rightarrow d + \bar{b}$

Figure 3.2. Schematic illustration of a t-channel Regge pole in line reversed reactions.

For spinless particles the amplitude for (II) is obtained from (I) by changing $z_t \rightarrow -z_t$ in the t-channel partial wave expansion. Hence

$$f_I^J \sim P_J(-z_t) + \tau P_J(z_t)$$

$$f_{II}^J \sim P_J(z_t) + \tau P_J(-z_t)$$

or equivalently for integral J

$$f_{II}^J \sim \tau[P_J(-z_t) + \tau P_J(z_t)]$$

As a consequence, a t-channel Regge pole contributes the same amplitude to both reactions, within a factor of $\tau = \pm 1$, which is just the signature of the Regge exchange. Figure 3.2 illustrates a Regge pole in the two line reversed reactions.

A similar connection exists for the Regge pole contribution to line reversed reactions involving external particles with spin. The line reversed factors are determined by the Lorentz transformation property of the couplings. The meson Regge pole contribution to the amplitude for the process $\pi^+ + p \to K^+ + \Sigma^+$ is multiplied by τ in the amplitude for the reaction $K^- + p \to \pi^- + \Sigma^+$. Line reversal of two spin 1/2 particles multiplies the meson Regge pole amplitude by the factor $\tau \epsilon$ where $\epsilon = -1$ if $\tau = -1$, $P = +1$, and $\epsilon = +1$ otherwise. Strange meson Regge pole contributions to the reactions $\Lambda + p \to \Lambda + p$ and $\bar{p} + p \to \bar{\Lambda} + \Lambda$ would therefore differ only by a factor of $\tau \epsilon$. In Chapters 4 and 5 we shall discuss various applications and experimental tests of line reversal for Regge pole exchange models of scattering processes.

3.3 FERMION REGGE POLES

Kinematics

The treatment of fermion Regge poles introduces several new problems and features that were not encountered in our discussion of meson Regge poles in πN elastic scattering. In this section we will concentrate on these different aspects of Regge theory. Again we shall consider the s-channel reaction $\pi N \to \pi N$. The fermion Regge poles occur in the u-channel that represents the crossed process $\bar{\pi} N \to \bar{\pi} N$. In the physical region for the u-channel we have

$$u = [(p_u^2 + M^2)^{1/2} + (p_u^2 + \mu^2)^{1/2}]^2$$

where p_u is the c.m. momentum. The cosine of the u-channel scattering angle is given by

$$z_u = \cos \theta_u = -\frac{[s - t - (M^2 - \mu^2)^2/u]}{4p_u^2} = -\frac{[s - M^2 - \mu^2 + u/2 - (M^2 - \mu^2)^2/2u]}{2p_u^2}$$

Daughter Trajectories

For the s-channel physical region, $-1 \leqslant \cos \theta_s \leqslant +1$, the range of the momentum transfer u is

$$(M^2 - \mu^2)^2/s \geqslant u \geqslant 2M^2 + 2\mu^2 - s$$

For the backward cone defined by $(M^2 - \mu^2)^2/s \geqslant u \geqslant 0$, it is easy to verify that $|z_u| \leqslant 1$ for any value of s. This bound on $|z_u|$ occurs as a result of unequal masses, $M \neq \mu$.

Since in the backward cone $|z_u|$ does not become large with increasing s, the conventional Regge representation, $P_\alpha(z_u)$ for spinless particles, does not lead to an $(s - t)^{\alpha(u)}$ asymptotic limit. If $P_\alpha(z_u)$ is expanded in powers of $(s - t)$

$$P_\alpha(z_u) = \sum_{m=0}^{\infty} C_m(s - t)^{\alpha(u) - m}$$

then C_0 is regular at $u = 0$ but all the other C_m are singular there. In order to restore the asymptotic $(s - t)^{\alpha(u)}$ dependence in the unequal mass problem and have Mandelstam analyticity of the complete amplitude at $u = 0$, Freedman and Wang proposed that there must exist a sequence of "daughter" trajectories $\alpha_m(u)$ passing through

$$\alpha_m(0) = \alpha(0) - m, \; m = 1, 2, \ldots$$

and having singular residues that cancel the singular behavior of the C_m for $m \neq 0$. The daughter trajectories have the same internal quantum numbers of the parent, with signature and parity related to those of the parent by $\tau_m = (-1)^m \tau_0$ and $P_m = (-1)^m P_0$. The existence of such daughter trajectories can be established in certain field theory models. These models indicate that it is unlikely that the daughter trajectories will rise for $u > 0$ to intersect physical J values and therefore should not lead to particle manifestations. The present phenomenological importance of daughter trajectories appears to be limited to the reinstatement of the $(s - t)^{\alpha(u)}$ asymptotic behavior of the parent trajectory. The daughter trajectories also contribute nonsingular terms of order $(s - t)^{\alpha(u) - m}$ with $m = 1, 2, \ldots$. However, these powers are of the same order as the secondary contributions from the parent trajectory that are usually neglected in high energy data analysis. Hereafter in writing the asymptotic Regge term in unequal mass situations we use the mnemonic:

$$\left(\frac{p_u^2}{s_0}\right)^\alpha P_\alpha(z_u) \to \frac{1}{\Gamma(1/2)} \cdot \frac{\Gamma(\alpha + 1/2)}{\Gamma(\alpha + 1)} \cdot \left(\frac{s - t}{2s_0}\right)^\alpha$$

Parity-Conserving Helicity Amplitudes

In the t-channel $\pi\pi \to \bar{N}N$, the coupling of the meson Regge pole to the $\pi\pi$ state restricts the exchange quantum numbers to $\tau P = +1$. The u-channel $\pi N \to \pi N$ permits both $\tau P = +1$ and $\tau P = -1$ exchanges. In this case it is convenient to use parity-conserving helicity amplitudes $F^{(\tau P)}$ whose asymptotic limit involves only exchanges with definite (τP) quantum number.

The Feynman amplitude in the u-channel is

$$\bar{u}_{\lambda'}(p')\left[-A - i\gamma\cdot\left(\frac{\bar{q}+\bar{q}'}{2}\right)B\right]u_{\lambda}(p)$$

The parity-conserving amplitudes are defined by

$$F^{\pm} = \frac{1}{\sqrt{2}}\left[\frac{h_{++}}{\cos(\theta_u/2)} \mp \frac{h_{+-}}{\sin(\theta_u/2)}\right]$$

where the $h_{\lambda'\lambda}$ are the u-channel helicity amplitudes. In terms of the invariant amplitudes $A(s, t, u)$ and $B(s, t, u)$, the $F^{\pm}$ are given by

$$F^+(\sqrt{u},s) = \frac{[(\sqrt{u}-M)^2 - \mu^2]}{\sqrt{2u}}[-A - (\sqrt{u}+M)B]$$

$$F^-(\sqrt{u},s) = \frac{[(\sqrt{u}+M)^2 - \mu^2]}{\sqrt{2u}}[A - (\sqrt{u}-M)B]$$

The factors in front are kinematic singularities and must be removed before Reggeization. An appropriate set of amplitudes, which have no kinematic singularities in the $\sqrt{u}$ plane, is

$$\tilde{F}^{\pm}(\sqrt{u},s) = [\mp A - (\sqrt{u}\pm M)B]$$

These amplitudes are related by the MacDowell symmetry

$$\tilde{F}^-(\sqrt{u},s) = -\tilde{F}^+(-\sqrt{u},s)$$

Because of the MacDowell symmetry, the combinations

$$F_1(u,s) = (\tilde{F}^- - \tilde{F}^+)/2$$

$$F_2(u,s) = (\tilde{F}^- + \tilde{F}^+)/(2\sqrt{u})$$

are kinematic singularity-free functions of u and s.

The s-channel differential cross section and polarization are expressed in terms of these u-channel amplitudes as

$$\frac{d\sigma}{du}(s,u) = \frac{1}{64\pi p_s^2 s}\{|F_1|^2(s+u+2D^2) + |F_2|^2[u(-s+4M^2)+D^4]$$

$$+ 4M\,\mathrm{Re}(F_1^*F_2)[u+D^2]\}$$

$$P_{\hat{n}}(s,u) = \left(\frac{-\sin\theta_s}{16\pi\sqrt{s}}\right)\mathrm{Im}(F_1^*F_2)\Big/\left(\frac{d\sigma}{du}\right)$$

where $D^2 \equiv M^2 - \mu^2$ and $n = (\mathbf{p}_i \times \mathbf{p}_f)/|\mathbf{p}_i \times \mathbf{p}_f|$.

MacDowell Symmetry and Fermion Conspiracy

The u-channel partial wave expansion is

$$\bar{F}^+(\sqrt{u}, s) = \sum_J \{F^+(J, \sqrt{u})P'_{J+1/2}(z_u) - F^-(J, \sqrt{u})P'_{J-1/2}(z_u)\}$$

$$\bar{F}^-(\sqrt{u}, s) = \sum_J \{F^-(J, \sqrt{u})P'_{J+1/2}(z_u) - F^-(J, \sqrt{u})P'_{J-1/2}(z_u)\}$$

The MacDowell symmetry relates partial wave amplitudes $F^{(\tau P)}(J, \sqrt{u})$ with the same total angular momentum (same signature) but opposite parity

$$F^+(J, \sqrt{u}) = -F^-(J, -\sqrt{u})$$

This reflection symmetry holds for complex J also and places a significant restriction on fermion Regge trajectories. If the amplitude $F^+(J, \sqrt{u})$ has a Regge pole (quantum numbers $\tau P = +1$) with position $\alpha^+(\sqrt{u})$ and residue $\beta^+(\sqrt{u})$

$$F^+(J, \sqrt{u}) = \frac{\beta^+(\sqrt{u})}{J - \alpha^+(\sqrt{u})}$$

then the amplitude $F^-(J, \sqrt{u})$ must also have a Regge pole (quantum numbers $\tau P = -1$)

$$F^-(J, \sqrt{u}) = \frac{\beta^-(\sqrt{u})}{J - \alpha^-(\sqrt{u})}$$

to satisfy the requirements of MacDowell symmetry. The trajectories and residues of the two poles are related by

$$\alpha^-(\sqrt{u}) = \alpha^+(-\sqrt{u})$$

$$\beta^-(\sqrt{u}) = -\beta^+(-\sqrt{u})$$

These conspiracy conditions were first derived by Gribov.

The requirement of a pair of opposite parity Regge poles, with trajectory functions $\alpha^\pm(\sqrt{u})$ that intersect at $u = 0$, is a consequence of the usual analyticity assumptions for the A and B amplitudes. Such a relationship at $u = 0$ between Regge poles with different internal quantum numbers (in this case parity) is usually called a "conspiracy."

The doubling of trajectories does not necessarily require fermion recurrences of both parities. An asymmetric functional dependence on $\sqrt{u}$ could allow $\alpha^+(\sqrt{u})$ to rise through physical J values for $u > 0$ without $\alpha^-(\sqrt{u})$ doing so. Nevertheless, it remains a very interesting possibility that particle recurrences will be realized for both the α^+ and α^- trajectories. This conjecture will be examined in Section 6.1.

Fermion Regge Exchange Amplitude

The technique of performing the Sommerfeld–Watson transform and isolating the asymptotic Regge pole contributions parallels the treatment for meson poles in Section 3.2 and will not be repeated here. Including both the Regge pole and its MacDowell reflection, we obtain the results

$$\tilde{F}^+(\sqrt{u}, s) = \gamma^+(\sqrt{u})\, R(\alpha^+(\sqrt{u}), s)$$
$$\tilde{F}^-(\sqrt{u}, s) = \gamma^-(\sqrt{u})\, R(\alpha^-(\sqrt{u}), s)$$

where

$$R(\alpha(\sqrt{u}), s) = \frac{1}{\Gamma(\alpha + 1/2)} \frac{1 + \tau e^{-i\pi(\alpha - 1/2)}}{\sin \pi(\alpha - 1/2)} \left(\frac{s - t}{2s_0}\right)^{\alpha - 1/2}$$

It is interesting to note that the $\tau P = \pm 1$ Regge poles play equally important roles in the Regge exchange amplitude at $u = 0$, regardless of whether both have particle recurrences. The trajectories and reduced residues appearing above are understood to obey the symmetry conditions

$$\alpha^+(\sqrt{u}) = \alpha^-(-\sqrt{u})$$
$$\gamma^+(\sqrt{u}) = -\gamma^-(-\sqrt{u})$$

These functions are presumed to be real analytic in the cut $\sqrt{u}$ plane with cuts $[-\infty, -(M + \mu)]$ and $[(M + \mu), \infty]$.

In the s-channel physical region the momentum transfer u ranges from small positive values at $\cos \theta_s = -1$ to negative values. For u negative, $\sqrt{u} = i\sqrt{|u|}$, so the fermion trajectories and residues will be, in general, complex functions in the scattering region unlike meson trajectories. The residues and trajectories of the MacDowell pairs are related for $u < 0$ by complex conjugation:

$$\gamma^+(\sqrt{u}) = -[\gamma^-(\sqrt{u})]^*$$
$$\alpha^+(\sqrt{u}) = [\alpha^-(\sqrt{u})]^*$$

Nucleon Trajectory

As a concrete example, suppose we are interested in the contribution of the Regge pole associated with the nucleon, $N_\alpha(938, J^P = 1/2^+)$. Since the quantum numbers of this pole are $\tau = +1, P = +1$, it contributes to the $\tilde{F}^+$ amplitude

$$\alpha^+(\sqrt{u}) = \alpha_N(\sqrt{u})$$
$$\gamma^+(\sqrt{u}) = \gamma_N(\sqrt{u})$$

and its MacDowell partner ($\tau = +1, P = -1$) contributes to the $\bar{F}^-$ amplitude

$$\alpha^-(\sqrt{u}) = \alpha_N(-\sqrt{u})$$
$$\gamma^-(\sqrt{u}) = -\gamma_N(-\sqrt{u})$$

For $\sqrt{u} = M_N$ the nucleon trajectory satisfies the constraint Re $\alpha_N(M_N) = 1/2$, and the nucleon residue is related to the $\pi \bar{N} N$ coupling constant $\gamma_N(M_N) \sim g_{\pi \bar{N} N}{}^2$. From a classification of $N_\alpha(1688, J^P = 5/2^+)$ and $N_\beta(1650, J^P = 5/2^-)$ particles on MacDowell reflected trajectories, we will argue in Chapter 6 that the nucleon trajectory is approximately an even function of $\sqrt{u}$; that is, $\alpha_N(\sqrt{u}) \approx \alpha_N(-\sqrt{u})$. Assuming this to be the case, we have for $\sqrt{u} = \bar{M} \approx M_N$,

$$\text{Re } \alpha^-(\bar{M}) = \text{Re } \alpha_N(-\bar{M}) = \tfrac{1}{2}$$

which implies the existence of a $J^P = 1/2^-$ particle of mass $\bar{M}$ *unless* the residue vanishes at $\sqrt{u} = \bar{M}: \gamma^-(\bar{M}) = -\gamma_N(-\bar{M}) = 0$. Since no $1/2^-$ particles with mass about M_N are observed, we are left with this stringent restriction on the nucleon residue function if our premise on the functional form of the trajectory is correct.

Fermion Exchange Dips

For fermion trajectories the right and wrong signature points are half-integral values of Re $\alpha(\sqrt{u}) = J_0$ at which $(-)^{J_0 \mp 1/2} = \tau_0$, respectively. Provided that Im $\alpha(\sqrt{u}) \approx 0$ (or, equivalently, that the trajectory is approximately an even function of $\sqrt{u}$), the factor $1/\Gamma(\alpha + 1/2)$ gives rise to zeros in the fermion exchange amplitudes when the trajectory passes through wrong signature, nonsense points. The first wrong signature, nonsense point is Re $\alpha_N(\sqrt{u}) = -1/2$ for nucleon Regge exchange ($\tau = +1$) and Re $\alpha_\Delta(\sqrt{u}) = -3/2$ for Δ_δ Regge exchange ($\tau = -1$). The possibility of dips in πN elastic differential cross sections at these values of u is one of the most interesting predictions of Regge theory. The presence of fixed poles at the wrong signature, nonsense points would modify these predictions (cf. the corresponding discussion in Section 3.2).

Cross Section and Polarization

In an extreme high energy limit kinematical factors of order $1/s$ can be neglected and the differential cross section expression for $u \leqslant 0$ can be written as

$$\frac{d\sigma}{du}(s, u) = \frac{1}{32\pi s} \{ |\gamma^+(\sqrt{u}) R(\alpha^+(\sqrt{u}), s)|^2 + |\gamma^-(\sqrt{u}) R(\alpha^-(\sqrt{u}), s)|^2 \}$$

In this approximation the cross terms between the $\alpha^+(\sqrt{u})$ and $\alpha^-(\sqrt{u})$ amplitudes are absent and the energy dependence of the differential cross section is simply given by

$$\frac{d\sigma}{du}(s,u) = F(u)\left(\frac{s}{s_0}\right)^{[\alpha^+(\sqrt{u})+\alpha^-(\sqrt{u})]-2}$$

Thus the odd $\sqrt{u}$ terms in the trajectory function do not enter in the high s energy dependence of $d\sigma/du$.

The polarization in the high energy limit due to the $\alpha^\pm(\sqrt{u})$ Regge poles is

$$P_{\hat{n}}(s,u) = \frac{\sqrt{s}\sin\theta_s}{i2\sqrt{u}}\tanh\left\{-\frac{i\pi}{2}\left[\alpha^+(\sqrt{u})-\alpha^-(\sqrt{u})\right]\right\}$$

in the direction $\hat{n} = (\mathbf{P}_i \times \mathbf{P}_f)/|\mathbf{P}_i \times \mathbf{P}_f|$. Thus the phase difference between the MacDowell reflected trajectories leads to a polarization in backward πN scattering that is independent of the Regge residues. In reactions like $\pi^- p \to \pi^- p$ where the Δ_δ Regge pole and its MacDowell partner are thought to be the only exchanges, a polarization measurement in the backward hemisphere would yield valuable information on the importance of odd terms in $\sqrt{u}$ in the Δ_δ trajectory function.

3.4 SUMMARY

We have reviewed in this chapter the procedures by which meson and baryon Regge pole exchange contributions to πN scattering amplitudes are derived. The results and discussion here will form the basis for most of the Regge phenomenology in Chapters 4, 5, and 7.

The methods introduced in this chapter also apply to the Regge treatment of inelastic reactions. In some reactions the technical problems associated with (i) kinematic singularities, (ii) threshold or pseudothreshold relations, (iii) daughter trajectories, and (iv) conspiracy will all be encountered. Fortunately definite rules now exist in the literature for the kinematic singularities and threshold relations of the helicity amplitudes in the general case, so that a great deal of labor can be circumvented. The daughter trajectories do not play a large role in present phenomenology beyond the reinstatement of the s^α asymptotic behavior. We devote Chapter 9 to the conspiracy problem for meson Regge poles.

Chapter 4

Inelastic Reactions: Meson Exchanges

4.1 QUALITATIVE ASPECTS

A broad class of qualitative predictions of Regge pole theory can be experimentally verified without the necessity of resorting to detailed fits to the scattering data. In this section we briefly review some successful qualitative predictions for (i) energy dependences of cross sections, (ii) shrinkage of forward peaks, (iii) phases of scattering amplitudes, and (iv) dips at wrong signature, nonsense values of trajectories. The predictions can be most readily quantitatively evaluated for inelastic reactions that are mediated by a single t-channel meson exchange.

Energy Dependence

The shapes of Regge trajectories found from classification of particle recurrences are approximate straight lines as a function of (mass)^2:

$$\alpha(t) \simeq \alpha(0) + \alpha'(0)\,t \qquad \text{for mesons}$$

$$\alpha(\sqrt{u}) \simeq \alpha(0) + \alpha'(0)\,u \qquad \text{for baryons}$$

Continuity of the trajectories leads us to expect similar linear behaviors for $t \lesssim 0$ or $u \lesssim 0$, at least for small values of these variables. These negative momentum transfer regions correspond to physical s-channel scattering proceeding via t- or u-channel Regge pole exchanges. The energy dependence of the s-channel scattering is determined by

$$\frac{d\sigma}{dt}(s,t) = F(t)\,s^{2\alpha(t)-2}$$

or

$$\frac{d\sigma}{du}(u,t) = F(u)\,s^{2\alpha(u)-2}$$

for exchange of a single trajectory. Since the scattering is highly peripheral the integrated cross sections are roughly given by $\sigma(s) \sim s^{2\langle\alpha\rangle-2}$, where $\langle\alpha\rangle$ denotes a mean value for the trajectory over the momentum transfer region of the peak. Using $s \to 2M_T P_{\text{Lab}}$ at high energy, this result can be conveniently rewritten as $\sigma \sim (P_{\text{Lab}})^{2\langle\alpha\rangle-2}$.

We can make some crude estimates of cross section energy dependences from the information on Regge trajectories obtained from particle classification. We begin by considering *representative* trajectories associated with the particles

$$\rho\,(750, 1^-) \quad Y = 1 \qquad I = 1$$
$$K^*\,(890, 1^-)\; Y = \pm 1 \quad I = \tfrac{1}{2}$$
$$N\,(938, \tfrac{1}{2}^+) \quad Y = 1 \qquad I = \tfrac{1}{2}$$

The mass inequalities $M_\rho < M_{K^*} < M_N$ leads us to expect

$$\alpha_\rho(0) > \alpha_K{}^*(0) > \alpha_N(0)$$

for straight-line trajectories. In fact from particle assignments like those in Chapter 1, we have

$$\alpha_\rho(t) \simeq 0.5 + t \qquad \alpha_K{}^*(t) \simeq 0.3 + t \qquad \alpha_N(u) \simeq -0.3 + u$$

If we estimate that $\langle \alpha \rangle$ corresponds to momentum transfer -0.2, we obtain

$$\langle \alpha_\rho \rangle \simeq 0.3 \qquad \langle \alpha_K{}^* \rangle \simeq 0.1 \qquad \langle \alpha_N \rangle \simeq -0.5$$

Thus we expect the characteristic momentum dependences:

$$\sigma \sim (P_{\text{Lab}})^{-1.4} \qquad \text{nonstrange meson exchange}$$
$$\sigma \sim (P_{\text{Lab}})^{-1.8} \qquad \text{strange meson exchange}$$
$$\sigma \sim (P_{\text{Lab}})^{-3.0} \qquad \text{nonstrange baryon exchange}$$

These approximate power law behaviors for inelastic cross sections are in good accord with the observed behaviors compiled in Figure 2.23. The empirical separation of energy dependences according to crossed-channel quantum numbers follows naturally in Regge pole theory. We defer to the next chapter a discussion of the energy dependence of elastic-like reactions for which $\sigma \sim (P_{\text{Lab}})^{-0.2}$.

Shrinkage

The reaction $\pi^- p \to \pi^0 n$ is ideal from the standpoint of Regge phenomenology in that only one trajectory is known to have particle recurrences with quantum numbers appropriate for t-channel exchange ($I = 1$, $G = +1$, $Y = 0$, $P = (-1)^J$). This is the ρ meson trajectory (ρ_V) with functional form $\alpha_\rho\,(t) \simeq 0.5 + t$ deduced from the mass spectra. With this t dependence for the trajectory, the differential cross section due to the ρ Regge pole is

$$\frac{d\sigma}{dt} = F(t)\,(E_{\text{Lab}})^{-1}\exp(t\,2\ln E_{\text{Lab}})$$

The exponential is the Regge shrinkage factor. As noted in Section 2.2 (cf. Figure 2.17), the $\pi^-p \to \pi^0 n$ cross section data show just this decrease and shrinkage with energy. Similar agreement has been found for inelastic reactions with more than one exchanged Regge pole.

Amplitude Phase

The $\pi^-p \to \pi^0 n$ reaction also provides a simple test of the Regge prediction for the phase of the scattering amplitude. Since $\tau = -1$ for the ρ trajectory the prediction at $t = 0$ is

$$\frac{\text{Re }f}{\text{Im }f} = \tan\left[\frac{\pi\alpha_\rho(0)}{2}\right]$$

From the energy dependence of the $t = 0$ cross section we know that $\alpha_\rho(0) \sim 1/2$. Thus we expect $\text{Re }f/\text{Im }f \sim 1$. The magnitude of this ratio can be directly determined from the data by the relation

$$\left|\frac{\text{Re }f}{\text{Im }f}\right|^2 = \frac{(d\sigma/dt)^{\text{observed}}_{t=0}}{(d\sigma/dt)^{\text{optical}}} - 1$$

where $(d\sigma/dt)^{\text{optical}}$ is the contribution of $\text{Im }f$ to the $t = 0$ differential cross section, as obtained from the optical theorem

$$\left(\frac{d\sigma}{dt}\right)_{\text{optical}} = \frac{1}{32\pi}[\sigma_t(\pi^-p) - \sigma_t(\pi^+p)]^2$$

Experimentally, the above relation gives $|\text{Re }f/\text{Im }f| \simeq 1$, independent of energy as predicted. Later we shall examine some Regge phase predictions for reactions that involve simultaneous exchanges of several Regge poles.

Dips at Wrong Signature, Nonsense Points

The presence of a minimum in $d\sigma/dt$ at a wrong signature, nonsense point was first observed in the $\pi^-p \to \pi^0 n$ reaction for the t value at which $\alpha_\rho(t) = 0$.

As discussed in Section 3.2, the t-channel helicity amplitudes for ρ exchange have the essential structure

$$f_{++} \sim \left(\tan\frac{\pi\alpha}{2} + i\right)s^{\alpha-1}$$

$$f_{+-} \sim \sqrt{t}\,\alpha\left(\tan\frac{\pi\alpha}{2} + i\right)s^{\alpha-1}$$

The value $\alpha = 0$ is an unphysical angular momentum for f_{+-} and the amplitude vanishes there. Furthermore, since f_{+-} is proportional to $\sqrt{t}$, it also vanishes at $t = 0$. The relative size of f_{+-} and f_{++} can be inferred from the shape of the $\pi^- p \to \pi^0 n$ differential near $t = 0$. The experimental values of $d\sigma/dt$, shown in Figure 4.1 for $P_{\text{Lab}} = 5.9$ BeV/c, rise near $t = 0$, thus indicating the dominance of the f_{+-} contribution to the cross section. Then at $t \simeq -0.5$ (BeV/c)^2, $d\sigma/dt$ shows a minimum. This dip is correlated with the point where the ρ trajectory passes through zero. In this connection recall that the trajectory $\alpha_\rho(t) \simeq 0.5 + t$ is deduced independently from the energy dependence of $d\sigma/dt$. The data in Figure 2.17 indicate that the dip remains at fixed t for all energies as predicted.

Inasmuch as $d\sigma/dt$ is nonzero at the position of the dip, the f_{++} amplitude presumably does not vanish there. Hence the ρ chooses the sense mechanism at $\alpha = 0$, as used above. (Both f_{++} and f_{+-} vanish at $\alpha = 0$ for the other mechanisms.) This latter conclusion is dependent on the assumed absence of contributions other than ρ exchange.

The ρ-trajectory values determined from the energy dependence of

$$d\sigma/dt(\pi^- p \to \pi^0 n)$$

are shown in Figure 4.1. The trajectory seems to deviate from a straight-line form at large negative t. However, this conclusion is not definite because of the size-able experimental errors on the large $|t|$ measurements. The actual behavior of meson trajectories for $-t > 1$ (BeV/c)^2 is still open to speculation. Linearly falling trajectories should lead to a series of minima in $d\sigma/dt$ versus t, correlated with the exceptional points of the trajectories at negative integral angular momentum values. If instead trajectories level off, the energy dependence at large $|t|$ will be more gradual. We shall discuss the possibility of falling trajectories further in Chapter 5 for elastic processes on which some large $|t|$ data are presently available.

Right Signature Zeros

The reaction $\pi^- p \to \eta n$ has also received a great deal of phenomenological attention. Here π_T is the only established trajectory with the quantum numbers of the t-channel ($I = 1$, $G = -1$, $P = (-)^J$). We subsequently label this trajectory by α_A since the $A_2(1310, 2^+)$ is the lowest particle member. In the literature the symbol R has sometimes been used to denote the π_T trajectory.

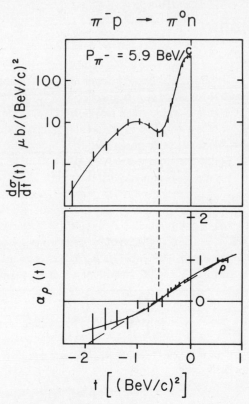

Figure 4.1. ρ-meson trajectory determined from the experimental energy dependence of $d\sigma/dt(\pi^- p \rightarrow \pi^0 n)$. Data on $d\sigma/dt(\pi^- p \rightarrow \pi^0 n)$ at 5.9 BeV/c are shown for comparison: from O. Guisan, SUNY Report (1968).

The A trajectory deduced from the energy dependence of the $\pi^- p \rightarrow \eta n$ reaction is shown in Figure 4.2. The shape appears to deviate appreciably from a linear form and does not seem to cross $\alpha = 0$ out to $t \simeq -1$. Such behavior is quite anomalous in comparison with the approximate linear forms with slope about equal to 1 $(\text{BeV}/c)^{-2}$ at small $|t|$ found for most other meson trajectories. This result is also surprising in view of the approximate linearity of the π_T trajectory in the time-like region indicated by the particle classifications in Section 1.3. Further experiments on reactions involving A exchange will be necessary to confirm whether this trajectory is really atypical.

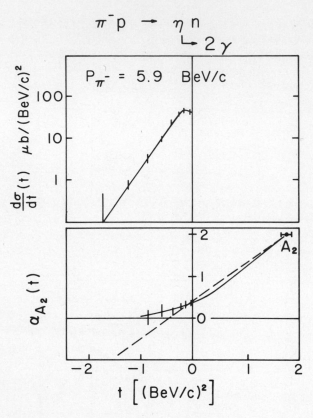

Figure 4.2. A-meson trajectory deduced from the $d\sigma/dt(\pi^-p \to \eta n)$ energy dependence. Data on the differential cross section at 5.9 BeV/c are also shown: from O. Guisan, SUNY Report (1968).

The uncertainty in the A trajectory makes it difficult to decide which sense-nonsense mechanism is chosen at $\alpha = 0$. The essential α dependences of the t-channel amplitudes for the three possible mechanisms discussed in Section 3.2 are

nonsense

$$f_{++} \sim \frac{\alpha}{\sin \pi\alpha} \qquad f_{+-} \sim \frac{\alpha}{\sin \pi\alpha}$$

Chew

$$f_{++} \sim \frac{\alpha}{\sin \pi\alpha} \qquad f_{+-} \sim \frac{\alpha^2}{\sin \pi\alpha}$$

no-compensation

$$f_{++} \sim \frac{\alpha^2}{\sin \pi\alpha} \qquad f_{+-} \sim \frac{\alpha^2}{\sin \pi\alpha}$$

The flattening of $d\sigma/dt(\pi^-p \to \eta n)$ near $t = 0$ is evidence for an appreciable f_{+-} amplitude. Hence had $\alpha \to 0$ at $t \simeq -0.5$, the absence of a dip in $d\sigma/dt$ there would have decided in favor of the nonsense mechanism. However for the flatter trajectory found from the energy dependence of the data, $\alpha \to 0$ for $t \simeq -1$. Since the present measurements do not extend beyond this value of t, we cannot yet decide which mechanism the A trajectory chooses at this right signature point.

4.2 SU(3) FOR REGGE RESIDUES

In order to realistically incorporate SU(3) symmetry into the description of scattering processes, it is necessary to employ a suitable dynamical framework. Then symmetry breaking effects such as nondegenerate masses can be taken into account. Historically SU(3) symmetry was applied to the complete scattering amplitude with no consideration of the inherent dynamics, but many of the derived relations were in substantial disagreement with experiment. These unsuccessful relations are generally not obtained when SU(3) symmetry is assumed only for the three-particle vertices of exchange models. Furthermore, some new predictions result that are experimentally verified.

In the context of the Regge pole exchange model, SU(3) symmetry is applied to the Regge residues. Since the residue factors into parts associated with the vertices of the scattering amplitude, SU(3) symmetry can be used for the vertex factors to relate the contributions of a given Regge pole in different processes. Symmetry breaking effects are taken into account by allowing nondegenerate masses for the external particles and nondegenerate trajectories for Regge exchanges belonging to the same multiplet.

Charge Exchange Reactions

A particularly simple illustration of the application of SU(3) symmetry to meson Regge pole residues involves the pseudoscalar meson–nucleon charge exchange reactions. Here the baryon vertex $p \to n$ is fixed and symmetry of the trilinear meson vertex can be evaluated. Since the meson exchange must be $I = 1$, only octet trajectories are involved; we are assuming that 1 and 8 SU(3) multiplets are the only candidates for meson exchange, in accordance with the particle classifications in Chapter 1. The external particles $\pi, \eta, K, \overline{K}$ presumably form an octet representation of SU(3). If we label the meson exchange amplitudes of definite G parity by

$$F(s,t) \quad \text{for} \quad G = +1 \quad I = 1$$
and
$$D(s,t) \quad \text{for} \quad G = -1 \quad I = 1$$

then SU(3) symmetry for the meson vertex residue factor leads to the following expressions for the charge exchange amplitudes

$$\langle \pi^- p | \pi^0 n \rangle = -\sqrt{2}\, F(s,t)$$

$$\langle K^- p | \overline{K^0} n \rangle = F(s,t) + D(s,t)$$

$$\langle K^+ n | K^0 p \rangle = -F(s,t) + D(s,t)$$

$$\langle \pi^- p | \eta n \rangle = (\tfrac{2}{3})^{1/2}\, D(s,t)$$

The F and D amplitudes may also depend on the masses of the external mesons, but we ignore that dependence for the moment. Helicity indices are suppressed in the equations since corresponding relations hold for both helicity amplitudes. The ρ_V and π_T are presently the only known trajectories that contribute to the F and D amplitudes, but these results are valid in a more general context with multiple exchanges of $I = 1$ octet trajectories. The preceding expressions can be verified by inspection of the SU(3) Lagrangian for the meson couplings:

$$= g_F \{ -\sqrt{2}\, \pi^- \pi^0 \rho_V{}^+ + K^- K^0 \rho_V{}^+ - K^+ \bar{K}^0 \rho_V{}^- \}$$

$$+ g_D \{ K^- K^0 \pi_T{}^+ + (\tfrac{2}{3})^{1/2} \pi^- \eta \pi_T{}^+ + K^+ \bar{K}^0 \pi_T{}^- \}$$

Since the four physical processes are given in terms of only two amplitudes (F and D) we obtain two sum values

$$\langle K^- p | \bar{K}^0 n \rangle - \langle K^+ n | K^0 p \rangle = -\sqrt{2} \langle \pi^- p | \pi^0 n \rangle$$

$$|\langle K^- p | \bar{K}^0 n \rangle|^2 + |\langle K^+ n | K^0 p \rangle|^2 = |\langle \pi^- p | \pi^0 n \rangle|^2 + 3|\langle \pi^- p | \eta n \rangle|^2$$

These equations hold separately for the real and imaginary components of the amplitudes. Applying the optical theorem to the linear relation, we obtain a sum rule for total cross section differences:

$$[\sigma_t(K^- p) - \sigma_t(K^- n)] - [\sigma_t(K^+ p) - \sigma_t(K^+ n)] = [\sigma_t(\pi^- p) - \sigma_t(\pi^+ p)]$$

For the π and K projectiles, the factors of c.m. momentum from the optical theorem are essentially equal for $P_{\text{Lab}} > 3$ BeV/c and therefore have not been retained. This sum rule is compared with experiment in Figure 4.3. The agreement is quite satisfactory.

The other sum rule obtained above relates the four differential cross sections for charge exchange reactions:

$$\frac{d\sigma}{dt}(K^- p \to \bar{K}^0 n) + \frac{d\sigma}{dt}(K^+ n \to K^0 p) = \frac{d\sigma}{dt}(\pi^- p \to \pi^0 n) + 3\frac{d\sigma}{dt}(\pi^- p \to \eta n)$$

Accurate data have existed for some time for the $K^-p \to \bar{K}^0 n$, $\pi^-p \to \pi^0 n$, and $\pi^-p \to \eta n$ differential cross sections. The $K^+n \to K^0 p$ differential cross section can be predicted from the data on the other three reactions. The predictions for the forward differential and integrated cross sections are shown in Figure 4.4. Recent data on $K^+n \to K^0 p$ at 5.5 BeV/c are consistent with the predicted values, as indicated in the figure.

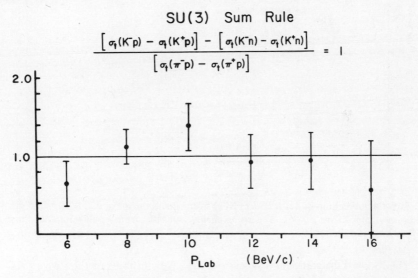

Figure 4.3. Experimental evaluation of the SU(3) sum rule for total cross sections: from V. Barger, CERN Report 68-7.

To proceed further and actually fit the $t = 0$ differential cross sections, we use the explicit forms for ρ and A Regge exchanges. The amplitudes are given by

$$F = \left[\tan\left(\frac{\pi\alpha_\rho}{2}\right) + i\right]R_\rho \qquad D = \left[-\cot\left(\frac{\pi\alpha_A}{2}\right) + i\right]R_A$$

where

$$R_E = \frac{\gamma_M^E \gamma_N^E}{\sqrt{s}}\left[\frac{(s - (1/2)\sum_{i=1}^{4} m_i^2)}{s_E}\right]^{\alpha_E}$$

The γ_M^E and γ_N^E are SU(3) invariant residue factors at the meson and nucleon vertices for the exchange E. For compactness of notation all sense–nonsense factors of α have been absorbed into these residues. The application of SU(3) to the residue factors assumes that the scaling factor s_E is associated only with the exchange, with no dependence on masses of external particles. In fitting the $t = 0$ data the actual numerical normalizations used for the s_E are irrelevant.

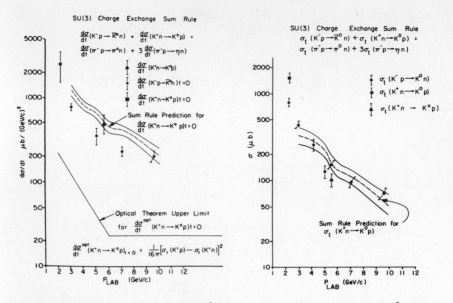

Figure 4.4. Predictions of $d\sigma/dt(K^+n \to K^0p)$ at $t = 0$ and the integrated $K^+n \to K^0p$ cross section obtained from the SU(3) charge exchange sum rule: from V. Barger and D. Cline, *Phys. Rev.* **156**, 1522 (1967).

The forward differential cross sections are given in terms of the Regge parameters by

$$\frac{d\sigma}{d\Omega}(\pi^- p \to \pi^0 n) = 2\left[1 + \tan^2\left(\frac{\pi\alpha_\rho}{2}\right)\right]R_\rho^2$$

$$\frac{d\sigma}{d\Omega}(\pi^- p \to \eta n) = \frac{2}{3}\left[1 + \cot^2\left(\frac{\pi\alpha_A}{2}\right)\right]R_A^2$$

$$\frac{d\sigma}{d\Omega}(K^- p \to \bar{K}^0 n) = [R_\rho + R_A]^2 + \left[R_\rho\tan\left(\frac{\pi\alpha_\rho}{2}\right) - R_A\cot\left(\frac{\pi\alpha_A}{2}\right)\right]^2$$

$$\frac{d\sigma}{d\Omega}(K^+ n \to K^0 p) = [-R_\rho + R_A]^2 + \left[-R_\rho\tan\left(\frac{\pi\alpha_\rho}{2}\right) - R_A\cot\left(\frac{\pi\alpha_A}{2}\right)\right]^2$$

The results of fitting the data to these expressions are shown in Figure 4.5. The fit in terms of the four parameters α_ρ, α_A, $(\gamma_\rho^M \gamma_\rho^N)$, and $(\gamma_A^M \gamma_A^N)$ is adequate, thus indicating that the data are consistent with SU(3) for the residue factors.

The values for the trajectories obtained in the fit are $\alpha_\rho(0) = 0.57$ and $\alpha_A(0) = 0.34$. For $\alpha_\rho = \alpha_A = 1/2$ the curves in Figure 4.5 would have been flat.

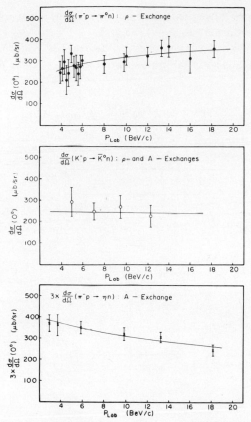

Figure 4.5. Differential cross section data used in testing the validity of SU(3) symmetry for the ρ and A residues. Solid curves represent the Regge fits: from V. Barger and M. Olsson, *Phys. Rev. Letters* **18**, 294 (1967).

The positive or negative slopes reflect whether the corresponding α is greater than or less than $1/2$, respectively.

Exchange Degeneracy

The amplitudes for the KN and $\bar{K}N$ charge exchange processes in the ρ, A Regge model are

$$\langle K^- p | \bar{K}^0 n \rangle = \frac{\exp\left[-(i\pi/2)(\alpha_\rho - 1)\right]}{\cos(\pi\alpha_\rho/2)} R_\rho + \frac{\exp\left[-(i\pi/2)(\alpha_A - 2)\right]}{\sin(\pi\alpha_A/2)} R_A$$

$$\langle K^+ n | K^0 p \rangle = \frac{-\exp\left[-(i\pi/2)(\alpha_\rho - 1)\right]}{\cos(\pi\alpha_\rho/2)} R_\rho + \frac{\exp\left[-(i\pi/2)(\alpha_A - 2)\right]}{\sin(\pi\alpha_A/2)} R_A$$

Some simple qualitative predictions can be made in the approximation of exchange degenerate trajectories, $\alpha_\rho(t) \approx \alpha_A(t)$.

In this limit the ρ and A amplitudes are 90° (or 270°) out of phase and no interference terms appear in the cross sections above. Thus we directly obtain the prediction

$$\frac{d\sigma}{dt}(K^- p \to \bar{K}^0 n) \approx \frac{d\sigma}{dt}(K^+ n \to K^0 p)$$

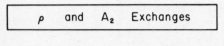

Estimates: $a_\rho(0) \sim a_A(0) \sim \frac{1}{2}$ $\gamma_\rho(0) \sim \gamma_A(0)$

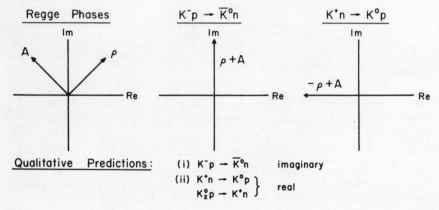

Qualitative Predictions: (i) $K^- p \to \bar{K}^0 n$ imaginary

(ii) $K^+ n \to K^0 p$
$K_2^0 p \to K^+ n$ } real

Figure 4.6. Phase diagrams for ρ and A Regge amplitudes in $\bar{K}N$ and KN scattering: from V. Barger, *Rev. Mod. Phys.* **40**, 129 (1968).

At $t = 0$ with $\alpha_\rho \sim \alpha_A \sim 1/2$ the amplitudes are

$$\langle K^- p | \bar{K}^0 n \rangle = (R_\rho - R_A) + i(R_\rho + R_A)$$

$$\langle K^+ n | K^0 p \rangle = -(R_\rho + R_A) - i(R_\rho - R_A)$$

For ρ and A residues of comparable magnitude and the same sign

$$\frac{\gamma_M{}^\rho \gamma_N{}^\rho}{\gamma_M{}^A \gamma_N{}^A} \approx +1$$

the $K^-p \to \bar{K}^0 n$ forward amplitude is pure imaginary and the $K^+n \to K^0p$ forward amplitude pure real. This qualitative result is illustrated in the phase diagram of Figure 4.6. The optical theorem provides a direct check of these estimates since

$$\text{Im}\langle K^-p|K^0 n\rangle = \frac{4\pi}{q_{cm}}[\sigma_t(K^-p) - \sigma_t(K^-n)]$$

$$\text{Im}\langle K^+n|K^0 p\rangle = \frac{4\pi}{q_{cm}}[\sigma_t(K^+p) - \sigma_t(K^+n)]$$

The high energy experimental data (cf. Figure 2.14) give

$$[\sigma_t(K^-p) - \sigma_t(K^-n)] \sim 2 \text{ or } 3 \text{ mb}$$

whereas

$$[\sigma_t(K^+p) - \sigma_t(K^+n)] \sim 0$$

as anticipated. Only approximate exchange degeneracy is required to reproduce these experimental results.

Line Reversal

The reactions $K^-p \to \bar{K}^0 n$ and $K^+n \to K^0p$ provide a simple example of line reversal (cf. Section 3.2). The line reversed reaction corresponding to $K^-p \to \bar{K}^0 n$ is $K^0p \to K^+n$. Under line reversal the ρ contribution ($\tau = -1$) changes sign and the A contribution ($\tau = +1$) remains unchanged. We then use isospin invariance to equate the $K^0p \to K^+n$ and $K^+n \to K^0p$ amplitudes.

Simple polarization predictions can be made for line reversed reactions. For the KN charge exchange processes the polarization is essentially given by

$$P \sim \text{Im}[F^{\rho}_{++} D^{A*}_{+-} + D^{A}_{++} F^{\rho*}_{+-}]\sin\theta_s\left(\frac{d\sigma}{dt}\right)^{-1}$$

Since the ρ contribution changes sign between the above two reactions, we can predict that

$$P(K^-p \to \bar{K}^0 n) = -P(K^+n \to K^0p).$$

For exchange degenerate trajectories the polarization is energy independent and proportional to

$$P \propto [\gamma^{\rho}_{++}\gamma^{A}_{+-} - \gamma^{A}_{++}\gamma^{\rho}_{+-}]$$

Thus, if the residues happen to be in the ratio

$$\frac{\gamma_{++}^\rho}{\gamma_{++}^A} \approx -\frac{\gamma_{+-}^\rho}{\gamma_{+-}^A}$$

then the contributions from the two terms reinforce and the polarization becomes large. No polarization measurements have been made for the $K^-p \to \bar{K}^0 n$ reaction. However, these qualitative remarks can be generalized to hypercharge exchange reactions where some polarization data do exist.

Data Fitting

With appropriate parametrizations for the t dependence of the ρ and A residues, remarkably accurate fits to the charge exchange differential cross sections have been obtained. We record below a typical parametrization of the ρ residues that reproduce the $d\sigma/dt(\pi^-p \to \pi^0 n)$ data. The t-channel helicity amplitudes for ρ exchange are given by

$$f_{++} = -\sqrt{2}\frac{\gamma_{++}}{(t-4M^2)^{1/2}}(\alpha+1)\left[\tan\left(\frac{\pi\alpha}{2}\right) + i\right]\left(\frac{E_{\text{Lab}}}{E_0}\right)^\alpha$$

$$f_{+-} = -\sqrt{2}\frac{\gamma_{+-}}{(t-4M^2)^{1/2}}\frac{(-t)^{1/2}}{2M}\,\alpha(\alpha+1)\left[\tan\left(\frac{\pi\alpha}{2}\right) + i\right]\left(\frac{E_{\text{Lab}}}{E_0}\right)^\alpha$$

This form is intended for use only in the range $|t| \leqslant 1$ (BeV/c)^2. The function $1/\Gamma(\alpha+1)$ appearing in the Regge amplitudes of Section 3.2 has been approximated as $(\alpha+1)$. The factor $-\sqrt{2}$ appearing in front of both amplitudes is an isotopic spin Clebsch-Gordan coefficient. The residues and trajectories are parameterized as

$$\gamma_{++}(t) = a[(1+b)\,e^{ct} - b]$$

$$\gamma_{+-}(t) = g e^{ht}$$

$$\alpha(t) = \alpha(0) + \alpha'(0)\,t$$

Taking $E_0 = 1$ BeV, the numerical values of the parameters found in the data analysis are $a = 14.0$ BeV, $b = 2.0$, $c = 2.0$ (BeV)$^{-1}$, $g = 260.0$ BeV, $h = 0.1$ (BeV)$^{-1}$, $\alpha(0) = 0.58$, and $\alpha'(0) = 1.0$ (BeV)$^{-2}$.

The dominance of the helicity flip amplitude is apparent from these parameters. The sign change in $\gamma_{++}(t)$ at $t \simeq -0.15$ is required by the crossover of $d\sigma/dt(\pi^-p)$ and $d\sigma/dt(\pi^+p)$ at this t value. A more detailed discussion of the crossover phenomena in the context of the Regge model will be given in Section 5.3. The threshold condition at $t = 4M^2$ has not been imposed on the residues, but since the threshold is far from the scattering region, the condition is expected to bear little significance to phenomenological parametrizations for $t \leqslant 0$.

The single ρ-exchange description of the $\pi^- p \to \pi^0 n$ reaction would have been completely satisfactory had the polarization turned out to be zero at high energy. However an average polarization of about 10–15% has been found at 5.9 and 11.0 BeV/c for the momentum transfer range $t = 0$ to $t = -0.4$ (BeV/c)^2. Thus although the ρ-exchange contribution apparently dominates, another J-plane singularity is required to explain the finer details of the data. In Chapter 10 we study this additional ρ singularity by dispersion relation techniques.

Finally the SU(3) predictions for the meson residue factors in the charge exchange reactions have also been checked for $t \neq 0$. The t dependence of the residue for a given exchange is assumed to be a universal SU(3) invariant function; the SU(3) equalities

$$\frac{\gamma_{\rho RK}(t)}{\gamma_{\rho\pi\pi}(t)} = \frac{1}{2} \qquad \frac{\gamma_{A\bar{K}K}(t)}{\gamma_{A\pi\eta}(t)} = \frac{\sqrt{3}}{\sqrt{2}}$$

are assumed for all t. The differential cross section data on the charge exchange reactions are well described by Regge parameterizations using these SU(3) ratios.

The usefulness of SU(3) symmetry in correlating data on high energy reactions has been exploited only for a few simple examples like those described above. As more data on inelastic reactions become available, we can expect that approximate SU(3) relations for residue factors will play an increasingly important role in unifying our descriptions of scattering data.

4.3 SU(3) FOR REGGE EXCHANGES

The classification of particles in Chapter 1 led us to expect approximately parallel Regge trajectories for the individual members of an SU(3) multiplet. In the scattering region we expect this feature of nondegenerate trajectories with similar shapes to be maintained for the multiplet members. As a working hypothesis, the knowledge of the ρ and A trajectories is sometimes used as input information for the shapes of the other vector and tensor nonet trajectories $[\rho, K^*, \phi, \omega]$ and $[A, K^{**}, f', f_0]$. Analyses of data do favor similar shapes for the ω and ρ trajectories. However, evidence on the f_0 trajectory indicates a roughly linear shape, $\alpha \simeq 0.55 + t$, in contrast to the empirical form for the A trajectory discussed in Section 4.1. Accurate data on a variety of inelastic reactions will be required to test the above hypothesis.

If SU(3) is a meaningful symmetry in relating properties of *different* exchanges, then the sense–nonsense factors should be the same for all trajectories in a given multiplet. This is apparently the case for the ρ and ω trajectories, which both appear to choose the sense mechanism at $\alpha = 0$. In Chapter 5 we present evidence that the f_0 trajectory chooses the no-compensation mechanism at $\alpha = 0$ ($t \simeq -0.5$). Whether the no-compensation mechanism is also consistent for the A trajectory is not established.

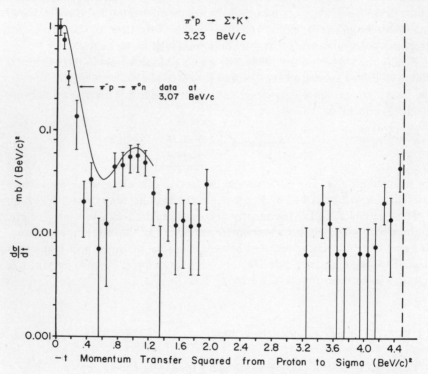

Figure 4.7. Experimental data on $d\sigma/dt(\pi^+ p \to K^+ \Sigma^+)$ at 3.2 BeV/c. The solid curve represents $d\sigma/dt(\pi^- p \to \pi^0 n)$ data: from R. Kofler *et al.*, *Phys. Rev.* **163**, 1479 (1967).

Eventually we may hope to use SU(3) to relate vertices of different exchanges, as for example, the $\rho\pi\pi$ and $K^*K\pi$ residue factors. To do so will require an additional assumption about the scaling factors; a natural possibility is to try $s_\rho = s_{K^*}$, and so forth.

Hypercharge Exchange Reactions

The hypercharge exchange reactions will provide a suitable proving ground for investigations of the SU(3) properties of trajectories and residues. Some of the pseudoscalar meson-spin 1/2-baryon hypercharge reactions that allow t-channel exchanges are

$$\pi^+ p \to K^+ \Sigma^+ \qquad \pi^- p \to K^0 \Sigma^0 \qquad K^- p \to \pi^- \Sigma^+$$

$$\pi^- p \to K^0 \Lambda \qquad K^- p \to \pi^0 \Lambda$$

Aside from the technical complications of unequal masses, the Regge treatment proceeds in an analogous fashion to the charge exchange processes. The exchanges are associated with the $K^*(890, 1^-)$ (q trajectory) and the $K^{**}(1410, 2^+)$ (Q trajectory) mesons. Since there is no analog of G parity for strange mesons, both trajectories are allowed as exchanges in all reactions listed above.

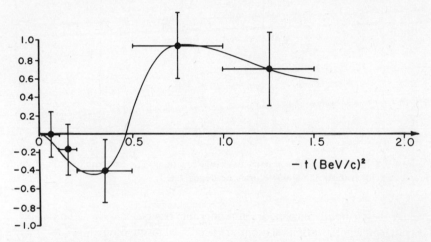

Figure 4.8. Polarization measurements of $\pi^+ p \to K^+ \Sigma^+$ at 3.2 BeV/c: from R. Kofler *et al.*, *Phys. Rev.* **163**, 1479 (1967).

At the moment the available experimental data on these reactions are fragmentary and primarily limited to laboratory momenta less than about 6 BeV/c. A considerable accumulation of data will be required for sophisticated phenomenological analyses like those that have been made for the charge exchange reactions. Nevertheless some qualitative checks of Regge pole models can be made. The first crude check is the energy dependence of the integrated cross sections. As noted in Section 4.1, the power law dependence on P_{Lab} compares favorably with that estimated from extrapolations of the q and Q trajectories.

In the way of orientation the data on $d\sigma/dt(\pi^+ p \to K^+ \Sigma^+)$ at 3.2 BeV/c are shown in Figure 4.7. The solid curve represents $d\sigma/dt(\pi^- p \to \pi^0 n)$ measurements at a similar momentum. The similarity in the two cross sections is striking. In

particular, the $\pi^+ p \to K^+ \Sigma^+$ data also show a dip at $t \simeq -0.5$ $(\text{BeV}/c)^2$. The necessity for both q and Q exchange contributions to this reaction is indicated by the
presence of a sizeable polarization, as shown in Figure 4.8. The polarization
changes sign around $t \simeq -0.5$ $(\text{BeV}/c)^2$. It is tempting to associate the dip in
$d\sigma/dt$ and the change in sign of polarization with sense-nonsense factors at $\alpha = 0$.
Such an association has not been established yet because of the difficulty in dis-
entangling the q and Q trajectories and residues from the limited amount of data.

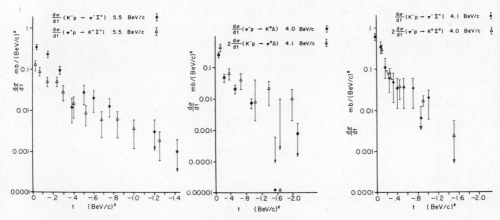

Figure 4.9. Typical data on hypercharge exchange reactions. The compared values of $d\sigma/dt$
should coincide if the q and Q trajectories are degenerate.

Since the q amplitude changes sign under line reversal and the Q amplitude
does not, some polarization relations are predicted in the model:

$$P(\pi^+ p \to K^+ \Sigma^+) = -P(K^- p \to \pi^- \Sigma^+)$$

$$P(\pi^- p \to K^0 \Lambda) = -P(K^- p \to \pi^0 \Lambda)$$

In writing these relations we have ignored differences in phase space that are
negligible at high energy but can be taken into account at intermediate energies.
If we make the additional assumption that the q and Q trajectories are degenerate, then the following cross section relations are obtained

$$\frac{d\sigma}{dt}(\pi^+ p \to K^+ \Sigma^+) = \frac{d\sigma}{dt}(K^- p \to \pi^- \Sigma^+)$$

$$\frac{d\sigma}{dt}(\pi^- p \to K^0 \Lambda) = 2 \frac{d\sigma}{dt}(K^- p \to \pi^0 \Lambda)$$

$$2 \frac{d\sigma}{dt}(\pi^- p \to \Sigma^0 K^0) = \frac{d\sigma}{dt}(K^- p \to \pi^- \Sigma^+)$$

Comparisons of available experimental data on the left- and right-hand sides of these equalities are presented in Figure 4.9. The relations do not seem to be in gross disagreement with experiment. Some deviations resulting from nonexact degeneracy of the trajectories and phase space differences are expected in any event.

As a final remark we note that the application of SU(3) to the baryon vertex is far more involved than for the meson vertex. For the exchange of a given octet multiplet, both F and D types of SU(3) invariant couplings exist at the baryon vertex. The F/D coupling ratio will be different, in general, for vector and tensor exchanges and also different in helicity flip and helicity nonflip amplitudes. As a final complication the F/D ratios may be t dependent. Thus attempts to relate charge and hypercharge reactions necessarily involve considerable input information or assumptions regarding the F/D ratios.

4.4 RESONANCE PRODUCTION REACTIONS

The applications of Regge pole theory to inelastic processes involving the production of particles with high spin are technically more complex because of the presence of additional helicity amplitudes. Moreover, a greater degree of arbitrariness is encountered since more residues must be parametrized. To offset these limitations, data on the spin density matrix elements supplement the data on $d\sigma/dt$. Here we wish to mention briefly a relatively simple class of inelastic reactions that will likely play an important role in future Regge phenomenology. The reactions and the contributing meson exchanges are

$$\pi^+ p \to \pi^0 \Delta_\delta^{++} \qquad (\rho)$$

$$\pi^+ p \to \eta \Delta_\delta^{++} \qquad (A)$$

$$K^+ p \to K^0 \Delta_\delta^{++} \qquad (\rho, A)$$

$$K^- p \to \bar{K}^0 \Delta_\delta^0 \qquad (\rho, A)$$

$$\pi^+ p \to K^+ \Sigma_\delta^+ \qquad (q, Q)$$

$$K^- p \to \pi^- \Sigma_\delta^+ \qquad (q, Q)$$

These reactions are analogs of the processes considered in previous sections, with the produced $1/2^+$ baryon replaced by the corresponding member of the $3/2^+$ decuplet. Since the trajectories can be determined from the processes discussed in Sections 4.2 and 4.3, only the residues remain as parameters here.

Some of the available data on these reactions are shown in Figure 4.10. A dip has been observed in high energy data on the $\pi^+ p \to \pi^0 \Delta_\delta^{++}$ reaction at $t \simeq -0.5$ $(\text{BeV}/c)^2$ corresponding to $\alpha_\rho(t) \simeq 0$. Data on reaction $K^+ p \to K^0 \Delta_\delta^{++}$ show no dip, similar to the $K^-p \to \bar{K}^0 n$ data. Energy dependences of $d\sigma/dt$ for these re-actions, where known, fall into the expected trajectory patterns. Thus we have reason to believe that Regge predictions will continue to be borne out by these reactions.

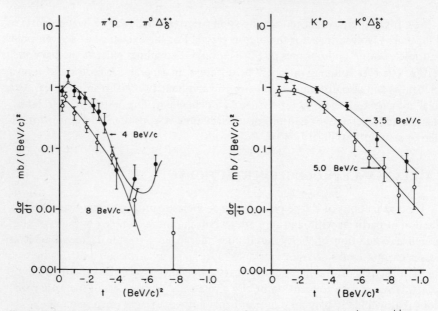

Figure 4.10. Representative data on the resonance production reactions $\pi^+ p \to \pi^0 \Delta_\delta^{++}$ and $K^+ p \to K^0 \Delta_\delta^{++}$.

There are still numerous questions to be answered by phenomenological studies in even the simplest of inelastic reactions. Nonetheless the overall picture seems quite encouraging. The prominent features of the accumulated data on inelastic scattering apparently fit rather nicely into the framework of the Regge pole theory.

Chapter 5

Total Cross Sections and Forward Elastic Scattering

5.1 MESON EXCHANGES

The spirit of the Regge approach is to associate, insofar as possible, the t-channel Regge poles with observed mesons. A possible exception to this rule is encountered in the description of elastic processes. With conventional slopes $\alpha' \approx 1$ (BeV/c)$^{-2}$, extrapolations of trajectories through known mesons to $t = 0$ give $\alpha(0) \leq 0.6$. For such intercepts the elastic and total cross sections would decrease rather rapidly with increasing energy. Experimentally the trends of total cross section and $t = 0$ elastic differential cross section ($d\sigma/dt$) data are toward constant limiting values at high energy (cf. Figure 2.14). This empirical behavior requires the leading trajectory to have $\alpha(0) = 1$ and $\tau = +1$. Thus if the leading trajectory has particle recurrences, it apparently has a small slope so that the 2^+ meson occurs at high mass. The label "Pomeranchuk trajectory" or simply "Pomeron" is customarily used to describe this trajectory since the Pomeranchuk theorem on asymptotic total cross sections, $\sigma_t^{\bar{A}B}(\infty) = \sigma_t^{AB}(\infty)$, must be realized by the leading Regge singularity. The exceptional nature of the Pomeron is not theoretically understood. Whether $\alpha_P(0)$ is exactly 1 or whether $\alpha_P'(0)$ is nonzero remain unsolved questions. Nonetheless the Pomeron plays an essential role in high energy phenomenology. In the subsequent discussion we assume that $\alpha_P(0) = 1$.

The important Regge exchanges for elastic amplitudes are thought to be the Pomeron, and the neutral nonstrange members of the vector and tensor nonets. The trajectory notation and the association with mesons in the 1^- and 2^+ SU(3) nonets are given in the table below. The S and ϕ Regge exchanges are believed to be uncoupled from the $\bar{N}N$ vertex and consequently do not contribute to the πN, KN, or NN elastic amplitudes. (This coupling ansatz can be verified from studies of reactions like $\pi N \rightarrow \phi N$ and $\pi N \rightarrow f^0 N$ at backward angles, cf. Section 7.2.)

The contributing poles to the $\bar{p}p$, K^-p, and π^-p elastic amplitudes are

$$f(\bar{p}p) = \tfrac{3}{2}P_N + \tfrac{3}{2}P_N' + \tfrac{1}{6}A_N + \tfrac{3}{2}\omega_N + \tfrac{1}{6}\rho_N$$

$$f(K^-p) = P_K + \tfrac{1}{2}P_K' + \tfrac{1}{6}A_K + \tfrac{1}{2}\omega_K + \tfrac{1}{6}\rho_K$$

$$f(\pi^-p) = P_\pi + P_\pi' + \tfrac{1}{3}\rho_\pi$$

Trajectory label	Particle (mass, J^P, I^G)	Signature and SU(3) multiplet
P	??	$\tau = +1$, singlet
P'	$f_0(1250, 2^+, 0^+)$	
S	$f'(1500, 2^+, 0^+)$	$\tau = +1$, nonet
A	$A_2(1320, 2^+, 1^-)$	
ω	$\omega(783, 1^-, 0^-)$	
ϕ	$\phi(1020, 1^-, 0^-)$	$\tau = -1$, nonet
ρ	$\rho(750, 1^-, 1^+)$	

The numerical coefficients are extracted so that certain of the residues would be equal in symmetry limits to be discussed later. Helicity indices have been suppressed since a similar expression holds for each helicity amplitude. The trajectory symbol as used above denotes the corresponding Regge exchange amplitude. Representative forms of the spin-averaged nonflip amplitudes are

$$P_K = \frac{1}{\sqrt{s}} \gamma_{P\bar{K}K} \gamma_{P\bar{N}N} \left(-\cot\frac{\pi\alpha_P}{2} + i \right)\left(\frac{E_{\text{Lab}}}{E_0}\right)^{\alpha_P}$$

for Pomeron or tensor nonet exchanges and

$$\omega_K = \frac{1}{\sqrt{s}} \gamma_{\omega\bar{K}K} \gamma_{\omega\bar{N}N} \left(\tan\frac{\pi\alpha_\omega}{2} + i \right)\left(\frac{E_{\text{Lab}}}{E_0}\right)^{\alpha_\omega}$$

for vector nonet exchanges. Line reversal and isotopic spin invariance enable us to generate the other NN, KN, and πN amplitudes without introducing additional residues. Under line reversal the odd signature amplitudes change sign and under the interchange $p \to n$, the $I = 1$ exchange amplitudes change sign. Thus, the four elastic amplitudes for KN scattering are

$$f(K^- p) = P_K + \tfrac{1}{2}P'_K + \tfrac{1}{6}A_K + \tfrac{1}{2}\omega_K + \tfrac{1}{6}\rho_K$$

$$f(K^+ p) = P_K + \tfrac{1}{2}P'_K + \tfrac{1}{6}A_K - \tfrac{1}{2}\omega_K - \tfrac{1}{6}\rho_K$$

$$f(K^- n) = P_K + \tfrac{1}{2}P'_K - \tfrac{1}{6}A_K + \tfrac{1}{2}\omega_K - \tfrac{1}{6}\rho_K$$

$$f(K^+ n) = P_K + \tfrac{1}{2}P'_K - \tfrac{1}{6}A_K - \tfrac{1}{2}\omega_K + \tfrac{1}{6}\rho_K$$

Similarly the πN amplitudes are

$$f(\pi^- p) = P_\pi + P'_\pi + \tfrac{1}{3}\rho_\pi$$

$$f(\pi^+ p) = P_\pi + P'_\pi - \tfrac{1}{3}\rho_\pi$$

5.2· TOTAL CROSS SECTIONS AND SYMMETRIES

The most direct application of this Regge model for elastic amplitudes is to total cross sections via the optical theorem:

$$\sigma_t(s) = \frac{4\pi}{q_{cm}} \operatorname{Im} f(s, t = 0)$$

From the line reversal and isotopic spin results, certain of the meson exchange contributions can be directly isolated from the data. For example, with the notation

$$\Delta(AB) = \sigma_t(\bar{A}B) - \sigma_t(AB)$$

the ρ contributions to πN, KN, and NN total cross sections are

$$\rho_\pi = \tfrac{3}{2}\Delta(\pi^+ p)$$

$$\rho_K = \tfrac{3}{2}[\Delta(K^+ p) - \Delta(K^+ n)]$$

$$\rho_N = \tfrac{3}{2}[\Delta(pp) - \Delta(pn)]$$

where the symbol ρ is now used to denote the ρ-Regge pole contribution to σ_t. Similarly the ω contributions are

$$\omega_K = \tfrac{1}{2}[\Delta(K^+ p) + \Delta(K^+ n)]$$

$$\omega_N = \tfrac{1}{6}[\Delta(pp) + \Delta(pn)]$$

Sum rules relating these contributions can be derived from SU(3) or universality principles.

If the couplings of the exchanges obey SU(3) symmetry, then a single sum rule is predicted: $\rho_\pi/\rho_K = 1$. This sum rule is consistent with the data on total cross section differences (cf. Figure 4.3).

If, on the other hand, both the ρ and ω couplings are universal (i.e., F type in analogy with the isovector and isoscalar couplings of the photon), then three equalities are predicted:

$$\frac{\rho_\pi}{\rho_K} = 1 \qquad \frac{\rho_\pi}{\rho_N} = 1 \qquad \frac{\omega_K}{\omega_N} = 1$$

Unfortunately, with the large errors on existing $\sigma_t(\bar{p}n)$ data the latter two universality relations cannot be directly checked. However an equality related to ω_K/ω_N using a deuteron target

$$\frac{[\tfrac{1}{2}\Delta(K^+ d)]}{[\tfrac{1}{6}\Delta(pd)]} = 1$$

agrees very well with experiment, as shown in Figure 5.1. The success of this relation based on ω exchange substantiates the assumption that the ϕ exchange is decoupled from the $\bar{N}N$ vertex.

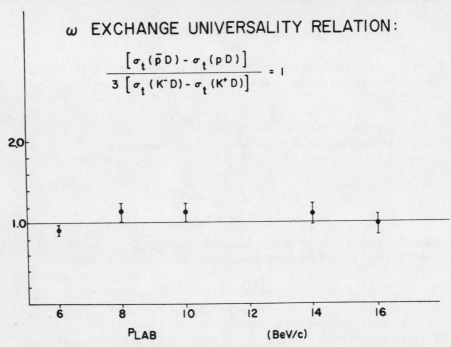

Figure 5.1. Experimental evaluation of ω universality sum rule: from V. Barger, CERN Report 68-7.

SU(3) versus Universality Dilemma

When both SU(3) and universality are assumed for the couplings of ρ and ω exchanges, a series of predictions are obtained that systematically disagree with experiment by 40 to 80%, with uncertainties in the data of about 5%. Some of these relatively unsuccessful predictions are

$$\tfrac{1}{2}\Delta(K^+ p) = \Delta(K^+ n) = \Delta(\pi^+ p)$$

$$\Delta(pp) = 5\Delta(\pi^+ p) = \tfrac{5}{4}\Delta(pn)$$

It is therefore clear that we must give up *some part* of the universality hypothesis or alternatively abandon approximate SU(3) symmetry for the residues. On the face of it, neither alternative seems very attractive. SU(3) apparently works well for other couplings (such as $A\pi\eta/A\bar{K}K$), whereas the ω universality relation for deuterons is well obeyed.

A theoretical answer to the above puzzle is suggested by the Regge pole model. The t-channel helicity nonflip Regge residue for vector meson exchange in πN or KN scattering has the structure

$$\beta_{++}(t, \alpha) \sim \gamma\left[g + \frac{t}{4M^2}h + (\alpha - 1)(g + h)\right]$$

where γ denotes the coupling to the pseudoscalar mesons; g and h are the charge and anomalous moment couplings to baryons, respectively: $g\gamma_\mu$ and $-h\sigma_{\mu\nu}q_\nu/2M$. From the vector meson–photon analogy, the g coupling is presumably pure F type at $t = 0, \alpha \equiv 1$, whereas h contains an appreciable D-type coupling. Now the vector meson exchange contribution to the total cross section is determined by $\beta_{++}(t = 0, \alpha(0))$. Thus, we have

$$(\sigma_t)_V \propto \gamma\{g + [\alpha(0) - 1](g + h)\}$$

From this expression, it is apparent that universality holds only if $\kappa = (g + h)/g \ll 1$ at $t = 0, \alpha(0)$. An estimate of this ratio from nucleon electromagnetic form factors gives $\kappa_\rho = 4.7, \kappa_\omega = 0.9$ at $t = 0, \alpha = 1$. It seems reasonable to expect $\kappa_\rho \gg \kappa_\omega$, $\kappa_\omega \ll 1$ at $t = 0, \alpha(0)$, in which case *universality would be valid for ω exchange but not for ρ exchange*. The present data are consistent with having both SU(3) and ω universality for the couplings. An interesting sidelight of this speculation is a prediction for the ρ, ω t-channel helicity flip amplitudes. The flip residue has the general structure

$$\beta_{+-}(t, \alpha) \sim (-t)^{1/2}\alpha\gamma[g + h]$$

Consequently we expect $\beta_{+-}^\rho/\beta_{+-}^\omega \gg 1$ for $t \leqslant 0$. Charge exchange differential cross sections and elastic polarization data for πN scattering indicate that β_{+-}^ρ is large. The size β_{+-}^ω has not been established yet by phenomenological analyses of KN scattering.

Exchange Degeneracy

Some qualitative predictions for total cross sections and real parts of the $t = 0$ elastic amplitudes can be obtained from the following assumptions about the trajectories and residues:

$$\alpha_{P'}(0) \approx \alpha_\omega(0) \approx \alpha_A(0) \approx \alpha_\rho(0) \approx \tfrac{1}{2}$$

$$\gamma_{P'\bar{K}K} \approx \gamma_{\omega\bar{K}K} \qquad \gamma_{P'\bar{N}N} \approx \gamma_{\omega\bar{N}N}$$

$$\gamma_{A\bar{K}K} \approx \gamma_{\rho\bar{K}K} \qquad \gamma_{A\bar{N}N} \approx \gamma_{\rho\bar{N}N}$$

where the γ's are the residue factors for the nonet exchanges. These approximate equalities lead to the relations

$$\sigma_t(K^+ p) \approx \sigma_t(K^+ n) = \frac{4\pi}{q}\operatorname{Im}P_K \approx \text{const}$$

$$\sigma_t(pp) \approx \sigma_t(pn) = \frac{4\pi}{q}\operatorname{Im}P_N \approx \text{const}$$

$$\operatorname{Re}f(K^- p) \approx \operatorname{Re}f(K^- n) \approx \operatorname{Re}P_K = 0$$

$$\operatorname{Re}f(\bar{p}p) \approx \operatorname{Re}f(\bar{p}n) \approx \operatorname{Re}P_N = 0$$

The approximate experimental equality and constancy of these total cross sections is a well-known empirical fact (cf. Figure 2.14). The real part of the $\bar{p}p$ amplitude has been measured at 12 BeV/c and found to be essentially zero.

Still using the above exchange degeneracy relations and taking $\alpha_{P'}(0) \approx \alpha_A(0) \approx \frac{1}{2}$, we obtain the following prediction

$$\left[\frac{\operatorname{Re}f(pp)}{\operatorname{Im}f(pp)}\right]_{t=0} = -\frac{[\sigma_t(\bar{p}p) - \sigma_t(pp)]}{\sigma_t(pp)}$$

This result is also in qualitative agreement with the high energy data.

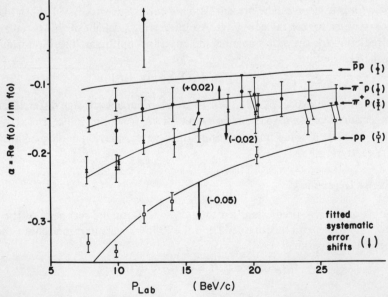

Figure 5.2. Regge pole model fits to the experimental data on the ratio of real to imaginary parts of the scattering amplitude at $t = 0$: from V. Barger *et al.*, *Nucl. Phys.* B5, 411 (1968).

Data Fitting: σ_t and $(\mathrm{Re}\,f/\mathrm{Im}\,f)_{t=0}$

The total cross section data in the 5–30 BeV/c range were shown in Figure 2.14. Data on $\mathrm{Re}\,f/\mathrm{Im}\,f$ at $t = 0$ are plotted in Figure 5.2. The curves in the two figures represent the results of a simultaneous fit to σ_t, $(\mathrm{Re}\,f/\mathrm{Im}\,f)_{t=0}$, and $t = 0$

Table 5.1

Regge parameters determined from a fit to data on total cross sections, $(\mathrm{Re}\,f/\mathrm{Im}\,f)_{t=0}$, and forward charge exchange data. For comparison, the predictions of various symmetry schemes for the Regge residues are indicated: from V. Barger *et al., Nucl. Phys.* **B5**, 411 (1968).

Regge Model for Total Cross Sections

Fitted Trajectory Intercept	Regge Residue	Fitted Residue	SU(3)	ρ,ω Universality	SU(3) Quark Model	(ρ, A) Exchange Degeneracy
$\alpha_P = 1$	$(P\pi\pi)(P\bar{N}N)$	2.16 ± 0.03	a		g	
	$(P\bar{K}K)(P\bar{N}N)$	1.77 ± 0.04	a		g	
	$(PNN)^2$	2.45 ± 0.05			g	
$\alpha_{P'} = .51 \pm .03$	$(P'\pi\pi)(P'NN)$	2.03 ± 0.08	b ⎫		h ⎫	
	$(P'\bar{K}K)(P'\bar{N}N)$	1.77 ± 0.31	b ⎬		h ⎬	
	$(P'\bar{N}N)^2$	3.02 ± 0.18			h	
$\alpha_A = .34 \pm .03$	$(A\pi\eta)(A\bar{N}N)$	1.6 ± 0.03	c ⎫		h ⎫	
	$(A\bar{K}K)(A\bar{N}N)$	1.7 ± 0.23	c ⎬		h ⎬	j
	$(A\bar{N}N)^2$	$0\ {}^{+1.7}_{-0}$			h	k
$\alpha_\omega = .38 \pm .04$	$(\omega\bar{K}K)(\omega\bar{N}N)$	2.5 ± 0.3		e ⎫	i ⎫	
	$(\omega\bar{N}N)^2$	2.8 ± 0.4		e ⎬	i ⎬	
$\alpha_\rho = .54 \pm .01$	$(\rho\pi\pi)(\rho\bar{N}N)$	1.1 ± 0.06	d ⎫	f ⎫	i ⎫	
	$(\rho\bar{K}K)(\rho\bar{N}N)$	1.2 ± 0.1	d ⎬	f ⎬	i ⎬	j
	$(\rho\bar{N}N)^2$	$0\ {}^{+0.9}_{-0}$		f	i	k

$\chi^2 = 122$ Repeated letter denotes predicted equality

No. Data = 165   } Denotes verification from fit

charge exchange differential cross section data using the (P, P', A, ω, ρ) exchange model. The theoretical curves reproduce the data well. The fitted parameters from this analysis are listed in Table 5.1. The P' couplings to $\pi\pi$ and $\bar{K}K$ differ by 20% from exact SU(3). Predictions of universality and exchange degeneracy can also be evaluated from the table. The trajectories and residues of the (ρ, A) or (ω, P') poles are less degenerate than the success of our previous qualitative arguments might have led us to believe. Nevertheless the approximate imaginary amplitude equalities

$$\text{Im}\,\rho \approx \text{Im}\,A \qquad \text{Im}\,P' \approx \text{Im}\,\omega$$

over the presently explored momentum range are maintained by the fitted parameters.

5.3 ELASTIC SCATTERING

General Character of Exchange Amplitudes

Studies of hadron scattering over the past five years suggest that small angle elastic scattering is theoretically the most complex of two-particle collision phenomena. Whereas selection rules limit the variety of exchanges in inelastic processes, no such simplification occurs for elastic scattering. As a consequence of this intrinsic complexity, present Regge pole descriptions of elastic scattering are not unique. Despite this limitation, phenomenological Regge pole analyses have been exceedingly useful in the formation of a probable dynamical picture of the elastic scattering mechanism. The basic appeal of the Regge pole theory is the treatment of elastic scattering and inelastic reactions on an equal footing. Thus characteristic features of Regge exchange amplitudes determined from studies of elastic scattering processes apply also in inelastic reactions, and vice versa. The discussion here will be limited to the practical state of the art, and will not include consideration of cuts or other complex Regge phenomena.

The dominant t-channel helicity amplitudes for P and P' exchanges must be nonflip inasmuch as the elastic differential cross sections show no sign of flattening near $t = 0$, which would result from a large flip amplitude. The ρ exchange flip amplitude is large since the $\pi^- p \to \pi^0 n$ differential cross section has a turnover at small $t\,[t \simeq -0.1\ (\text{BeV/c})^2]$. Our previous theoretical arguments suggest that the ω is primarily nonflip. Finally the basic similarity of pp and pn differential cross section data (cf. Figure 2.18) and the marked difference in pp and $\bar{p}p$ angular distributions (cf. Figure 2.16) imply that ρ and A exchange amplitudes in NN scattering are small and ω is large. The approximate isospin independence of high energy elastic differential cross sections implies that *isoscalar exchange amplitudes are considerably larger than those for isovector exchange.* In summary, the dominant t-channel helicity amplitudes for elastic processes are as tabulated below. Using only P, P', ω, and ρ exchanges, the elastic differential cross sections have been adequately parameterized. A common feature of the various parameterizations is the necessity for a distinctively smaller slope for the Pomeranchuk trajectory than for the other trajectories. In order to account for

	Nonflip	Flip
πN	P, P'	ρ
KN	P, P', ω	?
NN	P, P', ω	?

the nonshrinking πp forward peak, the Pomeranchuk slope must be constrained in the interval

$$0 \leqslant \frac{d\alpha_P}{dt} \leqslant 0.5 (\text{BeV}/\text{c})^2$$

with the smaller values preferred. In contrast, the (P', ω, ρ) trajectories are normally found to have more conventional slopes: $d\alpha/dt \simeq 1 \ (\text{BeV}/\text{c})^2$.

Right Signature Dips

Striking minima have been observed in $d\sigma/dt$ at $t \approx -0.5 \ (\text{BeV}/\text{c})^2$ for some elastic processes. However interpretations of minima in elastic scattering are not so direct as in inelastic reactions like $\pi^- p \to \pi^0 n$. The contributions of several contributing trajectories must first be disentangled in a model-dependent analysis of the elastic scattering data.

Representative data on $\pi^\pm p$ elastic scattering are shown in Figure 5.3. A break occurs in both angular distributions around $t \simeq -0.8$. The data at large t show rapid shrinkage with increasing energy as would result from negative values of Regge trajectories. The $\bar{p}p$ data in Figure 5.4 also go through a marked dip near $t \simeq -0.5 \ (\text{BeV}/\text{c})^2$. However the pp data appear to be very smooth throughout this momentum transfer range.

The construction of a Regge model to explain these data is somewhat simplified by the approximate empirical equalities

$$\frac{d\sigma}{dt}(\pi^+ p) \simeq \frac{d\sigma}{dt}(\pi^- p) \qquad \frac{d\sigma}{dt}(pp) \simeq \frac{d\sigma}{dt}(pn)$$

indicating very little isospin dependence. Accordingly only P, P', and ω Regge exchanges are necessary to account for the dominant features of the data. Moreover, neglecting the small high energy polarizations, only spin-nonflip amplitudes need be considered. Then, the various scattering amplitudes have the forms

$$f_{\pi^+ p} = f_{\pi^- p} = f_{\pi N}(P) + f_{\pi N}(P')$$

$$f_{pp} = f_{pn} = f_{NN}(P) + f_{NN}(P') + f_{NN}(\omega)$$

$$f_{\bar{p}p} = f_{\bar{p}n} = f_{NN}(P) + f_{NN}(P') - f_{NN}(\omega)$$

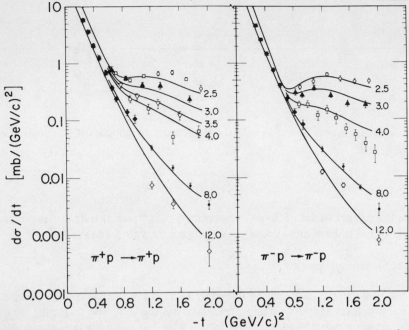

Figure 5.3. $\pi^{\pm}p$ elastic scattering data. The curves represent a Regge pole fit with P, P', and ρ exchanges: from C. Chiu *et al., Phys. Rev.* **161**, 1563 (1967).

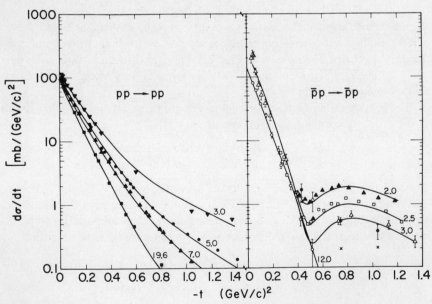

Figure 5.4. pp and $\bar{p}p$ elastic differential cross section data. The curves represent a fit with P, P', and ω Regge pole amplitudes: from C. Chiu *et al., Phys. Rev.* **161**, 1563 (1967).

Corresponding formulas for KN and $\bar{K}N$ scattering are similar to the NN and $\bar{N}N$ expressions.

For small t the trajectories are expected to have the approximate linear shapes

$$\alpha_P(t) \simeq 1 + \epsilon t \qquad (\epsilon < \tfrac{1}{2})$$

$$\alpha_{P'}(t) \simeq 0.5 + t$$

$$\alpha_\omega(t) \simeq 0.5 + t$$

The elastic scattering dip–bump structures for $t \simeq -0.5$ have been successfully interpreted in terms of the no-compensation mechanism for the P' trajectory and the sense mechanism for the ω trajectory at $\alpha = 0$:

$$f_{\pi N}(P') \sim f_{NN}(P') \sim \frac{(\alpha_{P'})^2}{\sin(\pi\alpha_{P'}/2)}$$

$$f_{NN}(\omega) \sim \frac{1}{\cos(\pi\alpha_\omega/2)}$$

The $f_{\pi N}(P')$ amplitude vanishes at $\alpha_{P'}(t) = 0$ causing the break in $d\sigma/dt(\pi N)$. The marked dip in $d\sigma/dt(\bar{p}p)$ is caused by destructive interference of P and ω imaginary amplitudes, whereas for $d\sigma/dt(pp)$ these contributions interfere constructively. The solid curves in Figures 5.3 and 5.4 represent the results of a fit to the data using these mechanisms. [The ρ helicity flip amplitude was included in the fit to account for the $\pi^\pm p$ polarization data and the slight splitting of $d\sigma/dt(\pi^+ p)$ and $d\sigma/dt(\pi^- p)$.] In this fit to the $\pi^\pm p$ data, $\alpha_{P'} = 0$ at $t = -0.5$ whereas the actual minimum in the theoretical curve occurs at $t = -0.8$. This shift in the dip position is due to the presence of the Pomeranchuk amplitude which falls smoothly with increasing t. Moreover, as the momentum increases, the dip position moves out slightly in t. In general we should expect the position of a minimum in an elastic differential cross section to be shifted somewhat from the t value at which one of the trajectories passes through a nonpositive integer. The position of such a minimum may migrate slightly to larger $|t|$ with increasing momenta.

The above interpretation of the structure in the elastic data can be simply demonstrated by the following picture. The P trajectory is taken to be flat; the P' and ω trajectories are assumed linear and approximately degenerate, as in Figure 5.5. The individual contributions (suppressing subscripts πN, etc.) then have the forms

$$f(P) = \gamma i$$

$$f(P') = -\beta \frac{\exp(-i\pi\alpha/2)}{\sin(\pi\alpha/2)} s^{\alpha-1}$$

$$f(\omega) = i\bar{\beta} \frac{\exp(-i\pi\alpha/2)}{\cos(\pi\alpha/2)} s^{\alpha-1}$$

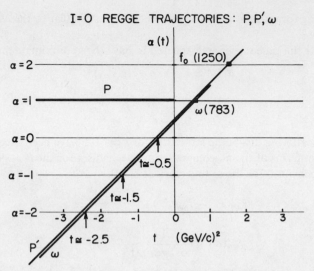

Figure 5.5. Speculative straight-line plot of P, P', and ω Regge trajectories: from V. Barger and R. J. N. Phillips, *Phys. Rev. Letters* **20**, 564 (1968).

where $\gamma(t)$, $\beta(t)$, and $\bar{\beta}(t)$ are the residue functions and $d\sigma/dt = |f|^2$. A suitable dynamical ansatz, which reproduces the gross features of the data, is the cyclic residue structure

$$\beta(t) \approx \lambda(t)\sin^2\left(\frac{\pi\alpha}{2}\right) \qquad \bar{\beta}(t) \approx \lambda(t)\cos^2\left(\frac{\pi\alpha}{2}\right)$$

for the range of t considered ($0 \leqslant -t \leqslant 1$). The double zero of the P' residue at $\alpha = 0$ corresponds to the no-compensation mechansim. With the above forms the magnitudes of the two residues are correlated. The resulting cross sections are

$$\frac{d\sigma}{dt}(\pi N) = \bar{\gamma}^2 + [2\bar{\gamma}\bar{\lambda}s^{\alpha-1} + \bar{\lambda}^2 s^{2\alpha-2}]\sin^2\left(\frac{\pi\alpha}{2}\right)$$

$$\frac{d\sigma}{dt}(NN) = \gamma^2 + 2\gamma\lambda s^{\alpha-1} + \lambda^2 s^{2\alpha-2}$$

$$\frac{d\sigma}{dt}(\bar{N}N) = \gamma^2 - 2\gamma\lambda s^{\alpha-1}\cos\pi\alpha + \lambda^2 s^{2\alpha-2}$$

In this model dips occur in πN and $\bar{N}N$ at $\alpha = 0$ whereas NN is smooth. The dips come from terms that decrease rapidly as s increases. At small t, $d\sigma(NN)/dt$ approaches its asymptotic limit from above (shrinks) and $d\sigma(\bar{N}N)/dt$ approaches from below (antishrinks). Corrections to the model must be invoked to explain the crossover of the diffraction peaks at $t \simeq -0.15$ (BeV/c)^2.

Recurring Minima in Elastic Scattering

Data at larger momentum transfers reveal the presence of additional dips in $\pi^{\pm}p$ and $\bar{p}p$ elastic scattering differential cross sections. The $\pi^{\pm}p$ data in Figure 5.6 show a second dip at $t \simeq -2.7$ $(\text{BeV}/c)^2$. The approximate equality

$$\frac{d\sigma}{dt}(\pi^- p) \simeq \frac{d\sigma}{dt}(\pi^+ p)$$

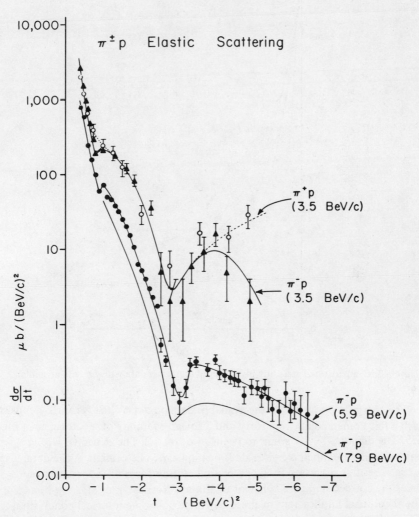

Figure 5.6. Structure in $\pi^{\pm}p$ elastic scattering data at large momentum transfers.

appears to hold out to the second dip in the 3.5-BeV/c momenta data, thus suggesting dominance of P and P' exchanges. The deviation from equality beyond the second dip at this low momentum is presumably due to u-channel baryon exchanges.

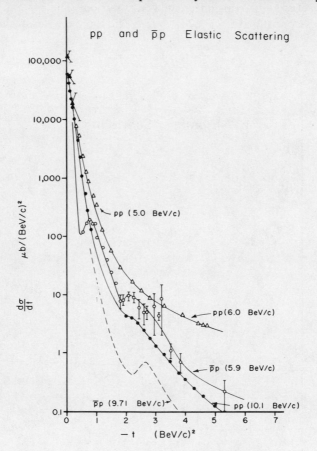

Figure 5.7. Comparison of structure in $\bar{p}p$ elastic scattering data with pp data at similar momenta.

The energy dependence of the available data on $d\sigma(\pi N)/dt$ is roughly consistent with a flat Pomeranchuk trajectory and a linearly falling P' trajectory, as in Figure 5.5. The dip at $t \simeq -2.7$ seems to occur at $\alpha_{P'} \approx -2$. The expected wrong signature, nonsense dip at $\alpha_{P'} = -1$ does not appear to be present in the data. The cyclic P' residue discussed in the preceding section for $\alpha = 0$ apparently reproduces the correct empirical behavior of the πN cross sections at $\alpha = -1$ and -2. The theoretical implications of these tentative phenomenological conclusions deserve further attention.

Representative large momentum transfer data on pp and $\bar{p}p$ scattering are plotted in Figure 5.7. The $\bar{p}p$ data show dips at $t \simeq -0.5$ and $-1.8\,(\text{BeV/c})^2$. The $d\sigma(\bar{p}p)/dt$ data lie below $d\sigma(pp)/dt$ for all $t \lesssim -0.2$. A quantitative analysis of the energy dependence of the large t data in terms of P, P', and ω exchanges has not yet been carried out.

The elastic data have provided the first indication for linearly falling Regge trajectories in the region $-t < 1\,(\text{BeV/c})^2$. This important result deserves further experimental confirmation. In addition, the accumulation of large momentum transfer data on elastic scattering should provide further clues as to the nature of the Regge dip mechanisms.

Polarization Data

In many instances accurate polarization data can provide a more sensitive guideline for the finer details of Regge models than is supplied by differential cross section data alone. Polarization in Regge models can arise only from interference between different poles since helicity flip and nonflip terms have the same phase for a given pole.

For πN scattering we have previously argued that the P and P' should be the dominant nonflip amplitudes and ρ the dominant flip amplitude. Thus the polarizations should be approximately given by

$$P(\pi^{\pm} p)\frac{d\sigma}{dt}(\pi^{\pm} p) \propto \pm \text{Im}\{\tilde{f}_{++}(P + P')\tilde{f}_{+-}^{*}(\rho)\}$$

The polarization data for $\pi^+ p$ and $\pi^- p$ do have opposite signs and about the same magnitudes, as shown in Figure 5.8. The solid curves in Figure 5.8 represent fits obtained from a conventional Regge parameterization. The change in sign of the curves at $t \simeq -0.5\,(\text{BeV/c})^2$ is due to the zero of $\tilde{f}_{+-}(\rho)$ at $\alpha_\rho = 0$.

High energy pp polarization data are plotted in Figure 5.9. Because the relative sizes of the P, P', and ω helicity flip amplitudes are not well established, it is not possible to make a clear-cut prediction for the $\bar{p}p$ polarization. Data on the $\bar{p}p$ polarization at lower energy (less than 3 BeV/c) have the same sign as the pp polarization at small t.

The measurement of polarization tensors may play an important role in the evolution of Regge models for elastic scattering. It has been suggested that such experiments can provide direct tests for the existence of Regge cuts.

Crossover Phenomenon

A common experimental feature of high energy $\pi^{\pm} p$, $K^{\pm} p$, $\bar{p}p$, and pp elastic scattering is the change in sign of the cross section differences:

$$D(AB) = \frac{d\sigma}{dt}(\bar{A}B) - \frac{d\sigma}{dt}(AB)$$

at momentum transfers $t = t_c \simeq -0.15 \,(\text{BeV}/c)^2$, as illustrated in Figures 2.15 and 2.16. This change in sign is commonly called the "crossover" phenomenon. In the Regge exchange model, $D(AB)$ can be expressed as

$$D(AB) = 2\,\text{Re}\,\Sigma_{[\lambda]}\,T^*_{[\lambda]}\,V_{[\lambda]}$$

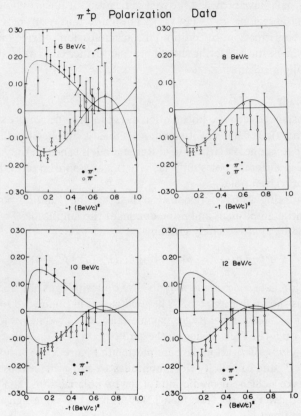

Figure 5.8. Polarization measurements for $\pi^{\pm}p$ elastic scattering. Solid curves represent the results of P, P', and ρ Regge pole fits: from W. Rarita *et al.*, *Phys. Rev.* **165**, 1615 (1968).

where $[\lambda]$ labels the particle helicities in the t-channel. The amplitude T represents the $\tau = +1$ exchanges (P, P') and V the $\tau = -1$ exchanges (ω, ρ). Since T is presumably dominantly nonflip and imaginary at small t, $D(AB)$ can be approximated by

$$D(AB) \sim \sum_{\text{nonflip}} \text{Im}\,T_{[\lambda]}\,\text{Im}\,V_{[\lambda]}$$

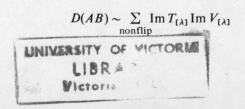

Since Im $T \neq 0$, the change in sign of $D(AB)$ must correspond to a change in sign of $(\text{Im } V)_{\text{nonflip}}$ for $t \sim t_c$.

In past Regge analyses, the crossovers have been explained by supposing that the helicity nonflip residue functions for the ρ and ω exchange amplitudes change sign at $t \simeq t_c$. This explanation in NN scattering becomes particularly restrictive when combined with the factorization theorem for the Regge residues and the requirement of real analyticity for the unfactored residues. It can then be shown that the ω-exchange residue functions vanish at $t \simeq t_c \sim -0.15 \ (\text{BeV/c})^2$ for every helicity amplitude in every reaction. Suppose for example that we parameterize the ω nonflip residue in NN elastic scattering as $\gamma(t) \sim (t - t_c)$. Since

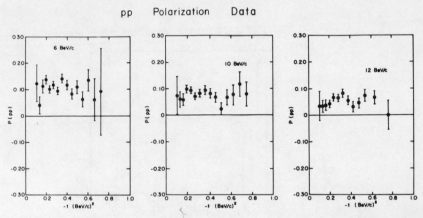

Figure 5.9. Polarization data for pp elastic scattering: from M. Borghini *et al.*, *Phys. Letters* **24B**, 77 (1967).

$\gamma(t) = (\gamma_{\omega \bar{N}N})^2$, the residue factor $\gamma_{\omega \bar{N}N}(t) \sim (t - t_c)^{1/2}$ becomes imaginary for $t < t_c$. Then real analyticity for complete residues like $(\gamma_{\omega A \bar{B}} \ \gamma_{\omega \bar{N}N})$ requires the behavior $\gamma_{\omega \bar{A} B} \sim (t - t_c)^{1/2}$.

If the usual explanation for the crossover in $\bar{p}p$ and pp scattering were correct, striking dips would appear at $t = t_c$ in all reactions in which ω exchange gives the dominant contribution. This conclusion is inconsistent with recent data on the reactions $\pi N \rightarrow \rho N$ and $\gamma p \rightarrow \pi^0 p$. The ω-exchange contribution to $\pi N \rightarrow \rho N$ can be directly isolated by the following combination of cross sections:

$$\left[\frac{d\sigma}{dt}(\pi^+ p \rightarrow \rho^+ p) + \frac{d\sigma}{dt}(\pi^+ p \rightarrow \rho^- p) - \frac{d\sigma}{dt}(\pi^- p \rightarrow \rho^0 n) \right]$$

In Figure 5.10 the results for this specific combination at 4 and 8 BeV/c are shown. The pronounced dip near $t = 0$ is a kinematic effect and the dip at $t \simeq -0.5$

$(\mathrm{BeV}/c)^2$ occurs where $\alpha_\omega(t) = 0$. However there is no indication of a dip at $t = t_c \simeq -0.15\ (\mathrm{BeV}/c)^2$ at either energy.

The difficulties with the foregoing explanation are a direct consequence of the assumption that the ω Regge pole gives the only significant $C = -1$ contribution to the $\bar{p}p$ and pp elastic scattering amplitudes. Therefore, extra ω-type contributions, which we denote by $\bar{\omega}$, presumably must be present such that $\mathrm{Im}(\omega + \bar{\omega})$ vanishes at $t = t_c$ to give the crossover. The presence of the $\bar{\omega}$ contribution avoids the prediction of dips in reactions like $\gamma p \to \pi^0 p$. The choice of the relevant mechanism for $\bar{\omega}$ (secondary Regge poles, Regge cuts, conspiring poles, or conspiring cuts) must come from detailed descriptions of a variety of scattering data.

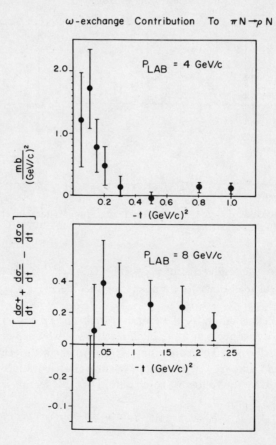

Figure 5.10. ω-exchange contribution to the reactions $\pi N \to \rho N$ at 4 and 8 BeV/c: from A. Contogouris *et al.*, *Phys. Rev. Letters* **19**, 1352 (1967).

5.4 DIFFRACTION MODELS

Unlike the development of nuclear physics, diffraction concepts have thus far not played a central role in the description of hadron elastic scattering processes at high energy. Nonetheless, many of the observed features of the forward elastic peaks can be crudely understood from the diffraction point of view, viz, dominantly imaginary amplitudes arise from absorption, dips occur as diffraction zeros; the crossover phenomenon is due to $d\sigma/dt \propto (\sigma_t)^2 \exp R^2 t$ where $\sigma_t \propto R^2$. The shrinkage or antishrinkage of forward peaks also can be qualitatively understood in the diffraction picture. In a certain sense the Regge pole treatments of elastic scattering represent an attempt to describe and understand more fully the intuitive picture of diffraction processes. Attempts at interpreting the pp elastic differential cross section data in terms of models that are more akin to the traditional diffraction formulations have recently been initiated by Yang and collaborators. We briefly discuss the point of view below and indicate some of the experimental consequences.

Extended Structure of the Proton

At high energy and small momentum transfer the pp differential cross section data are empirically related to the proton electromagnetic form factors by the relation

$$\left[\frac{(d\sigma/dt)^{pp}}{(d\sigma/dt)^{pp}_{t=0}} \right] = \left[\frac{G_E{}^p(t)}{G_E{}^p(0)} \right]^4$$

A comparison of experimental data for the left- and right-hand sides of this equality at small t is shown in Figure 5.11. The empirical scaling law $G_E{}^p(t)/G_E{}^p(0) = G_M{}^p(t)/G_M{}^p(0)$ has been used for the form factor data. Intuitively, a simple connection between pp scattering and the proton electromagnetic form factor suggests an equivalence of matter density (ρ_M) and charge density (ρ_c). From this point of view the pp scattering can be described as two absorptive spheres going through each other. In such a diffraction picture, the pp S-matrix element at impact parameter $b = (l + 1/2)\lambda$ is given by

$$S_{pp}(b) = \exp\left\{ -K \int dx\,dy\,dz\,dz'\,\rho_c(x,y,z)\rho_c(x-b,y,z') \right\}$$

The constant parameter K appearing in this formula is to be determined from $\sigma_t(pp)$. Using the dipole formula

$$G_E{}^p(t) = \frac{1}{(1 + t/0.71)^2}$$

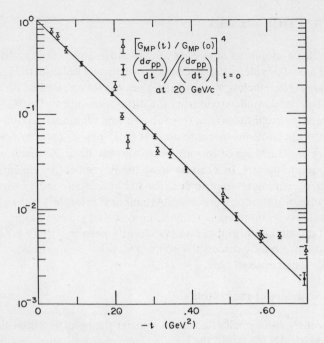

Figure 5.11. Experimental comparison of 20 BeV/c *pp* elastic scattering data with proton electromagnetic form factor data at small *t*: from R. Arnold and S. Fenster, CERN Report 68-7.

that approximately reproduces the observed proton electromagnetic structure, the qualitative predictions of this hadron density model for elastic *pp* differential cross sections can be simply explored. The results are shown in Figure 5.12. This diffraction model exhibits two particularly interesting features

(1) No shrinkage occurs at any value of *t*. Thus the calculation must be regarded as an asymptotic prediction. In experimental terms, the *pp* differential cross section is predicted to have a fixed lower bound at every *t*. In Regge language the energy dependence is like that of a fixed pole at $\alpha_P(t) \equiv 1$. This diffraction model presumably replaces the Pomeranchuk term of Regge models. The theoretical curve has the shape of $[G_E{}^P(t)]^4$ at large *t*, but falls below the form factor bound normalized at *t* = 0.

(2) The differential cross section has two diffraction zeros. Thus at higher energies the *pp* data should begin to show dips at these *t* values. This prediction is very different from the Regge model where the dips are due to exchange amplitudes whose contributions disappear at asymptotic energies.

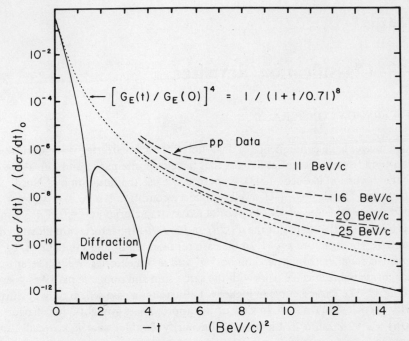

Figure 5.12. Predictions of the hadron density model for *pp* elastic scattering are shown by the solid curve. Experimental values of $(d\sigma/dt)/(d\sigma/dt)_{t=0}$ are represented by the dashed curves. The dotted curve denoted the dipole approximation to the proton electromagnetic structure data: from L. Durand, III and R. Lipes, *Phys. Rev. Letters* **20**, 637 (1968).

The unification of Regge pole and diffraction concepts for elastic amplitudes is clearly not complete. Nevertheless it is not unreasonable to expect a further merger of the two pictures as our understanding of the elastic scattering dynamics progresses. The outstanding problem in Regge models is the seemingly mysterious character of the Pomeranchuk trajectory. Why is it so different from the other trajectories? A complementary diffraction picture may provide the answer to this question.

Chapter 6

Classification Revisited

6.1 FERMION CONSPIRACY

An unavoidable consequence of analyticity for πN scattering is the occurrence of fermion Regge trajectories in pairs that have opposite parity and join at $u = 0$ (cf. the discussion in Section 3.3). As before, we use the notation $\alpha^{(\tau P)}$ for the trajectories. The Gribov–MacDowell symmetry condition is $\alpha^+(\sqrt{u}) = \alpha^-(-\sqrt{u})$, which results in a conspiracy of opposite parity trajectories at $u = 0$. Two of many possibilities for the shapes of the $\alpha^+(\sqrt{u})$ and $\alpha^-(\sqrt{u})$ trajectories are illustrated in Figure 6.1 for signature $\tau = +1$. In the case represented by the solid curves, particle recurrences will exist in general on both α^+ and α^- trajectories. We will refer to such correlated resonance pairs with the same spin and opposite parity as "parity doublets." The dashed curve in Figure 6.1 illustrates a case where only positive parity particles are realized. In view of the approximate straight-line behavior $\alpha(\sqrt{u}) \simeq a + bu$ found in Chapter 1, the parity doublet case is especially interesting.

In Chapter 1 only the dominant πN resonances were assigned to linear Regge trajectories. Numerous other N^* states also have been discovered through πN phase shift analyses. We attempt in the following to classify these additional resonances in the framework of MacDowell reflected trajectories.

(N_α, N_β) Trajectory

The N_α Regge trajectory has two established recurrences, $N(938, 1/2^+)$ and $N_\alpha(1688, 5/2^+)$. If we tentatively assume the *approximate* functional form

$$\alpha^+(\sqrt{u}) = \alpha_N(\sqrt{u}) \simeq -0.4 + 0.9(\sqrt{u})^2$$

for the N_α trajectory to be valid for both positive and negative values of u, then the reflected trajectory (N_β) is given by

$$\alpha^-(\sqrt{u}) = \alpha_N(-\sqrt{u}) \simeq -0.4 + 0.9(-\sqrt{u})^2$$

We would therefore expect particle recurrences $N_\beta(\sim 938, 1/2^-)$ and $N_\beta(\sim 1688, 5/2^-)$ provided that the residue $\gamma^-(\sqrt{u})$ does not vanish at these points. In fact an $I = 1/2$ πN resonance with $J^P = 5/2^-$ does exist at 1650 MeV. It is natural to associate this $N_\beta(1650, 5/2^-)$ state with the α^- trajectory. Since an $I = 1/2, J^P = 1/2^-$

106

particle of mass ~ 1 BeV does not exist, we assume that the N_β trajectory chooses nonsense at $\alpha^-(\sqrt{u}) = 1/2$ in order that the residue $\gamma^-(\sqrt{u})$ vanishes there. This speculation regarding the nucleon trajectory and residue function can be subject to indirect experimental test through its implications for backward πN elastic scattering. We will return to make this test in Section 7.4.

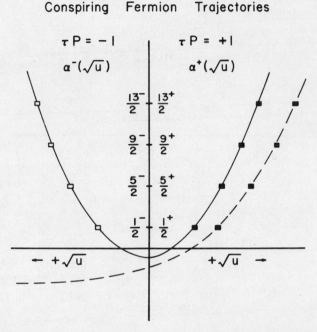

Figure 6.1. Illustration of two possibilities for the functional form of a MacDowell reflected trajectory.

$(\Delta_\delta, \Delta_\gamma)$ Trajectory

The five dominant $I = 3/2$ resonances fall nicely on a Δ_δ trajectory with no $\sqrt{u}$ terms, as illustrated in Figure 1.4

$$\alpha^-(\sqrt{u}) = \alpha_\Delta(\sqrt{u}) \simeq 0.15 + 0.9(\sqrt{u})^2$$

The lowest state on this trajectory is the well-known $\Delta_\delta(1236, 3/2^+)$ resonance. Again if this approximate functional form remains valid at negative $\sqrt{u}$, particle recurrences should also exist for the reflected trajectory (Δ_γ), with masses degenerate with the Δ_δ resonances. However, there is no D_{33} state with mass ~ 1236 for the MacDowell reflection of the $P_{33}(1236)$ and to retain the above trajectory hypothesis the residue must vanish to kill the state. The existence of a G_{37} state with mass close to the $F_{37}(1950)$ resonance provides a further test for the approximate symmetry in $\sqrt{u}$ of the Δ_δ trajectory. Until now this conjectured G_{37} resonance has not been found.

Small $\sqrt{u}$ terms in the Δ_δ trajectory function can shift the masses of the Δ_γ recurrences to higher values without appreciably modifying the interpolation through the Δ_δ resonance masses. As an example, the masses obtained from the trajectory forms

$$\text{(A)} \quad \alpha_\Delta(\sqrt{u}) = 0.15 + 0.9u$$

$$\text{(B)} \quad \alpha_\Delta(\sqrt{u}) = -0.12 + 0.35\sqrt{u} + 0.77u$$

are compared below.

Δ_δ masses

	$3/2^+$	$7/2^+$	$11/2^+$	$15/2^+$	$19/2^+$
Case (A)	1225	1929	2438	2858	3223
Case (B)	1236	1946	2476	2917	3304

Δ_γ masses

	$3/2^-$	$7/2^-$	$11/2^-$	$15/2^-$	$19/2^-$
Case (A)	1225	1929	2438	2858	3223
Case (B)	1691	2390	2930	3372	3758

A $D_{33}(1691)$ resonance has been discovered which might fit into case (B). Further information on πN resonance states from phase shift analyses and fits to backward πN scattering data should allow a determination of the importance of the $\sqrt{u}$ terms in the trajectory.

6.2 SECONDARY TRAJECTORIES

In addition to the dominant N^* resonances that have been classified as recurrences on N_α, Δ_δ, N_γ, and Δ_β Regge trajectories and their MacDowell reflections, other inelastic resonant states have been discovered in πN phase shift analyses. As an example, a P_{11} resonance exists at about 1460 MeV. Since this state has the same I and J^P as the nucleon, it cannot be accommodated on the leading N_α trajectory. Secondary trajectories are therefore essential if all particles are to be classified in simple Regge recurrence patterns. Inasmuch as secondary trajectories are commonplace in potential scattering, this development should not come as a surprise.

A tentative classification of all the presently known πN resonance states is shown in Figure 6.2. This classification involves secondary Regge trajectories

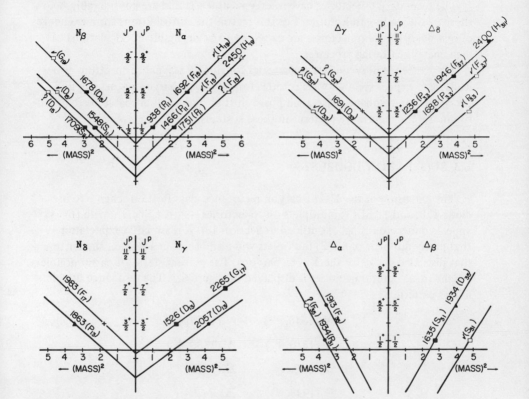

Figure 6.2. Tentative classification of πN resonances on MacDowell reflected trajectories: solid square—well-established resonance; solid circle—probable resonance; solid triangle—resonance interpretation still in doubt; open triangle—unconfirmed resonance; open square—predicted state; plus sign—extinguished state: from V. Barger and D. Cline, *Phys. Rev. Letters* **20**, 298 (1968).

which are displaced from the leading trajectories by approximately unit multiples of angular momentum. Furthermore, all trajectories in the scheme are approximately MacDowell symmetric; that is, trajectories with the same I and τ, but opposite P, are roughly degenerate. The assigments in Figure 6.2 are based on approximate straight-line trajectories: Re $\alpha(\sqrt{u}) \simeq a + bu$ and have been plotted versus (mass)^2 for convenience of straight-line representation. Fourteen of the known resonances are paired as MacDowell symmetric states with nearly degenerate masses. The experimental absence of the lowest particles on the leading trajectories with quantum numbers $J - L = 1 - I$ requires that the corresponding Regge residues vanish at the appropriate points to extinguish these states.

The secondary trajectories have intercepts at $u = 0$ that are considerably below those of the leading trajectories. For this reason the contributions from exchanges of secondary Regge trajectories are expected to be negligible in calculations of high energy scattering processes.

The existence of secondary trajectories for the N^* resonance spectrum also leads us to expect secondary trajectories for the $Y \neq 1$ baryon resonances and for the meson resonances. Detailed phase shift analyses will probably be required to unravel the recurrence patterns in these systems.

6.3 SU(3) PARITY DOUBLETS

The extension of the $Y = +1$ baryon recurrence classification scheme to include 1, 8, and 10 SU(3) multiplets on trajectories that rise linearly with $(mass)^2$ appears quite promising, as outlined in Section 1.4. A reasonable expectation is that parity doublets of SU(3) multiplets will also occur, in a fashion similar to that discussed above for the $Y = +1$ baryons. The present status of parity doublets for the (α, β) octet trajectories is displayed in Figure 6.3. The resonance doublets in this pattern are

$$N_\alpha(1688, \tfrac{5}{2}^+) \qquad N_\beta(1650, \tfrac{5}{2}^-)$$
$$\Lambda_\alpha(1810, \tfrac{5}{2}^+) \qquad \Lambda_\beta(1830, \tfrac{5}{2}^-)$$
$$\Sigma_\alpha \quad ? \qquad \Sigma_\beta(1765, \tfrac{5}{2}^-)$$
$$\Xi_\alpha(1930, ?) \qquad \Xi_\alpha \quad ?$$

The mass ordering $M[\Lambda_\beta(1830)] > M[\Sigma_\beta(1765)]$ for the $5/2^-$ states suggests a similar ordering $M[\Lambda_\alpha(1810)] > M[\Sigma_\alpha]$ for the $5/2^+$ states. The consequence of such an inversion of the masses (relative to the Λ_α and Σ_α masses of the $1/2^+$ particles) is to yield a value of $\alpha_\Sigma(0)$ much less than $\alpha_\Lambda(0)$. This conclusion can be experimentally checked eventually from the energy dependence of reactions that proceed via Σ_α and Λ_α exchanges.

Finally, in the realm of speculation, we can anticipate secondary trajectories for entire SU(3) multiplets. Figure 6.4 illustrates a possible pattern of the first secondary trajectories for the (α, β) octet multiplets. Clearly a great deal of accurate experimental data and refined phase shift analyses will be required to establish or disprove these expected recurrence patterns.

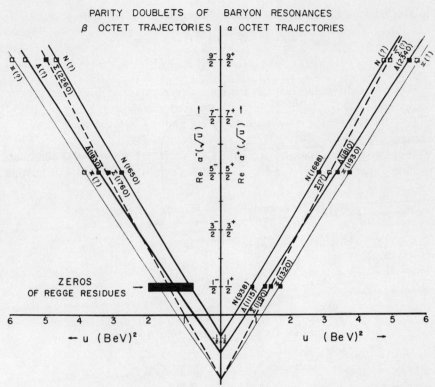

Figure 6.3. Tentative assignments of baryon resonances to parity doublets on MacDowell symmetric (α, β) octet trajectories: from V. Barger and D. Cline, *Phys. Letters* **26B**, 83 (1967).

6.4 EXCHANGE DEGENERACY

The $\Delta J = 2$ spacing of Regge recurrences is due to the existence of exchange forces that make the dynamics of even and odd J different. In the event that the exchange forces are weak, trajectories with $\tau = +1$ and -1 become approximately degenerate and the recurrence spacing becomes $\Delta J = 1$. Such a situation is called "exchange degeneracy."

As an example, suppose that mesons are primarily baryon–antibaryon bound states. The exchange forces resulting from dibaryon exchange would be expected to be weak compared to the meson exchange forces. The meson recurrences should then exhibit approximate exchange degeneracy. Although the actual bootstrap dynamics of meson states are presumably far more complex, the classifications of certain meson recurrences suggest an approximate exchange degeneracy.

In Section 1.3 we noted the approximate coincidence of the trajectories

$$\rho_V \qquad I = 1 \quad G = +1 \quad P = +1 \quad \tau = -1$$

$$\pi_T \qquad I = 1 \quad G = -1 \quad P = -1 \quad \tau = +1$$

Opposite G parity is necessary for exchange degenerate trajectories that are $\bar{N}N$ composites since $G = (-)^{L+S+I}$ for the $\bar{N}N$ system. The $\pi_P(I = 1, G = -1, \tau = +1)$ and $\rho_A (I = 1, G = +1, \tau = -1)$ trajectories are likewise possible candidates for an exchange degenerate pair.

If exchange degeneracy holds for the $I = 1$ members of two SU(3) multiplets, then we expect the other members to exhibit a similar degeneracy. For example,

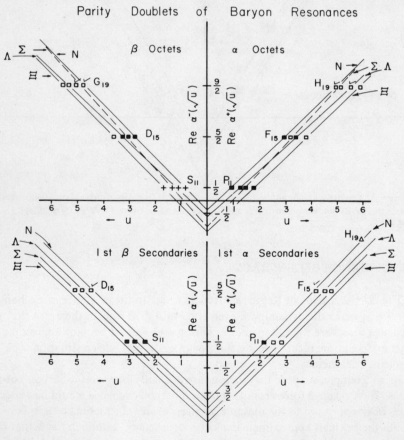

Figure 6.4. Proposed pattern for the leading and first secondary trajectories for the (α, β) octet multiplets.

the trajectories associated with the vector meson nonet [$\rho(750), K^*(890), \phi(1020)$, $\omega(780)$] should be degenerate with the corresponding trajectories of the tensor meson nonet [$A_2(1320), K^{**}(1410), f'(1500), f_0(1250)$]. Preliminary evidence on high mass $I = 0$ resonances suggests that (ω, f_0) exchange degeneracy is also approximately realized.

6.5 ABSENCE OF NON-$\bar{N}N$-TYPE MESONS

The mesons which couple to the nucleon–antinucleon system have quantum numbers given by

$$\mathbf{J} = \mathbf{L} + \mathbf{S} \qquad P = (-)^{L+1} \qquad G = (-)^{I+L+S}$$

where L and S are the orbital and spin angular momenta of the $N\bar{N}$ pair. The enumeration of meson trajectories with $I = 1$ that have an $N\bar{N}$ coupling are

$$\rho_V, \rho_A, \rho_P, \pi_T, \pi_A, \pi_P$$

where the symbols and subscripts denote

$$V(1^-, 3^-, \ldots)$$
$$\rho(I = 1, G = +) \qquad T(0^+, 2^+, \ldots)$$
$$\pi(I = 1, G = -) \qquad A(1^+, 3^+, \ldots)$$
$$P(0^-, 2^-, \ldots)$$

An exception to the above is the 0^- member of ρ_P that also does not couple to $N\bar{N}$. None of the mesons on the ρ_T and π_V trajectories have the quantum numbers of the $N\bar{N}$ system. Nevertheless, these non-$N\bar{N}$-type states can have allowed decays into simple final states. For example, some of the allowed decay modes of particles on the ρ_T and π_V trajectories are

$$\rho_T \to \pi\omega \qquad \pi_V \to \pi\rho$$
$$\to K_1 K_2 \qquad \to \pi\eta$$
$$\to \bar{K} K^*$$

In view of the existence of such common decay channels, *it is a remarkable experimental fact that no mesons have been discovered thus far with non-$\bar{N}N$-type quantum numbers.*

The above fact is frequently advanced as evidence for quark structure of matter. The quantum numbers of mesons built as $q\bar{q}$ composites correspond to the quantum numbers of the $N\bar{N}$ system. From the bootstrap point of view, it is possible that the forces are repulsive in the non-$\bar{N}N$-type states. Whatever the origin is for the nonexistence of these states, it is clearly an empirical fact that must be reckoned with in constructing an acceptable dynamical theory.

6.6 RESONANCE WIDTHS

By assignment of particles as Regge recurrences on Chew–Frautschi plots, we have learned something about the approximate behavior of Re $\alpha(t)$ for time-like values of t. Information on Im $\alpha(t)$ can be similarly obtained from resonance widths. The total width (Γ) of a resonance is related to the trajectory $\alpha(t) = \alpha_R(t) + i\alpha_I(t)$ by

$$\Gamma = \frac{\alpha_I(t)\,\alpha_R'(t)/\sqrt{t}}{[\alpha_R'(t)]^2 + [\alpha_I'(t)]^2}$$

where the primes denote differentiation with respect to t. All quantities on the right-hand side of this expression are understood to be evaluated at the resonance mass, $t = M^2$. For $\alpha_R'(t) \gg \alpha_I'(t)$ we have

$$\alpha_I(M^2) \approx M\Gamma\alpha_R'(M^2)$$

A similar formula can be written for the imaginary part of a fermion trajectory.

Present experimental results suggest that high mass meson resonances may be very narrow. Figure 6.5 shows the masses and widths of mesons indirectly observed in a "missing mass" experiment for the reaction $\pi^- p \rightarrow pX^-$. The widths of these meson states in the 1600–2400 MeV mass range are less than 40 MeV. In contrast, the widths of the $\rho(750)$ and $f_0(1250)$ mesons are greater than 100 MeV. The experimental indications for narrow high mass meson resonances imply that $\alpha_I(t)$ rapidly becomes small for increasing t. As a result, a twice-subtracted dispersion relation may be required to generate the linear behavior observed for $\alpha_R(t)$:

$$\alpha_R(t) = a + bt + \frac{1}{\pi}\int_{t_0}^{\infty} \frac{dt'\,\alpha_I(t')}{t' - t}$$

Here a and b are subtraction constants and $\sqrt{t_0}$ is the threshold energy. If two subtractions are indeed necessary, the two most important parameters for α_R (namely, the subtraction constants) cannot be determined from the resonance widths.

The widths of the $Y = +1$ baryon resonances are somewhat better known experimentally, and in fact increase with increasing mass. The values of $\alpha_I(M)$ determined from

$$\alpha_I(M) = \frac{\Gamma}{2}\left(\frac{d\alpha_R}{d\sqrt{u}}\right)_{\sqrt{u}=M}$$

are shown in Figure 6.6 for the Δ_δ and N_γ trajectories. For this plot the slope α'_R was calculated from the usual linear forms

$$\alpha_R(\sqrt{u}) = 0.15 + 0.9(\sqrt{u})^2 \qquad \text{for} \quad \Delta_\delta$$

$$\alpha_R(\sqrt{u}) = -0.9 + 0.9(\sqrt{u})^2 \qquad \text{for} \quad N_\gamma$$

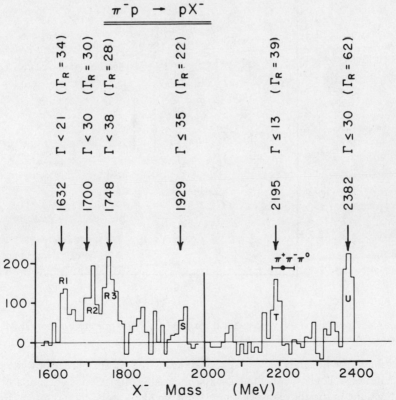

Figure 6.5. Masses and widths of mesons observed in a missing mass experiment for the reaction $\pi^- p \to p X^-$: from N. Barash-Schmidt *et al.*, UCLR-8030 (1968).

A single straight line roughly interpolates through the values of α_I for both trajectories $\alpha_I(\sqrt{u}) \simeq 0.12[u - u_0]$. Note that α_I must be zero at threshold where $u = u_0 = (M + \mu)^2$.

An unsubtracted dispersion relation for a fermion trajectory has the form

$$\alpha_R(\sqrt{u}) = \frac{1}{\pi} \int\limits_{\sqrt{u_0}}^{\infty} dx \frac{\alpha_I(x)}{x - \sqrt{u}} + \frac{1}{\pi} \int\limits_{-\sqrt{u_0}}^{-\infty} dx \frac{\alpha_I(x)}{x - \sqrt{u}}$$

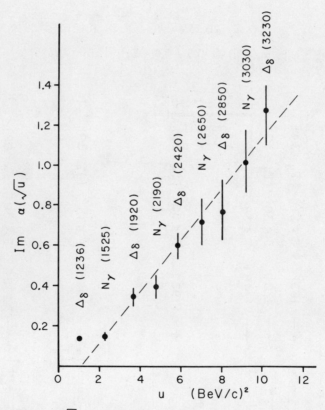

Figure 6.6. Plot of Im $\alpha(\sqrt{u})$ versus u for the Δ_δ and N_γ Regge trajectories: from R. M. Spector, *Phys. Rev.* **173**, 1761 (1968).

To evaluate the integrals we would need to know the widths of MacDowell reflected states as well, about which little experimental information is yet available. Subtractions in the above dispersion relation are likely to be required to reproduce the observed linear behavior in u of $\alpha_R(\sqrt{u})$.

Accurate experimental determinations of resonance widths may yield useful information concerning the possible termination of a series of particle recurrences. A Regge family of resonance states will terminate if the trajectory function turns around and moves towards decreasing values of $\alpha_R(\sqrt{u})$. A careful study of the trajectory shape in the complex α plane might provide evidence for such a turn-around. Projections of possible behaviors for the Δ_δ trajectory in the complex α plane are sketched in Figure 6.7.

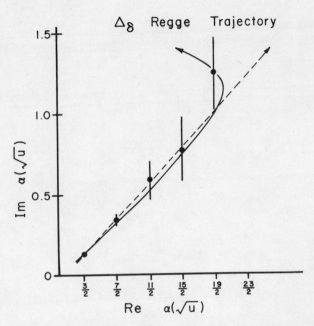

Figure 6.7. Plot of Im $\alpha(\sqrt{u})$ versus Re $\alpha(\sqrt{u})$ for the Δ_δ trajectory. Possible projected behaviors are indicated.

6.7 SUMMARY

Questions regarding the ultimate classification patterns of the fundamental particles are clearly far from answered. Nevertheless it is encouraging that simple extensions of Regge ideas, such as fermion conspiracy and secondary trajectories, can seemingly account for many observed aspects of the particle spectrum. The accumulation of data in the next few years on the existence of particles and the determinations of masses, widths, and quantum numbers of these states should go far toward clarifying the points that are now obscure. In the meantime, the analysis of scattering data can tell us much about the trajectories in the space-like momentum transfer region. In the following chapter we discuss in detail information obtained on the $Y = +1$ fermion Regge trajectories from analysis of backward πN scattering data.

Chapter 7

Baryon Exchange

7.1 INTRODUCTION

The appealing feature of the Regge pole theory of hadron interactions is the conjectured connection between particle mass spectra and particle exchange amplitudes as expressed by the trajectory function. In order to establish this connection a great deal of data are needed both on scattering processes and on the particle spectrum. Without a doubt the best known hadron spectrum at present (and for the foreseeable future) is the $Y = 1, B = 1$ fermion spectrum. This is due to richness of low energy πN scattering data and the extensive phase shift analyses performed over the past few years. At the same time precise high energy data on $\pi^{\pm} p$ elastic scattering near $180°$ have become available. Thus a test of the Regge concept for fermion trajectories is possible.

In this chapter we review experimental data that bear on the phenomenon of baryon exchange for elastic and inelastic two-body channels. The features of the theoretical models for fermion Regge pole exchange are compared with experimental πN scattering data and we attempt an evaluation of the extent to which the Regge trajectory concept has been tested through the study of baryon exchange reactions.

7.2 EXPERIMENTAL STUDIES OF BARYON EXCHANGE

As discussed in Section 2.1 detection of baryon exchange is accomplished by studying meson–baryon scattering events in which the baryon is scattered through approximately $180°$ in the c.m. system. The baryon exchange mechanism gives rise to a "backward peak" in the differential cross section. However, direct channel resonances can also give backward peaks at low energies since the dominance of a single Legendre polynomial gives a symmetric angular distribution, with peaks in the angular distribution at $0°$ and $180°$. In order to unambiguously separate baryon exchange from the effects of direct channel resonances the incident energy must be sufficiently high so that direct channel resonances do not play an important role or the system must be devoid of direct channel resonances. Alternatively, certain inelastic two-body channels have initial or final states that couple weakly to direct channel resonances.

119

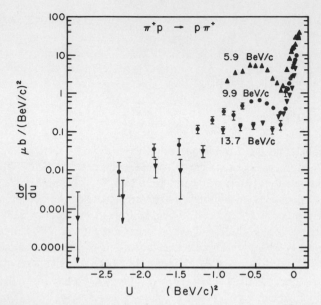

Figure 7.1. High energy π^+p elastic scattering data in the backward hemisphere: from J. Orear *et al.*, *Phys. Rev. Letters* **21**, 389 (1968).

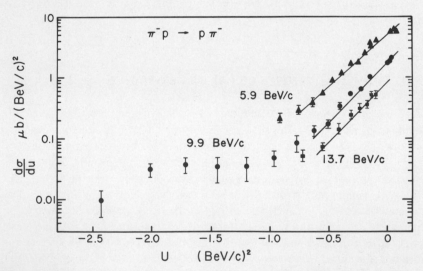

Figure 7.2. High energy π^-p elastic scattering data in the backward hemisphere: from J. Orear *et al.*, *Phys. Rev. Letters* **21**, 389 (1968).

The most carefully studied examples of baryon exchange to date are the backward $\pi^+ p$ and $\pi^- p$ elastic processes. A compilation of high energy πN backward cross sections is shown in Figures 7.1 and 7.2. Present data cover the u range out to about -1.2 $(\text{BeV}/\text{c})^2$. There are striking differences between the $\pi^+ p$ and $\pi^- p$ differential cross sections. The $\pi^+ p$ angular distribution is very sharp near $180°$,

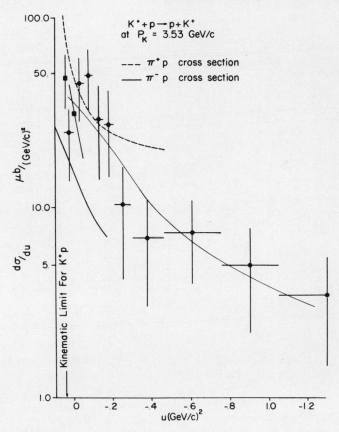

Figure 7.3. Comparison of $K^+ p$, $\pi^+ p$, and $\pi^- p$ backward elastic scattering data at 3.5 BeV/c: from D. Cline *et al.*, *Phys. Rev. Letters* **19**, 675 (1967).

falling through a dip at $u \simeq -0.15$ and rising again at larger u values. The slope of the near backward $\pi^+ p$ angular distribution is approximately twice the slope of forward $\pi^+ p$ elastic scattering. The $\pi^+ p$ cross section is considerably larger than the $\pi^- p$ cross section very near to $180°$ at all momenta above 2 BeV/c. Both the $\pi^+ p$ and $\pi^- p$ angular distributions shrink with increasing energy.

Another example of baryon exchange is provided by K^+p backward scattering data at 3.5 BeV/c. As pointed out in the second chapter, the K^+p backward cross section is much greater than K^-p, thus indicating the dominance of baryon exchange over direct channel resonance contributions. Figure 7.3 shows a comparison between the backward cross sections for K^+p, π^+p, and π^-p scattering. The K^+p cross section falls between π^+p and π^-p.

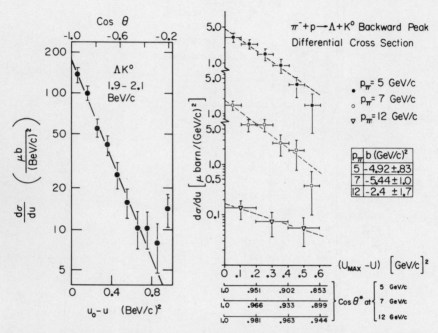

Figure 7.4. Data on the reaction $\pi^-p \to K^0\Lambda$ at backward angles: from O. I. Dahl *et al.*, *Phys. Rev.* **163**, 1430 (1967) and M. Pepin *et al.*, *Phys. Letters* **26B**, 35 (1967).

A number of inelastic two-body channels show striking backward peaks. In some cases the complete angular distribution is backward peaked over a wide range of energies because *t*-channel exchanges are not present. Two reactions which show this behavior are $\pi^-p \to K^+\Sigma^-$ and $K^-p \to K^+\Xi^-$, as illustrated in Figure 2.8. In both of these cases the backward peaking persists down to energies near threshold suggesting that baryon exchange is dominant even at very low energies. Neither of these channels appear to be strongly coupled to direct channel resonances.

Another inelastic reaction for which backward scattering data has been recently collected is $\pi^-p \to K^0\Lambda$. The angular distributions for beam momentum above

5 BeV/c are shown in Figure 7.4. One striking feature of this process is the existence of nearly maximal polarization for the Λ over the narrow backward angular range studied so far. The existence of such a large polarization is a severe constraint on theoretical baryon exchange models. A further fact of interest about

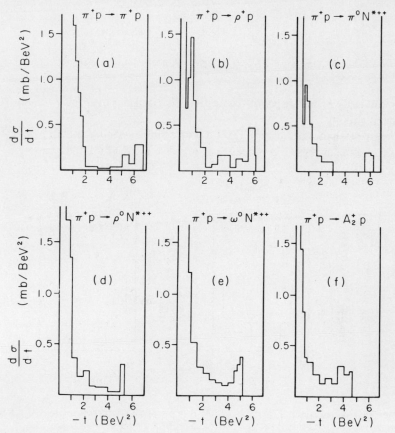

Figure 7.5. Data for several inelastic π^+p processes that have backward peaks: from Aachen *et al.*, collaboration, *Phys. Rev.* **138**, B897 (1965).

this reaction is that baryon exchange again seems to dominate down to rather low energy. Figure 7.4 also shows the angular distributions in the backward hemisphere for 1.9–2.1 BeV/c laboratory momenta. The angular distributions have been fitted to the empirical form:

$$\frac{d\sigma}{du} = A \exp\left[-b(u_{max} - u)\right]$$

The following values of b were obtained:

$$b = 4.2 \pm 0.6 \qquad 2 \text{ BeV/c}$$

$$b = 4.9 \pm 0.8 \qquad 5 \text{ BeV/c}$$

$$b = 5.4 \pm 1 \qquad 7 \text{ BeV/c}$$

$$b = 2.4 \pm 1.7 \qquad 12 \text{ BeV/c}$$

The similarity of the shapes of the angular distributions over the 2–12 BeV/c range is striking.

Many resonance production reactions also show evidence for baryon exchange. Data on some of these $\pi^+ p$ processes at 4 BeV/c are displayed in Figure 7.5.

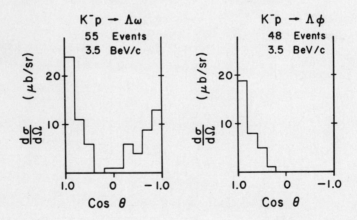

Figure 7.6. Comparison of $K^- p \rightarrow \omega \Lambda$ and $K^- p \rightarrow \phi \Lambda$ production cross sections at 3.5 BeV/c: from M. Derrick, "Backward Peaks," CERN Report 68-7, Vol. I.

The experimental comparison of various inelastic processes dominated by baryon exchange can suggest the relative strengths of couplings of meson states to the $\bar{N}N$ system. A case in point is the study of $K^- p \rightarrow \omega \Lambda$ and $K^- p \rightarrow \phi \Lambda$ near 180°. Figure 7.6 shows the angular distribution for these two processes at 3 BeV/c. The absence of backward ϕ production relative to backward ω production indicates that the ϕ meson is decoupled from $\bar{N}N$ while the ω meson is strongly coupled.

7.3 FERMION REGGE EXCHANGE

The basic formulas for the πN elastic differential cross section due to fermion Regge exchange were derived in Section 3.3. When kinematical factors of order $1/s$ are neglected (an approximation that is not advisable in actual data fitting), the contribution of a MacDowell trajectory pair to the differential cross section for $u \leqslant 0$ is

$$\frac{d\sigma}{du} = \frac{1}{32\pi s} \{|\gamma^+(\sqrt{u}) R(\alpha^+(\sqrt{u}), s)|^2 + |\gamma^-(\sqrt{u}) R(\alpha^-(\sqrt{u}), s)|^2\}$$

where

$$R(\alpha(\sqrt{u}), s) = (\alpha + \tfrac{1}{2})(\alpha + \tfrac{3}{2}) \frac{1 + \tau e^{-i\pi(\alpha - 1/2)}}{\cos \pi\alpha} \left(\frac{s}{s_0}\right)^{\alpha - 1/2}$$

The factor of $1/\Gamma(\alpha + 1/2)$ in the exact expression for R has been replaced above by $(\alpha + 1/2)(\alpha + 3/2)$ for the limited range of negative u values to be considered. At $u = 0$ the conspiring trajectories make equal contributions to $d\sigma/du$. Interference terms in the differential cross section between the $\alpha^+(\sqrt{u})$ and $\alpha^-(\sqrt{u})$ trajectories occur to order $1/s$ of the above terms (cf. exact expression for $d\sigma/du$ in Section 3.3).

Energy Dependence and Shrinkage

At fixed u, the energy dependence of $d\sigma/du$ obtained from the above expression is

$$\frac{d\sigma}{du} = F(u)\left(\frac{s}{s_0}\right)^{[\alpha^+(\sqrt{u}) + \alpha^-(\sqrt{u})] - 2}$$

As noted in Section 3.3 the odd $\sqrt{u}$ terms in the trajectory play no role in determining the energy dependence at high s. If we parameterize the trajectory by

$$\alpha^+(\sqrt{u}) = a + bu + c\sqrt{u}$$

then the shrinkage is determined in the usual way by the parameter b:

$$\frac{d\sigma}{du} = F(u)\left(\frac{s}{s_0}\right)^{2a} \exp\left[2bu \ln\left(\frac{s}{s_0}\right)\right]$$

At high s it is therefore possible with sufficiently accurate data to determine $\operatorname{Re} \alpha^+(\sqrt{u})$ by the comparison

$$\frac{(d\sigma/du)(s_2, u)}{(d\sigma/du)(s_1, u)} = \left(\frac{s_2}{s_1}\right)^{2(a+bu)-2}$$

At moderate energies the exact s behavior is also dependent on Im $\alpha^+(\sqrt{u})$, that is, the parameter c above. In reactions where more than one pair of trajectories is exchanged, the values of $\alpha^+(\sqrt{u})$ obtained in the above way represent the collective behavior of the trajectories and have little intrinsic interest.

The elastic π^-p process provides a suitable application for the above results. The Δ_δ trajectory is the only leading trajectory with appropriate quantum numbers for the u-channel, which requires $Q = 2$. Analysis of the high energy data on this process using the above formulas yields $a = 0.1 \pm 0.15$ and $b = 0.8 \pm 0.3$. These values are in reasonable agreement with the trajectory $a_\Delta = 0.15 + 0.9u$ found from assignments of particle recurrences (cf. Figure 1.4).

Connection with Particles

The similarity between the Δ_δ trajectory parameters deduced from the scattering region with the trajectory obtained from the Chew–Frautschi plot indicates that the trajectory continues smoothly between these two regions. This smooth behavior, while presently beyond the realm of theoretical prediction, nevertheless gives strong qualitative support of the Regge picture.

Backward Polarization

For processes with exchange of a single fermion pair, the polarization provides a direct measure of odd functional dependence on $\sqrt{u}$ in the trajectory. Thus for the Δ_δ trajectory parametrization

$$\alpha_\Delta^-(\sqrt{u}) = a + bu + c\sqrt{u}$$

the π^-p polarization at high s is given by

$$P(s,u) = \frac{\sqrt{s}\sin\theta_s}{i2\sqrt{u}}\tanh\{i\pi c\sqrt{u}\}$$

Representative predictions of the polarization at 5 and 12 BeV/c are shown in Figure 7.7 for the values $c = 1/2$ and $c = 1$. Sizeable polarizations are obtained in both cases. Such measurements will provide stringent tests for deviation of trajectories even from powers of $\sqrt{u}$. For processes in which more than one exchange occurs, the polarization depends both on the trajectories and the residues.

Amplitude Zeros

The Regge factor $R(\alpha(\sqrt{u}), s)$ vanishes at wrong signature, nonsense values of $\alpha(\sqrt{u})$ [i.e., negative half-integral values of α at which $(-)^{\alpha-1/2} = -\tau$]. Since $\sqrt{u}$ becomes imaginary in the scattering region, the Regge amplitude will have an appreciable dip near a wrong signature, nonsense point only if the trajectory is approximately an even function of $\sqrt{u}$. For the linear trajectories of Figure 1.4 the u values of the first wrong signature, nonsense points are

$$N_\alpha \qquad \alpha = -\tfrac{1}{2} \qquad u \simeq -0.11 \text{ (BeV/c)}^2$$

$$\Delta_\delta \qquad \alpha = -\tfrac{3}{2} \qquad u \simeq -1.8$$

$$N_\gamma \qquad \alpha = -\tfrac{3}{2} \qquad u \simeq -0.7 \text{ (uncertain trajectory form)}$$

$$\alpha_\Delta^-(\sqrt{u}) = a + bu + c\sqrt{u}$$

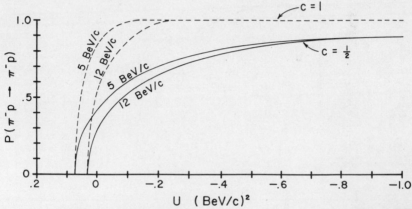

Figure 7.7. Polarization predictions for $\pi^- p \to p\pi^-$ backward scattering from $\sqrt{u}$ dependence of Δ_δ Regge trajectory, $\alpha_\Delta^-(\sqrt{u}) = a + bu + c\sqrt{u}$; solid curves are for $c = 1$, dashed curves for $c = 1/2$ (BeV/c)$^{-1}$.

The vanishing of the N_α amplitude at $\alpha = -1/2$ is essential to the Regge explanation of the dip at $u \simeq -0.15$ in backward $\pi^+ p$ scattering (cf. Figure 7.1), as discussed below.

The isotopic spin relations

$$f(\pi^- p) = f(\Delta)$$

$$f(\pi^+ p) = \tfrac{1}{3}[f(\Delta) + 2f(N)]$$

$$f(\pi^- p \to \pi^0 n) = \frac{\sqrt{2}}{3}[f(N) - f(\Delta)]$$

are used in adding up the $\Delta(I = 3/2)$ and $N(I = 1/2)$ fermion Regge exchange contributions to the πN elastic and charge exchange amplitudes. Some qualitative conclusions regarding N and Δ amplitudes can be made directly from the experimental data on $d\sigma/du(\pi^\pm p)$ at 9.9 BeV/c shown in Figure 7.8. At the backward direction ($u \simeq +0.03$), the ratio

$$\frac{(d\sigma/du)(\pi^+ p)}{(d\sigma/du)(\pi^- p)} \approx 4$$

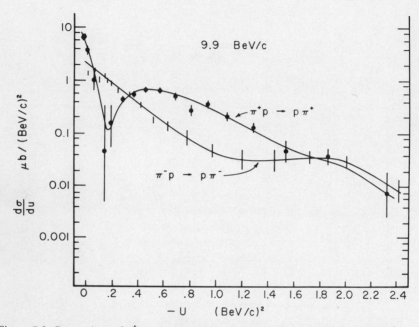

Figure 7.8. Comparison of π^+p and π^-p backward elastic scattering data at 9.9 BeV/c.

indicates the dominance of N exchanges. Away from 180°, $d\sigma/du(\pi^+ p)$ drops precipitously and the ratio is consistent with

$$\frac{(d\sigma/du)(\pi^+ p)}{(d\sigma/du)(\pi^- p)} \approx \tfrac{1}{9}$$

at $u \simeq -0.15$ (BeV/c)^2, suggesting a zero of the N exchange amplitude at this u value. These qualitative features are readily reproduced by an $N_\alpha + \Delta_\delta$ exchange model. The N_α amplitude zero at $\alpha = -1/2$ accounts for the π^+p dip. In this model the N_α trajectory can be allowed no appreciable $\sqrt{u}$ dependence and the N_γ amplitude contribution necessarily must be small.

Phase of Amplitude

The phase of the Regge factor $R(\alpha(\sqrt{u}), s)$ is completely determined once $\alpha(\sqrt{u})$ and τ are specified. However, the possible complex nature of the residue, such as $\gamma(\sqrt{u}) = f + g\sqrt{u}$, further complicates the prediction and determination of the overall amplitude phase (the $\sqrt{u}$ terms become pure imaginary in the $u \leqslant 0$ scattering region). An indirect check of the relative phase between the N_α and Δ_δ exchanges can be made by comparing differential cross section and polarization data on the three reactions

$$\pi^+ p \to \pi^+ p \qquad \pi^- p \to \pi^- p \qquad \pi^- p \to \pi^0 n$$

near $180°$. The prediction of the $\pi^- p \to \pi^0 n$ differential cross section turns out to be particularly sensitive to the interference of the Δ_δ and N_α exchange contributions.

7.4 DETAILED ANALYSIS OF $\pi^\pm p$ DATA

The qualitative features of the πN backward scattering data are consistent with the $N_\alpha + \Delta_\delta$ Reggeized baryon exchange model. A more detailed evaluation can be made by a χ^2 fit to the data. A simultaneous fit to all $\pi^\pm p$ backward scattering data above 5 BeV/c has been carried out. The N_α and Δ_δ residues were parameterized as

$$\gamma_N{}^+(\sqrt{u}) = \beta_N(1 + \delta_N\sqrt{u}) \qquad \gamma_\Delta{}^-(\sqrt{u}) = \beta_\Delta(1 + \delta_\Delta\sqrt{u})$$

where the β_i and δ_i are constants. For approximately linear trajectories in u, we expect $\delta_N \approx 1/M_N$ and $\delta_\Delta \approx 1/M_\Delta$ on the basis of the absence of the lowest lying particles on the MacDowell reflected trajectories (cf. discussions in Sections 3.3 and 6.1).

The resulting fits to the data using trajectories of the form $\alpha(\sqrt{u}) = a + bu$ are shown by the solid curves in Figure 7.9. The fits to the $\pi^+ p$ data could not distinguish the relative sign of β_Δ/β_N. The trajectory parameters obtained from this analysis of the data were

$$\left(\frac{\beta_\Delta}{\beta_N} > 0\right) \qquad\qquad \left(\frac{\beta_\Delta}{\beta_N} < 0\right)$$

$$N_\alpha: \quad \alpha = -0.38 + 0.88u \qquad \alpha = -0.35 + 0.86u$$

$$\Delta_\delta: \quad \alpha = 0.20 + 0.85u \qquad \alpha = 0.04 + 0.85u$$

These parameters are in good agreement with the values obtained from the Chew–Frautschi plot of the πN resonances:

$$N_\alpha: \quad \text{Re}\,\alpha = -0.39 + 1.0u$$

$$\Delta_\delta: \quad \text{Re}\,\alpha = +0.15 + 0.9u$$

The above results quantitatively substantiate the connection between the particle mass spectra and the particle exchange amplitudes, as expressed by the Regge trajectory functions.

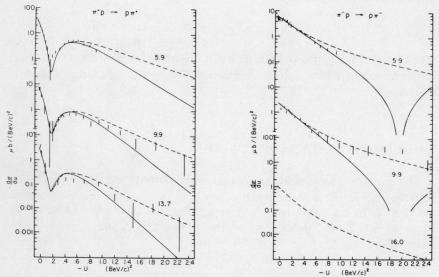

Figure 7.9. Results of a simultaneous fit to $\pi^+ p$ and $\pi^- p$ backward scattering data with the $(N_\alpha, \Delta_\delta)$ Reggeized baryon exchange model. Solid curves represent linear trajectories of the form $\alpha = a + bu$; dashed are curves based on nonlinear trajectories: from V. Barger and D. Cline, *Phys. Rev. Letters* **21**, 392 (1968).

The residue parameters δ_N and δ_Δ found from the fit were $\delta_N \simeq 1.6/M_N$ and $\delta_\Delta \simeq 1.5/M_\Delta$, corresponding to zeros of the residue functions rather close to expected mass values for the lowest particles on the N_β and Δ_γ trajectories. This result lends some support to a nonsense choosing mechanism for the N_β trajectory at $\alpha_N{}^-(\sqrt{u}) = 1/2$ and for the Δ_γ trajectory at $\alpha_\Delta{}^+(\sqrt{u}) = 3/2$ (cf. the discussions in Sections 3.3 and 6.1). For later use, we tabulate below the Regge parameters obtained from the fit with $\beta_\Delta/\beta_N > 0$:

$$\frac{\beta_N}{8\pi} = 32.0 \;\; (\text{BeV})^{-1} \qquad \frac{\beta_\Delta}{8\pi} = 0.10 \;\; (\text{BeV})^{-1}$$

$$s_0{}^N = 0.45 \;\; (\text{BeV})^2 \qquad s_0{}^\Delta = 2.85 \;\; (\text{BeV})^2$$

The principal defect of the fit shown by the solid curves in Figure 7.9 is a predicted dip in $d\sigma/du(\pi^-p)$ at $u \simeq -1.9$ corresponding to $\alpha_\Delta = -3/2$. Possible explanations for the experimental absence of this dip include:

(1) the existence of fixed pole at this wrong signature, nonsense point which removes or shifts the Δ_δ amplitude zero;

(2) a significant $\sqrt{u}$ dependence in the Δ_δ trajectory at large u, such that Im $\alpha(\sqrt{u}) \neq 0$ where Re $\alpha(\sqrt{u}) = -3/2$;

(3) a deviation of the Δ_δ trajectory from the linear form $\alpha = a + bu$, with the trajectory leveling off at large u.

Experimental measurements of the energy dependence of the π^-p differential cross section for $u < -1.5$ will be necessary to distinguish between these possibilities. In the meantime in order to investigate possibilities (ii) and (iii) above, fits have been made to the present π^-p data using two alternative Δ_δ trajectory parameterizations:

$$\text{(a)} \qquad \alpha^-(\sqrt{u}) = a + bu + c\sqrt{u}$$

$$\text{(b)} \qquad \alpha^-(\sqrt{u}) = \frac{a + bu}{1 - cu}$$

The χ^2 analysis with form (a) displayed a preference for small values of c/b, without eliminating the difficulty from the $\alpha = -3/2$ dip. Nevertheless a solution with somewhat higher χ^2 could be found with acceptable behavior at large u; the trajectory parameters for this solution were

$$\alpha_\Delta^-(\sqrt{u}) = -0.03 + 0.72u + 0.74\sqrt{u}$$

Good χ^2 fits to the $\pi^\pm p$ data were obtained with form (b). This construction reduces to the simple linear form at small u and tends to a constant value $\alpha \to -b/c$ at large u. The dashed curves in Figure 7.9 show results obtained with the Δ_δ and N_α trajectories

$$\alpha_\Delta = \frac{0.21 + 0.9u}{1 - 0.42u} \qquad \alpha_N = \frac{-0.37 + 0.9u}{1 - 0.12u}$$

In a similar vein, a smooth curve drawn through all resonances on the N_γ trajectory already shows indication of curvature (cf. Figure 1.4). Since the N_γ trajectory lies lower than the N_α and Δ_δ trajectories, it is natural to first expect a deviation from a straight-line trajectory in this case, if indeed the trajectories do level off as $u \to -\infty$.

Extrapolations to Particle Poles

If the assumed functional forms for the residues remain valid in the $u > 0$ region, additional information on the residue parameters can be obtained from extrapolation of the Regge amplitudes to the particle poles. At the mass of a physical particle, the Regge amplitude reduces to the lowest-order Feynman amplitude (or Breit–Wigner amplitude) and the residue is related to a product of coupling constants. Extrapolating $\bar{F}_N^+(\sqrt{u}, s)$ to the $N_\alpha(938, 1/2^+)$ pole and $\bar{F}_\Delta^-(\sqrt{u}, s)$ to the $\Delta_\delta(1238, 3/2^+)$ position, we find

$$\frac{\beta_N(1 + \delta_N M_N)}{8\pi} = \left(\frac{3\pi}{8}\right)\left(\frac{g^2}{4\pi}\right)\epsilon_N$$

$$\frac{\beta_\Delta(1 + \delta_\Delta M_\Delta)}{8\pi} \simeq \frac{\pi s_0}{32} \frac{M_\Delta}{M_N} \frac{\Gamma_\Delta}{q_\Delta^3} \epsilon_\Delta$$

where

$$\epsilon_N = \left(\frac{d\alpha_N}{d\sqrt{u}}\right)_{\sqrt{u} = M_N} \quad \text{and} \quad \epsilon_\Delta = \left(\frac{d\alpha_\Delta}{d\sqrt{u}}\right)_{\sqrt{u} = M_\Delta}$$

The πN coupling strength is $g^2/4\pi \simeq 14.6$. The width of the $\Delta_\delta(1238)$ is $\Gamma_\Delta = 120$ MeV and the decay momentum $q_\Delta = 231$ MeV.

The extrapolated residues from the best fits to the scattering data with linear trajectories $\alpha = a + bu$ are compared with the particle pole values in the following table.

Extrapolated residue	*Born residue*
$[\gamma_i/8\pi = \beta_i(1 + \delta_i M_i)/8\pi]$	
$(\text{BeV})^{-1}$	$(\text{BeV})^{-1}$
$\gamma_N^+/8\pi = 83.0$	$\gamma_N^+/8\pi = 28.0$
$\gamma_\Delta^-/8\pi = 0.25$	$\gamma_\Delta^-/8\pi = 7.6$

Considering the distance of the extrapolation in the J plane, the variations between the extrapolated and Born residue values may not be too unreasonable. Such extrapolations are highly dependent on the assumed parametric form of the residue functions.

The residues at the poles specify the relative sign choice $\beta_\Delta/\beta_N > 0$, provided that the residues do not change sign between $u = 0$ and the particle poles. The predicted $\pi^- p \to \pi^\circ n$ differential cross section is sensitive to the sign of β_Δ/β_N.

The solid curves in Figure 7.10 represent the cross section predictions for $\beta_\Delta/\beta_N > 0$, the dashed curves $\beta_\Delta/\beta_N < 0$. Verification of the preferred solution with $\beta_\Delta/\beta_N > 0$ would provide a partial confirmation of the extrapolation to the poles with the assumed functional forms of the residues.

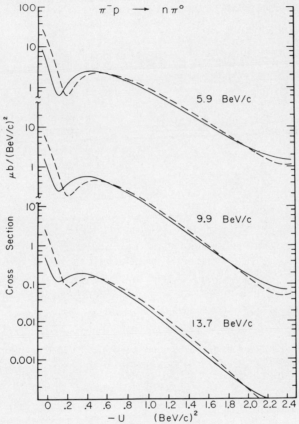

Figure 7.10. Predictions for $d\sigma/du$ ($\pi^-p \to \pi^0n$) from (N_α, Δ_δ) exchange model. Solid curves are for $\beta_\Delta/\beta_N > 0$, dashed curves for $\beta_\Delta/\beta_N < 0$: from V. Barger and D. Cline, *Phys. Rev. Letters* **19**, 1504 (1967).

7.5 $\bar{N}N \to \pi\pi$ ANNIHILATION PROCESS

Within the Regge pole framework, the amplitudes for baryon exchange in the annihilation process $\bar{N}_2 + N_1 \to \bar{M}_1 + M_2$ for c.m. scattering angles $\phi(\bar{N}_2M_2) \simeq 180°$ are related by line reversal to the amplitudes for the pseudoscalar meson–nucleon scattering process $M_1 + N_1 \rightarrow M_2 + N_2$ for $\theta(N_2M_2) \simeq 180°$ (see illustration in Figure 7.11). Thus a simultaneous study of baryon exchange in a meson–nucleon scattering process and the line reversed annihilation process should constitute a further critical test of the Regge model. In our subsequent discussion we use an adaptation of the notation of nuclear physics: N_1 $(\bar{N}_2, \bar{M}_1)M_2$ for the annihilation reaction with $\theta(\bar{N}_2M_2) \simeq 180°$ and $M_1(N_1, N_2)M_2$ for the meson–nucleon scattering process with $\theta(M_1M_2) \simeq 180°$.

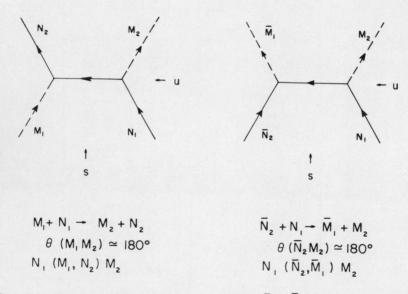

$$M_1 + N_1 \rightarrow M_2 + N_2$$
$$\theta\,(M_1 M_2) \simeq 180°$$
$$N_1\,(M_1, N_2)\,M_2$$

$$\bar{N}_2 + N_1 \rightarrow \bar{M}_1 + M_2$$
$$\theta\,(\bar{N}_2 M_2) \simeq 180°$$
$$N_1\,(\bar{N}_2, \bar{M}_1)\,M_2$$

Figure 7.11. Illustration of the line reversed reactions $N_1\bar{N}_2 \rightarrow \bar{M}_1 M_2$ and $M_1 N_1 \rightarrow M_2 N_2$.

Using the notation of Section 3.3 the line reversed amplitudes for exchange of a fermion trajectory pair of signature τ are related by

$$\bar{F}_1(u, s) = \tau F_1(u, s) \qquad \bar{F}_2(u, s) = \tau F_2(u, s)$$

where $(\bar{F}_1, \bar{F}_2)$ refer to the amplitudes for the annihilation process, and (F_1, F_2) are the amplitudes for the meson–nucleon scattering process. The complete u-channel amplitudes are obtained by summing over all the contributing trajectories. The differential cross section formulas are

$$\frac{d\sigma}{du} = \frac{1}{64\pi p^2 s}\{|F_1|^2\,[s + u + 2D^2] + |F_2|^2\,[u(-s + 4M^2) + D^4]$$

$$+ 4M\,\mathrm{Re}(F_1{}^* F_2)\,[u + D^2]\}$$

for the reaction $M_1 + N_1 \rightarrow M_2 + N_2$ and

$$\frac{d\bar{\sigma}}{du} = \frac{1}{128\pi p^2 s} \{|F_1|^2\,[s - 4M^2] + |F_2|^2\,[-us - (D^2 + u^2)]$$

$$- 4M\,\mathrm{Re}(F_1{}^* \bar{F}_2)\,[u + D^2]\}$$

for the reaction $\bar{N}_2 + N_1 \rightarrow \bar{M}_1 + M_2$. Here $D^2 = M^2 - \mu^2$ and p labels the appropriate c.m. momentum. For the exchange of a single MacDowell pair the relation $|\bar{F}_{1,2}| = |F_{1,2}|$ obtains and the analysis simplifies.

As $s \rightarrow \infty$ at fixed u, the cross sections approach the asymptotic values

$$\frac{d\sigma}{du} = \frac{1}{16\pi s}\,[|F_1|^2 - u|F_2|^2]$$

$$\frac{d\bar{\sigma}}{du} = \frac{1}{32\pi s}\,[|\bar{F}_1|^2 - u|\bar{F}_2|^2]$$

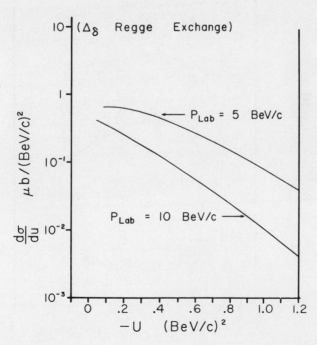

Figure 7.12. Δ_δ exchange model prediction for the reaction $p(\bar{p}, \pi^+)\pi^-$ at 5 and 10 BeV/c using a linear trajectory.

Assuming dominance of a single trajectory pair, we obtain the relation

$$\frac{d\bar{\sigma}}{du} = \frac{1}{2}\frac{d\sigma}{du} \qquad \text{for} \quad s \to \infty$$

In the nonasymptotic energy region, the Regge exchange amplitudes obtained from fitting backward meson–baryon scattering data can be used to predict the annihilation cross section. The predictions for

$$(d\sigma/du)[p(\bar{p}, \pi^+)\pi^-] \text{ and } (d\sigma/du)[p(\bar{p}, \pi^-)\pi^+]$$

from the $(N_\alpha, \Delta_\delta)$ Regge amplitudes of $\pi^\pm p \to \pi^\pm p$ backward scattering are shown in Figures 7.12 and 7.13. A dip is predicted in $(d\sigma/du)[p(\bar{p}, \pi^-)\pi^+]$ at $u \simeq -0.15$, due to the N_α trajectory passing through $\alpha = -1/2$. The solid curves in Figure 7.13 are for $\beta_\Delta/\beta_N > 0$, the dashed curves for $\beta_\Delta/\beta_N < 0$. The experimental confirmation of the $\bar{p}p \to \pi\pi$ predictions would provide strong support for the Regge picture of baryon exchange.

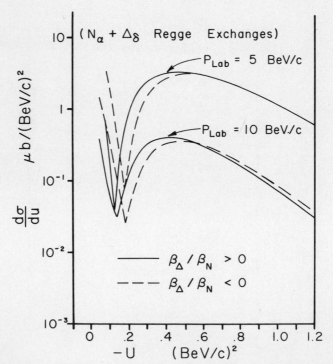

Figure 7.13. $(N_\alpha, \Delta_\delta)$ model predictions for the reaction $p(\bar{p}, \pi^-)\pi^+$ at 5 and 10 BeV/c: solid curve for $\beta_\Delta/\beta_N > 0$; dashed curve for $\beta_\Delta/\beta_N < 0$.

SU(3) for Baryon Exchange Residues

The successful application of SU(3) symmetry to baryon exchange residue factors would interrelate a number of backward scattering processes. As with meson exchanges, the nondegeneracy of trajectories within a SU(3) multiplet will induce a certain amount of symmetry breaking. Therefore, the most direct tests of SU(3) invariance of baryon exchange Regge residues will come from relations between processes mediated by the same trajectory. One such SU(3) equality is

$$\frac{d\sigma}{dr}(K^- p \to \pi^- \Sigma^+) = \frac{d\sigma}{d\Omega}(\pi^- p \to \pi^- p)$$

for backward angles. Both of these processes are expected to proceed via Δ_δ Regge exchange in the backward direction at high energy. The coupling strengths

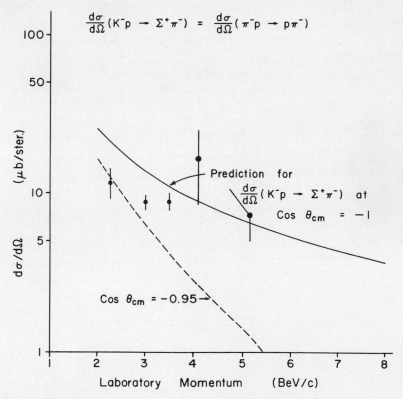

Figure 7.14. Experimental evaluation of SU(3) prediction relating Δ_δ baryon exchange processes: from V. Barger, *Rev. Mod. Phys.* **40,** 129 (1968).

of the Δ_δ exchange to the πp and $K\Sigma$ vertices are equal in the SU(3) symmetry limit. By using the explicit formula for the Δ_δ Regge amplitude, the corrections from mass differences of external particles to the above equality can be readily taken into account. Present data do not give a conclusive test of this SU(3) relation, but there is a strong suggestion that it is approximately satisfied, as shown in Figure 7.14.

The application of SU(3) to reactions involving different trajectories within the same SU(3) multiplet must be viewed in a somewhat more qualitative manner. Cross sections for processes mediated by $Y = 0$ baryon trajectories will have a different energy dependence than for processes where $Y = 1$ trajectories are exchanged because of the displacement of the trajectories (cf. Figures 1.6 and 6.3). However, two general qualitative predictions which follow from SU(3) are as follows:

(i) The sense–nonsense factors should be the same for all trajectories within a given SU(3) multiplet. Therefore, exchange amplitude zeros (which give rise to dips in differential cross sections) should be correlated. For example, since the N_α amplitude vanishes at $\alpha(N_\alpha) = -1/2$, the Λ_α exchange amplitude should likewise vanish at $\alpha(\Lambda_\alpha) = -1/2$.

(ii) The empirical ordering of the SU(3) multiplet trajectories in the resonance region will likely lead to a similar ordering in the scattering region (e.g., $\alpha_N > \alpha_\Sigma$). Thus, the energy dependence of reactions should be inversely related to the ordering of the exchange masses.

Chapter 8

Intermediate Energy Scattering

8.1 INTRODUCTION

The present view of hadron scattering processes regards high energy scattering as being governed by exchanges in the t- or u-channel. The intermediate energy region refers to that region between low energy where the s-channel resonances dominate the scattering process and high energy where the t- and u-channels dominate. As a rough rule of thumb, the intermediate region extends from approximately 1.5 to 5 BeV/c laboratory momentum.

The most successful theoretical descriptions of high energy scattering are given by the Regge pole model. It is natural to ask at what energy should the t- and u-channel exchanges, as described by the Regge theory, be expected to dominate the scattering amplitude? There is no simple answer to this question at present. In fact, conflicting viewpoints on this matter indicate that the next few years will see vigorous theoretical and experimental activity in the intermediate energy range.

8.2 DEFINITION OF s-, t-, or u-CHANNEL DOMINANCE

Of the three kinematic variables for a two-body process (s, t, u) only two are independent. Although the choice of independent variables is formally arbitrary, the amplitudes frequently show simple properties only when certain variables are used. For example, the s and t variables provide the simplest description of reactions where meson exchange processes are known to be dominant. In the Regge language the amplitude for the meson exchange takes the form

$$A(s, t) \sim \beta(t) s^{\alpha(t)-1}$$

where the s dependence is explicitly shown and the t dependence is contained in the β and α factors. Similarly reactions mediated by baryon exchange depend on s and u in a simple way, for example, $A(s, u) \sim \beta(\sqrt{u})(s)^{\alpha(\sqrt{u})-1}$. Several physical examples of fixed t and fixed u characteristics have been discussed in previous chapters. At very low energies some scattering amplitudes are simply described in terms of direct channel resonances by a small number of partial waves. In this case the appropriate variables are s and $\cos\theta$. In summary, the appropriate variables

139

to use are (s, t) for meson exchange, (s, u) for baryon exchange, and $(s, \cos \theta)$ for direct channel resonance dominance.

At high energy the t- and u-channel regions are widely separated and it is usually clear which set of variables to use for a particular angular region. At intermediate

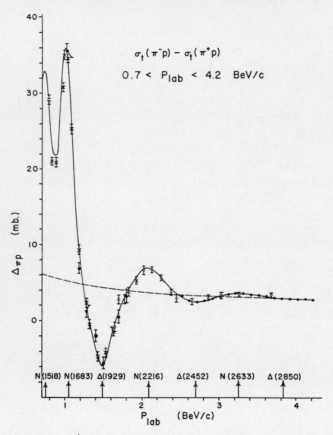

Figure 8.1. $[\sigma_t(\pi^-p) - \sigma_t(\pi^+p)]$ data in the laboratory momentum range from 0.7 to 4.2 BeV/c. Dashed curve represents an extrapolation of the Regge ρ-exchange amplitude from high energy. Solid curve is the result of an interference model calculation: from V. Barger and M. Olsson, *Phys. Rev.* **151**, 1123 (1966).

energies it is an open question as to which set of variables will describe the reaction in the simplest way. It may be appropriate to consider the different physical mechanisms for clues about the relevant variables and to contemplate interference between the amplitudes representing different mechanisms (e.g., interference between the meson exchange amplitude and the baryon exchange amplitude).

In this chapter we will first survey some experimental evidence for s-dependent fluctuations in the intermediate region along with evidence for fixed t and fixed u characteristics. Some initial theoretical attempts to describe intermediate energy scattering amplitudes will be discussed.

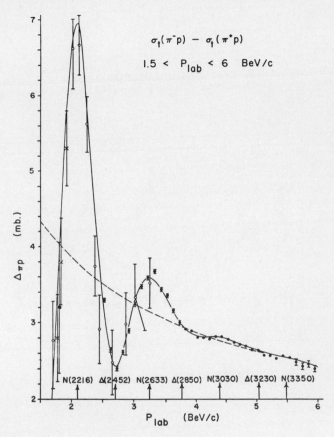

Figure 8.2. $[\sigma_t(\pi^-p) - \sigma_t(\pi^+p)]$ data for momenta between 1.5 and 6 BeV/c: from V. Barger and M. Olsson, *Phys. Rev.* **151**, 1123 (1966).

s-Dependent Structure

The $\pi^\pm p$ system has been extensively investigated in the intermediate energy region and shows clear evidence of s-dependent structure superimposed on background amplitudes. Structure in the total cross section difference

$$\Delta\sigma = \sigma_t(\pi^- p) - \sigma_t(\pi^+ p)$$

is shown in Figures 8.1 and 8.2 as a function of laboratory momentum. The dashed curves in the figures represent the Regge ρ-exchange contribution extrapolated from fits to high energy data. Since $\Delta\sigma$ can be expressed in terms of isotopic spin 1/2 and 3/2 cross sections as

$$\Delta\sigma = \tfrac{2}{3}[\sigma_t(I = \tfrac{1}{2}) - \sigma_t(I = \tfrac{3}{2})]$$

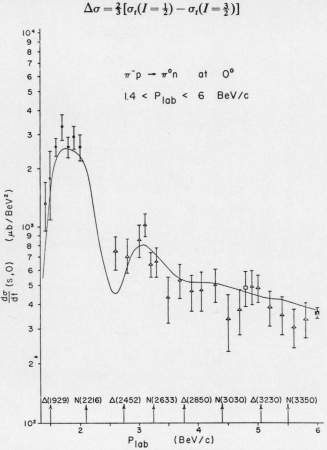

Figure 8.3. Forward $\pi^-p \to \pi^0 n$ scattering as a function of laboratory momentum. The solid curve represents a fit with the interference model: from V. Barger and M. Olsson, *Phys. Rev.* **151**, 1123 (1966).

a fluctuation that drives $\Delta\sigma$ down is likely to be associated with the $I = 3/2$ channel and a fluctuation that increases $\Delta\sigma$ with the $I = 1/2$ channel. The fluctuations in $\Delta\sigma$ have been long considered as evidence for the existence of high mass N^* resonances. Whether a fluctuation represents one resonance or a clustering of resonances is not clear from the total cross section data alone. However, from the

$\Delta\sigma$ structure the following pattern emerges: The $I = 1/2$ resonance contribution dominates in the $\sqrt{s}$ regions of 1700, 2200, and 2600 MeV whereas the $I = 3/2$ resonance contribution dominates in the $\sqrt{s}$ regions of 1950, 2400, and 2850 MeV. The magnitude of the fluctuations in $\Delta\sigma$ decreases rapidly with increasing $\sqrt{s}$ and are essentially unmeasurable above 5 BeV/c laboratory momentum.

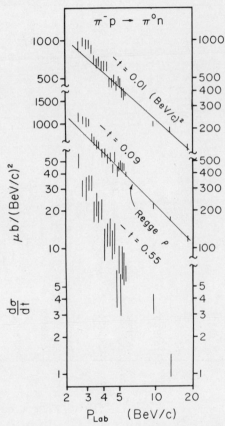

Figure 8.4. Data on $\pi^- p \to \pi^0 n$ at fixed t versus laboratory momentum. The solid curve is the Regge ρ-exchange contribution: from O. Guisan et al. (private communication).

Other evidence for s-dependent fluctuations in forward scattering can be seen in data on the reaction $\pi^- p \to \pi^0 n$ shown in Figures 8.3 and 8.4 as a function of P_{Lab} at fixed t.

Backward scattering data in the intermediate energy region are shown in Figures 8.5, 8.6, and 8.7 for the reactions $\gamma p \to \pi^0 p$ and $\pi^\pm p \to \pi^\pm p$. At 180° the structure in the three reactions has the same qualitative $\sqrt{s}$ dependence, with bumps in the $I = 3/2$ resonance regions (1950, 2450, 2850 MeV).

The interference of the resonance contributions with the background amplitude is sensitive to the angular region studied. This is particularly evident in
Figure 8.7. The $\pi^- p$ dip–bump structure changes considerably in going from
$\cos \theta = -1.0$ to $\cos \theta = -0.975$. A simple qualitative explanation can be given

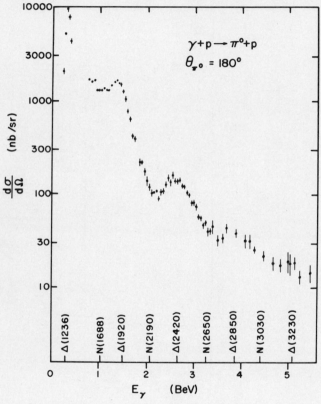

Figure 8.5. $\gamma p \to \pi^0 p$ differential cross section at $180°$ versus P_{Lab}: from G. Buschorn *et al.*,
Phys. Rev. Letters **20**, 230 (1967).

for the considerable changes in structure that occur over such a small range of
$\cos \theta$. Near $180°$ the dominant $I = 1/2$ resonances in $\pi^- p$ are approximately
parity doublets. Because of the property of Legendre polynomials that
$P_l(\cos \theta = -1) = (-1)^l$, the s-channel amplitudes owing to the $I = 1/2$ resonances
approximately cancel. Thus at $180°$ the $I = 1/2$ amplitude is greatly reduced and
the $I = 3/2$ structure is most evident. This also explains the similarity between
$\pi^+ p$ and $\pi^- p$ scattering at $180°$ as shown in Figures 8.6 and 8.7. Away from $180°$

(but still near the backward direction) the π^-p amplitude is dominated by $I = 1/2$ structure, and the structure in the cross section resembles the structure in $\Delta\sigma$ (Figures 8.1 and 8.2).

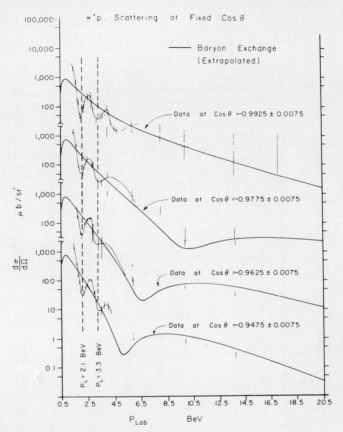

Figure 8.6. Backward π^+p elastic scattering differential cross sections for various cos θ cuts versus laboratory momentum. The solid curve is an extrapolation of the $(N_\alpha, \Delta_\delta)$ baryon exchange model: from V. Barger and D. Cline, *Phys. Letters* **27B**, 312 (1968).

Also shown in Figures 8.6 and 8.7 is an extrapolation of the Regge baryon exchange amplitudes from fits to the high energy data described in Section 7.4. The baryon exchange amplitude appears to adequately describe the mean value of the backward scattering cross section down to 2 BeV/c. In a similar way the Regge ρ charge exchange cross section as shown in Figures 8.1, 8.2, and 8.4 describes the average behavior of the intermediate energy cross section. The success of these extrapolations suggests that the t- and u-channel contributions are quite important in the intermediate region. Furthermore, if the local fluctuations are neglected (or averaged over) the t- and u-channel characteristics observed at high energy (sharp angular distributions, dips and bumps in the angular distribution) should also be observable in the intermediate region. Figure 8.8 compares

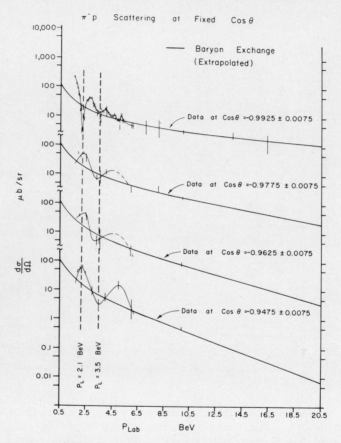

Figure 8.7. Data on $d\sigma/du(\pi^-p)$ versus P_{Lab} for various $\cos\theta$ cuts. Extrapolations of Reggeized baryon exchange model are shown by the solid curves: from V. Barger and D. Cline, *Phys. Letters* **27B**, 312 (1968).

recent data on $\pi^\pm p$ angular distributions in the intermediate energy range with the extrapolated Reggeized baryon exchange results. The overall agreement is quite remarkable. The dip in $d\sigma/du(\pi^+p)$ at $u \simeq -0.15$ is present, but apparently filled in somewhat by direct channel resonance contributions.

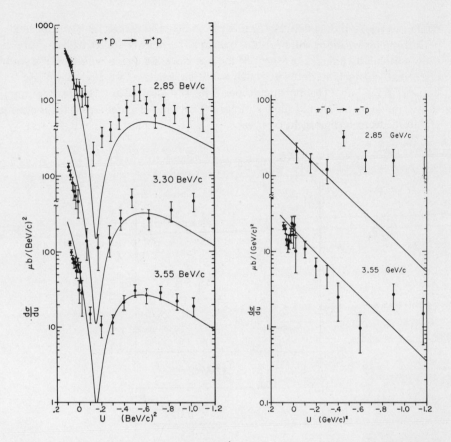

Figure 8.8. Angular distributions for $d\sigma/du(\pi^{\pm}p)$ at intermediate energies. Solid curves represent a $(N_\alpha, \Delta_\delta)$ exchange model that describes the high energy data.

t- and u-Dependent Structure

Figure 8.9 shows a schematic differential cross section with both fixed t and fixed u structure. The experimental data around 2 BeV/c show similar behavior, as illustrated in Figure 8.10. The interplay between the fixed t dip in $\pi^{\pm}p$ elastic scattering at $t \sim -2.7$ (BeV/c) (see Figure 5.6) and the fixed u dip caused by the N_α trajectory at $u \sim -0.15$ (BeV/c)^2 can be observed in Figure 8.10. This structure occurs in the same energy range where fixed $\cos\theta$, s-channel structure is also observed (Figures 8.6 and 8.7). Thus in the intermediate energy region for $\pi^{\pm}p$ scattering there is evidence of the interplay of the s-, t-, and u-channel amplitudes.

While this region promises to be formidable to describe theoretically, refined experimental observations will probably continue to uncover additional structure.

A particularly interesting aspect of the s–t–u overlap region would be the study of t- and u-channel interference, which could be sensitive to the relative phase between the t- and u-channel amplitudes. The $180°$ scattering π^-p cross section shown in Figure 8.7 should show structure from the t-channel dips if the u-channel amplitude were negligible. In fact, the $t = -2.7$ dip would cross $\cos \theta = -1$ at

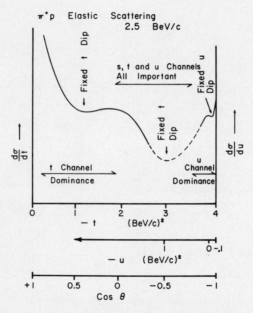

Figure 8.9. Illustration of t- and u-channel structure in differential cross sections.

about 2 BeV/c laboratory momentum. Figure 8.11 shows $d\sigma/dt(\pi^-p)$ for laboratory momenta near 2 BeV/c. It is evident from this figure that the t-channel dip does not cross $\cos \theta = -1$ at 2 BeV/c. The dip occurs essentially at fixed t since the u position of the dip changes appreciably over the small momentum range of 1.88–2.08 BeV/c. Finally, the fixed $\cos \theta$ dip seen in Figure 8.7 in the vicinity of 2.2 BeV/c laboratory momentum can be seen in Figure 8.10 as an additional decrease of $d\sigma/dt$ near $180°$ at $P_L = 2.08$ BeV/c. It is a remarkable fact that at the fixed t dip the cross section is so small; this indicates that all the participating amplitudes are destructively interfering. Since the dip occurs over a fairly wide range of u and $\cos \theta$ (as shown in Figure 8.11), the interference appears to be roughly independent of u and $\cos \theta$.

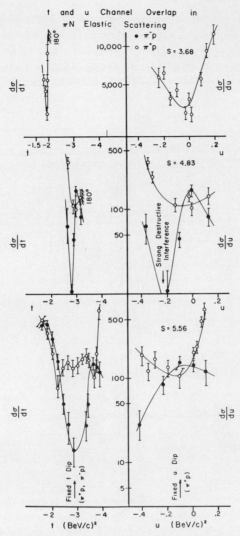

Figure 8.10. Backward π^+p and π^-p elastic scattering data plotted both as a function of t and as a function of u in order to reveal aspects of t- and u-channel structure. Note the occurrence of the fixed t dip in $\pi^{\pm}p$ at $t \simeq -2.7$ (BeV/c)^2 and the fixed u dip in $\pi^{\pm}p$ near $u \simeq -0.15$ (BeV/c)^2. The fixed u dip is present at $s = 3.68$ and 5.56 but is washed out for $s = 4.83$.

8.3 VERY LOW ENERGY SCATTERING

For some scattering processes even very low energy data show empirical regularities that are similar to that observed at high energies. The $\bar{p}p$ and $\bar{p}n$ elastic scattering data at approximately 1.4 BeV/c incident momentum provide a suitable illustration. As shown in Figure 8.12 the differential cross section for these processes show a striking dip for $t \simeq -0.4$ (BeV/c)^2. Similar structure for $\bar{p}p$ scattering has been observed up to the highest energies studied (5.9 BeV/c). Furthermore, the qualitative similarity of $\bar{p}n$ and $\bar{p}p$ scattering at this low momenta suggests, in terms of a meson exchange model, that the $I = 0$ meson exchanges dominate.

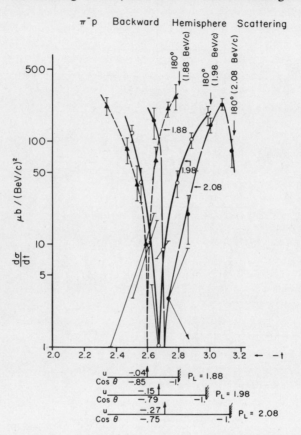

Figure 8.11. Plot of backward hemisphere $\pi^- p$ elastic scattering as a function of t, u, and $\cos\theta$ at three different energies. Note the striking dip that appears at approximately fixed t.

Low energy $K^- p$ elastic scattering also displays characteristics associated with high energy mechanisms. The proton polarization and angular distribution of the elastic scattering process have a simple fixed t behavior at as low a K^- momentum as 1.4 BeV/c. However, it seems likely that a large number of resonances contribute to the s-channel at such a low momentum. Similarly $\pi^\pm p$ elastic scattering and polarization show simple fixed t behavior down to relatively low momentum, again in the presence of many important s-channel resonances. These empirical behaviors have led to the suggestion that the resonances conspire in such a way as to "build up" the fixed t (or fixed u) structure. Just how such a conspiracy among resonances is actually realized is far from clear at present. However, the fact that similar simple and approximately energy-independent behaviors are found in the hadron scattering processes both for the resonance-dominated and resonance-free energy regions gives ample reason for further extensive experimental and theoretical studies of the scattering processes in the low and intermediate energy ranges.

In channels where resonances are not present or not strongly coupled there is the possibility that the models invoked to explain the high energy behavior will also apply at low energy. Two phenomenological approaches have been taken in investigating this question:

1. scrutinizing the available low energy data for the characteristics observed in the high energy data;
2. extrapolating the models which describe high energy data to very low energy and comparing with the available data.

An example of the former procedure was discussed in Chapter 2 where it was pointed out that the charge exchange process $np \to pn$ shows similar behavior from 90-MeV kinetic energy up to high energy. Other high energy characteristics appearing at low energy are as follows:

1. $\bar{p}p$ and $\bar{p}n$ elastic scattering differential cross sections show the same dip–bump pattern down to about 1 BeV/c. The pn and pp cross sections are similar suggesting approximate isospin independence down to about 1 BeV/c.
2. The dip–bump pattern in $\pi^{\pm}p$ elastic scattering continues down to at least 1.5 BeV/c, for both the t- and u-channel dips.
3. The total cross sections for K^+p and K^+n scattering are equal (to within 2 mb out of about 20 mb) and constant down to 1 BeV/c.
4. The pp and np elastic scattering cross sections at 90° are approximately equal from 1500 MeV/c up to 7 BeV/c.

An example of the extrapolation of theoretical models used to fit high energy data into the intermediate and low energy region was given in this chapter for $\pi^{\pm}p$ baryon exchange reactions. Other examples of such successful extrapolations are as follows:

1. Extrapolation of the Regge pole fit to high energy pp and $\bar{p}p$ total cross section data down to 1 BeV/c, as shown in Figure 8.13.
2. Evaluation of the ω universality sum rule (cf. Section 5.2) which is approximately satisfied even at 1 BeV/c, as shown in Figure 8.14.

3. Extrapolation of the K^+p and K^+n total cross section fits down to about 1 BeV/c.

From the standpoint of the Regge theory, the low and intermediate energy regions take on considerable importance for the study of secondary trajectories.

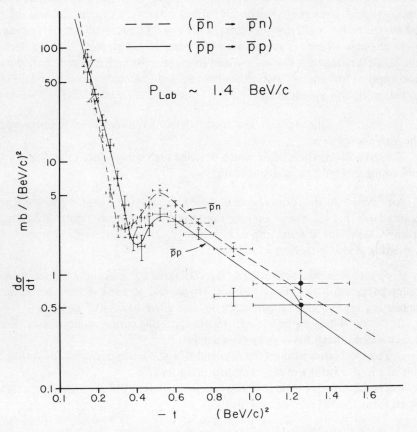

Figure 8.12. Comparison of $\bar{p}p$ and $\bar{p}n$ elastic scattering at low energy: from J. Berryhill and D. Cline, *Phys. Rev. Letters* **21**, 769 (1968).

The measurable effects of these trajectories die out rapidly as the energy is increased due to their smaller values of $\alpha(t)$ compared to the leading trajectories. Thus it is in the low and intermediate energy ranges that these trajectories are likely to make significant contributions to differential cross sections and polarization measurements.

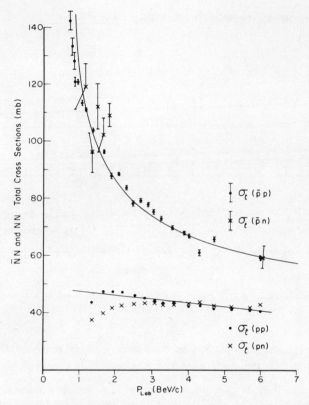

Figure 8.13. Intermediate energy $\bar{p}p$, $\bar{p}n$, pp, and pn total cross section data. The solid curves represent an extrapolation of a Regge pole model used to fit data above 5 BeV/c: from V. Barger and M. Olsson, *Phys. Rev.* **148**, 1428 (1966).

8.4 THEORETICAL DESCRIPTION

The earliest attempt to formulate a model for the intermediate energy region approximated the complete amplitude by a sum of Breit–Wigner resonance amplitudes and the u- or t-channel Regge exchange amplitude: $F \simeq F_{Regge} + F_{Resonance}$. This "interference model" reproduced with moderate success the s-dependent structure in π^-p backward scattering, $\Delta\sigma$, $\pi^-p \rightarrow \pi^0 n$ forward scattering. In the spirit of the model F_{Regge} is obtained from a fit to the high energy data (beyond the intermediate energy range) and extrapolated into the intermediate energy region. With the known Regge amplitude as background, the interference structure provides direct information on parities and spins of the direct channel resonances. While it has been possible to fit a great deal of intermediate energy data and

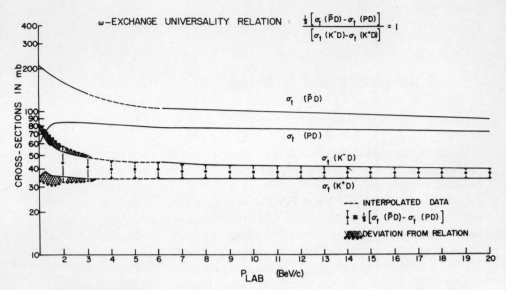

Figure 8.14. Experimental test of the ω universality sum rule down to low energies: from V. Barger and D. Cline, *Phys. Letters* **26B**, 591 (1968).

obtain some valuable information on resonance quantum numbers, there remain some problems with the model that have not been fully answered.

1. The simple Breit-Wigner resonance form is presumably not realistic for the broad, inelastic resonances encountered in the intermediate energy region. Ad hoc modifications have been introduced to gradually cut off the Breit–Wigner tails at energies far from the resonance positions.

2. F_{Regge} may already contain to some extent the energy-averaged contribution of $F_{\text{Resonance}}$ and double counting may occur in adding the two amplitudes.

3. The simple addition of two amplitudes may violate unitarity in some partial wave l.

The present experimental data are not adequate to allow a reliable test of the interference model. At the moment the interference model represents the only quantitative attempt towards a phenomenological description of intermediate energy scattering.

Chapter 9

Conspiracy and Evasion

9.1 CONSPIRING MESON POLES

Analyticity considerations necessarily impose a conspiracy at $u = 0$ between opposite parity fermion Regge poles (cf. Section 3.3). Similar conspiratorial relationships between meson Regge trajectories with different quantum numbers may sometimes exist at $t = 0$. However for meson poles conspiracy is not a necessity; the analyticity requirements can be met without demanding a relationship between trajectories by simply enforcing certain conditions on residue functions. In the latter circumstance the situation is called "evasion."

The consequence of a conspiracy between meson poles is to allow certain helicity amplitudes to be important at $t = 0$ when otherwise (with evasion) they would be small or vanish. There are usually striking differences in the predictions of evasive and conspiring Regge pole models. The reactions $\gamma p \to \pi^+ n$ and $np \to pn$ provide particularly suitable examples. The experimental differential cross sections for these reactions show extremely sharp forward peaks with widths $(\Delta t)^{-1} \sim 1/\mu_\pi^2$ that are highly suggestive of pion exchange. However, unless the pion trajectory conspires with a trajectory of opposite parity, the predicted π-exchange forward differential cross sections vanish, contrary to experimental fact. In the following section we will derive the conspiracy conditions for π exchange in the reaction $\gamma p \to \pi^+ n$.

Pion Conspiracy in Photoproduction

The pion photoproduction amplitude can be alternatively expressed in terms of four invariant amplitudes $A_i(s, t, u)$, $i = 1, \ldots, 4$, or four t-channel parity-conserving helicity amplitudes $\tilde{F}_i(t, s)$, $i = 1, \ldots, 4$. Both the A_i and $\tilde{F}_i$ are constructed to be free of kinematic singularities. We omit the precise definitions of the amplitudes except to record the connection between the two sets:

$$\tilde{F}_1 = -A_1 + 2MA_4$$

$$\tilde{F}_2 = A_1 + tA_2$$

$$\tilde{F}_3 = 2MA_1 - tA_4$$

$$\tilde{F}_4 = -A_3$$

155

The Reggeization proceeds from the t-channel partial wave expansions of the $\tilde{F}_i$. Constraints which must be imposed on the Regge pole forms of the $\tilde{F}_i$ can be readily deduced from the above relationship of the $\tilde{F}_i$ to the A_i. The relevant constraints are

$$\tilde{F}_3(4M^2, s) = -2M\tilde{F}_1(4M^2, s)$$

$$\tilde{F}_2(0, s) = 2M\tilde{F}_3(0, s)$$

The first restriction is a threshold condition analogous to that found for the $\pi\pi \to \bar{N}N$ amplitude in Chapter 3. Since $t = 4M^2$ is far from the s-channel scattering region $t \leqslant 0$, we will not bother to subsequently impose it. The second condition is the conspiracy constraint equation at $t = 0$.

The significance of the $t = 0$ constraint becomes apparent once we realize that $\tilde{F}_2$ and $\tilde{F}_3$ receive contributions from exchanges with different quantum numbers. The quantum numbers of the $\tilde{F}$'s can be found from their couplings to the $\bar{N}N$ system. They are listed in the following table.

	τP	GP	Example exchanges
$\tilde{F}_1$	+1	−1	ρ, A_2
$\tilde{F}_2$	−1	+1	π
$\tilde{F}_3$	+1	−1	ρ, A_2
$\tilde{F}_4$	−1	−1	A_1

Thus if the constraint equation at $t = 0$ is satisfied by *individual* Regge pole exchanges, we are forced to conclude that

$$\tilde{F}_2(0, s) = \tilde{F}_3(0, s) = 0$$

This is the so-called evasive solution which requires the residues of the Regge poles in $\tilde{F}_2$ and $\tilde{F}_3$ to vanish at $t = 0$. Since the differential cross section is given by

$$\frac{d\sigma}{dt} = \frac{1}{16\pi}\left[|\tilde{F}_2|^2 + \frac{1}{4M^2 - t}|\tilde{F}_3|^2 - \frac{t|\tilde{F}_1|^2}{4M^2 - t} - t|\tilde{F}_4|^2\right]$$

the evasive solution yields

$$\left(\frac{d\sigma}{dt}\right)_{t=0} = 0$$

Expressed in terms of the invariant amplitude $A_1(s, t, u,)$, evasion gives $A_1(s, t = 0) = 0$, which is not required by kinematics.

An alternative way of satisfying the $t = 0$ constraint equation, without a vanishing forward cross section, is to have a conspiring Regge pole. The pion contributes only to $\bar{F}_2$; its contribution is

$$\bar{F}_2(t,s) = \gamma_\pi(t)\,\alpha_\pi(t)\,\mathcal{S}^{+1}_{\alpha_\pi}\left(\frac{s-u}{2s_0}\right)^{\alpha_\pi(t)-1}$$

A conspiring Regge pole π_c contributing to $\bar{F}_3$ has the form

$$\bar{F}_3(t,s) = \gamma_c(t)\,\alpha_c(t)\,\mathcal{S}^{\tau}_{\alpha_c}\left(\frac{s-u}{2s_0}\right)^{\alpha_c(t)-1}$$

As the $t = 0$ conspiracy condition applies to both real and imaginary parts of the amplitudes, the π_c must have the same signature τ as the π. Hence the π_c has opposite parity from the π, but other quantum numbers are the same. The $t = 0$ constraint equation yields

$$\alpha_c(0) = \alpha_\pi(0)$$

$$\gamma_c(0) = -(1/2M)\,\gamma_\pi(0)$$

The pion and its conspirator must have degenerate trajectories at $t = 0$.

When we extrapolate the Regge form of $\bar{F}_2(t, s)$ to the pion pole ($t = \mu^2$, $\alpha_\pi = 0$), we must recover the Born approximation

$$\bar{F}_2^{\text{Born}} \approx \frac{2eG\mu^2}{(t-\mu^2)}\frac{1}{s - M^2}$$

Consequently the t variation of π residue function must be chosen as

$$\gamma_\pi(t) = \left(\frac{-1}{t-\mu^2}\right)\bar{\gamma}_\pi(t)$$

with $\bar{\gamma}_\pi(\mu^2) = -eG\pi\mu^2/s_0$. The final form of the cross section due to the π and π_c contributions is

$$\frac{d\sigma}{dt} = \frac{1}{16\pi}\left\{\left(\frac{1}{t-\mu^2}\right)^2\left[\frac{\bar{\gamma}_\pi\,\alpha_\pi}{\sin(\pi\alpha_\pi/2)}\right]^2\left(\frac{s-u}{2s_0}\right)^{2\alpha_\pi-2}\right.$$

$$\left. +\frac{1}{4M^2}\cdot\left[\frac{\gamma_c\,\alpha_c}{\sin(\pi\alpha_c/2)}\right]^2\left(\frac{s-u}{2s_0}\right)^{2\alpha_c-2}\right\}$$

The expected sharp spike in $(d\sigma/dt)$ near $t = 0$ due to pion exchange has been restored as a result of the conspiracy.

If the π_c trajectory has a positive slope, then it will intersect $J^P = 0^+$ at a value of $t > 0$. Then in order to avoid the embarrassing prediction of a very low mass 0^+

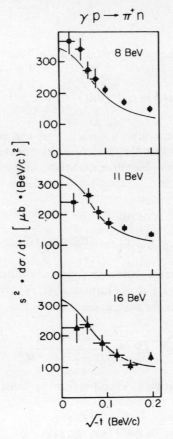

Figure 9.1. Representative fit to the $\gamma p \to \pi^+ n$ data at small t with the (π, π_c) conspiracy model: from P. DiVecchia *et al.*, Trieste preprint (1968).

meson, the π_c trajectory must choose the nonsense mechanism (cf. Section 3.2) in order that no scattering amplitude develops a pole at $\alpha_c(t) = 0$. The first particle manifestation would occur when (and if) the π_c trajectory intersected spin 2. A priori it is also possible that the π_c trajectory is flat or has a negative slope.

The high energy data on $\gamma p \to \pi^+ n$ at small t can be adequately described by the (π, π_c) conspiracy model. Figure 9.1 shows the results of one such fit for the experimental cross sections. Values of Regge parameters that can reproduce the small t data are

$$\bar{\gamma}_\pi(t) \simeq -(eG\pi\mu^2)\left[1 + 0.4\left(\frac{t - u^2}{\mu^2}\right)\right]$$

$$\gamma_c(t) \simeq \frac{1}{2M\mu^2}\bar{\gamma}_\pi(0)$$

$$\alpha_\pi(t) \simeq -0.02 + 0.7t$$

$$\alpha_c(t) \simeq -0.02 + 1.6t$$

with $s_0 = 1$ (BeV/c)^2 for the scale factor. The rapid variation of $\bar{\gamma}_\pi(t)$ is needed for fitting the data while maintaining consistency with the coupling constants at the pion pole. The zero of the pion residue at $t \simeq -1.5\mu^2$ should also show up in pion exchange residues for other reactions. If the zero of the pion residue at $t = t_0 \simeq -1.5\mu^2$ for the $\gamma p \to \pi^+ n$ reaction is associated entirely with the $\pi \bar{N} N$ vertex factor, then the pion residue for the $np \to pn$ reaction must have a double zero $(t - t_0)^2$. On the other hand, if both the $\gamma \pi \pi$ and πNN vertex factors have a square-root-type dynamical zero $\sim (t - t_0)^{1/2}$, then such a $(t - t_0)^{1/2}$ zero must be present in the π residue factors of every reaction (similar to the propagation of the crossover zero of the ω residue discussed in Section 5.3).

The pion and conspirator give the same amplitudes for both $\gamma p \to \pi^+ n$ and $\gamma n \to \pi^- p$. Experimentally the ratio

$$R = \frac{d\sigma/dt(\gamma n \to \pi^- p)}{d\sigma/dt(\gamma p \to \pi^+ n)}$$

is consistent with 1 for $t \approx 0$ but becomes appreciably less than 1 for $t \neq 0$. Interference terms in the cross section between $C = +1$ and -1 Regge exchanges are required to account for values of $R \neq 1$. Possible for $C = -1$ exchanges are are ρ_V and ρ_A. Regge models have been constructed to describe the $\gamma N \to \pi N$ data out to $t \simeq -0.5$ (BeV/c)^2, but they are decidedly nonunique.

Pion Conspiracy in np Charge Exchange

A conspiracy for the pion also seems necessary to reconcile Regge pole theory with data on the reaction $np \to pn$. Experimentally, the differential cross section for this reaction has an exceptionally sharp peak, with width $\Delta t \sim 0.02$ (BeV/c)^2,

that persists to very low energies (cf. Figures 9.2 and 2.19). It is natural to attri-
bute this narrow peak to the exchange of the pion whose mass is $m_\pi{}^2 \sim 0.02$.
However, if the pion does not conspire, kinematic constraints cause all of its
helicity amplitudes to vanish at $t = 0$, at variance with the narrow experimental
peak. Conspiracy with an opposite parity pole that intersects the pion trajectory

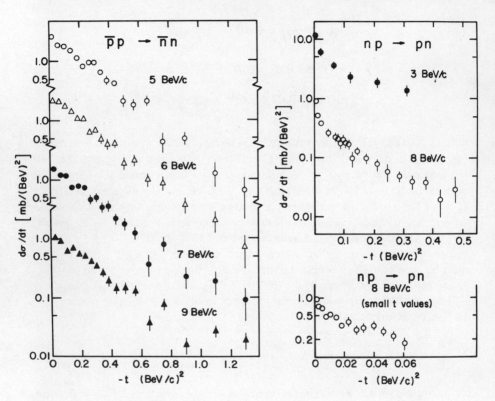

Figure 9.2. High energy differential cross section data on the reactions $np \rightarrow pn$ and
$\bar{p}p \rightarrow \bar{n}n$.

at $t = 0$ can remove the difficulty by allowing certain of the pion helicity amplitudes to contribute at the forward direction.

The expression for the $np \rightarrow pn$ differential cross section in terms of s-channel
helicity amplitudes ϕ_j is

$$\frac{d\sigma}{dt} = \tfrac{1}{2}\{|\phi_1|^2 + |\phi_2|^2 + |\phi_3|^2 + |\phi_4|^2 + 4|\phi_s|^2\}$$

The two amplitudes of particular interest are

$$\phi_2 = \langle p(-)n(-)|n(+)p(+)\rangle_i^f$$

$$\phi_4 = \langle p(+)n(-)|n(-)p(+)\rangle_i^f$$

since the t-channel pion Regge pole contributes only to these s-channel amplitudes. The ($\pm$) labels above refer to the particle helicities. As illustrated in Figure 9.3, the amplitude ϕ_4 involves net helicity flip and must therefore vanish at $t = 0$ for angular momentum conservation. The amplitude ϕ_2 is not constrained to vanish

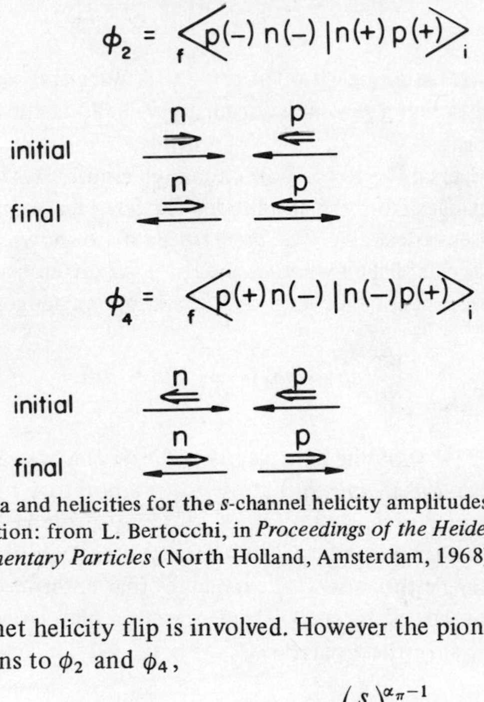

$$\phi_2 = \langle p(-)\, n(-) \,|n(+)\, p(+)\rangle_i^f$$

initial

final

$$\phi_4 = \langle p(+)n(-)\,|n(-)p(+)\rangle_i^f$$

initial

final

Figure 9.3. Momenta and helicities for the s-channel helicity amplitudes ϕ_2 and ϕ_4 at $t = 0$ in the $np \rightarrow pn$ reaction: from L. Bertocchi, in *Proceedings of the Heidelberg International Conference on Elementary Particles* (North Holland, Amsterdam, 1968), H. Filthuth, ed., p. 197.

at $t = 0$ since no net helicity flip is involved. However the pion Regge pole gives equal contributions to ϕ_2 and ϕ_4,

$$\phi_2{}^\pi = \phi_4{}^\pi = t\sqrt{s}\,\beta_\pi \mathscr{S}_{\alpha_\pi}^{+1}\left(\frac{s}{s_0}\right)^{\alpha_\pi - 1}$$

and the necessary constraint $\phi_4(t = 0) = 0$ forces the entire pion contribution to vanish at $t = 0$.

The vanishing of $\phi_2(t = 0)$ is no longer a necessary consequence of the constraint $\phi_4(t = 0) = 0$ when a conspirator trajectory (with $I = 1$, $G = -$, $\tau = +$, $P = +$) is also present. The contributions of π_c to ϕ_2 and ϕ_4 are related by

$$\phi_2{}^c = -\phi_4{}^c = t\sqrt{s}\,\alpha_c \beta_c \mathscr{S}_{\alpha_c}^{+1}\left(\frac{s}{s_0}\right)^{\alpha_c - 1}$$

The explicit form on the r.h.s. is intended only for $t \approx 0$; the factor of α comes from the assumption that the π_c chooses nonsense at $J = 0$. Singular behaviors for the π and π_c residues at $t = 0$, $\beta_\pi(t) \sim \bar{\beta}_\pi(t)/t$ and $\beta_c(t) \sim \bar{\beta}_c(t)/t$, allow $\phi_2(t = 0) \neq 0$ with $\phi_4(t = 0) = 0$, provided that $\alpha_\pi(0) = \alpha_c(0)$ and $\bar{\beta}_\pi(0) = \alpha_c(0)\bar{\beta}_c(0)$. With such a conspiracy, it has been possible to fit the $d\sigma/dt(np \rightarrow pn)$ forward peak. To maintain consistency of the height of the forward peak with the known value of the pion–nucleon coupling constant G^2, a rapidly varying pion residue function is required. The form used in one such fit was

$$\beta_\pi(t) \sim G^2\left[1 + \lambda\left(\frac{t - \mu_\pi^2}{\mu_\pi^2}\right)\right]$$

with $\lambda \sim 1/2$, which has a linear zero at $t \sim -\mu_\pi^2$. With this residue structure, factorization implies that a zero must occur universally in the pion residue functions for all reactions.

Since by line reversal the Regge pole exchange amplitudes for $np \rightarrow pn$ differ at most by sign changes from the amplitudes for $\bar{p}p \rightarrow \bar{n}n$, a unified description of the two processes is desirable. The $\bar{p}p \rightarrow \bar{n}n$ data are shown in Figure 9.2. It is not experimentally established whether the $\bar{p}p \rightarrow \bar{n}n$ differential cross section also has a sharp spike near $t = 0$. With only π and π_c exchanges the equality

$$\frac{d\sigma}{dt}(np \rightarrow pn) = \frac{d\sigma}{dt}(\bar{p}p \rightarrow \bar{n}n)$$

is obtained. For $|t| \gtrsim 0.05$ the data clearly indicate that $d\sigma/dt(\bar{p}p \rightarrow \bar{n}n)$ is substantially larger than $d\sigma/dt(np \rightarrow pn)$ at the same laboratory momentum. Thus $C = -1$ exchanges such as ρ_V and ρ_A must also play a role in the description of these reactions. Further phenomenological analysis and additional data will be required to disentangle the variety of exchanges that enter in the NN and $\bar{N}N$ charge exchange processes. Nevertheless at present a pion conspiracy seems essential to Regge models for these reactions.

9.2 EVASIVE MESON POLES

The meson poles that appear in total cross sections (through the optical theorem) cannot conspire in elastic scattering amplitudes. In order to demonstrate this, we write the residue of a t-channel Regge pole contributing to NN scattering in factorized form $\beta^N_{\lambda_1 \lambda_3}(t)\beta^N_{\lambda_2 \lambda_4}(t)$, where the λ_i denote t-channel helicities of nucleons or antinucleons. Similarly the residues for the πN scattering amplitudes are $\beta^\pi(t)\beta^N_{\lambda_2 \lambda_4}(t)$. Taking into account kinematic singularities, the required behaviors of the residues near $t = 0$ are

$$\beta^N_{++}(t)\,\beta^N_{++}(t) = \gamma_1(t)$$

$$\beta^N_{++}(t)\,\beta^N_{+-}(t) = \sqrt{t}\,\gamma_2(t)$$

$$\beta^N_{+-}(t)\,\beta^N_{+-}(t) = \gamma_3(t)$$

$$\beta^\pi(t)\,\beta^N_{++}(t) = \gamma_4(t)$$

$$\beta^\pi(t)\,\beta^N_{+-}(t) = \sqrt{t}\,\gamma_5(t)$$

where the $\gamma_i(t)$ are free of kinematic singularities at $t = 0$. These kinematic conditions on the residues of a given Regge pole can be satisfied in two simple ways:

(1) *evasive solution*

$$\beta^N_{++}(t) \sim C_1 \qquad \beta^N_{+-}(t) \sim \sqrt{t} \qquad \beta^\pi(t) \sim C_2$$

(2) *conspiring solution*

$$\beta^N_{++}(t) \sim \sqrt{t} \qquad \beta^N_{+-}(t) \sim C_3 \qquad \beta^\pi(t) \sim \sqrt{t}$$

The total cross sections are related to the t-channel helicity nonflip elastic amplitudes at $t = 0$ and thereby receive contributions only from Regge poles that satisfy the evasive solution. Thus the best known meson Regge poles $(\rho, \omega, A_2, P', P)$ do not conspire. The discussion of the $np \rightarrow pn$ process in the preceding section was based on the above conspiring solution for the π and π_c Regge poles. Another possible conspiracy that has been discussed in the literature involves a speculative ρ' trajectory $(I = 1, G = +, \tau = -, P = -)$ and the B trajectory $(I = 1, G = +, \tau = -, P = +)$. The evidence bearing on a $\rho' - B$ conspiracy is inconclusive.

9.3 LORENTZ POLE CLASSIFICATION OF CONSPIRACIES

The conspiracy relations among Regge poles at $t = 0$ can be alternatively obtained from considerations of Lorentz invariance. The scattering amplitude at $t = 0$ can be expanded in terms of irreducible representations of the homogeneous Lorentz group $0(3, 1)$. From a Sommerfeld–Watson transform, the scattering amplitude is then expressed in terms of Lorentz poles. The amplitudes of these "four-dimensional" angular momentum poles involve Gegenbauer polynomials, which, in turn, can be expanded in terms of the usual Legendre functions (i.e., Regge poles). The immediate result is that a single Lorentz pole at $J = \alpha$ corresponds to an infinite sequence of Regge poles (and also vice versa) at $J_n = \alpha - n$ with $n = 0, 1, 2, \ldots$. Definite relations (conspiracy relations) exist among the trajectories and residues of the Regge poles that correspond to the same Lorentz pole.

In addition to the usual quantum numbers we now have a Lorentz quantum number M to classify families of Regge poles at $t = 0$. The possible values of M are restricted by the external spins

$$M \leqslant \min(j_1 + j_3, j_2 + j_4)$$

where j_i labels the spins of the particles in the t-channel $1 + \bar{3} \to \bar{2} + 4$. In NN scattering there are three classes of Lorentz families:

Class I: $M = 0$, $\tau P = +1$, $\tau = C$
This class corresponds to evasive Regge poles such as P, P', ρ, ω, A_2. The daughters are spaced by two units, $J_n = \alpha, \alpha - 2, \alpha - 4, \ldots$.

Class II: $M = 0$, $\tau P = -1$, $\tau = (-)^{n+1} C$
This class corresponds to two different sequences of Regge poles:
   (i) $J_n = \alpha, \alpha - 2, \alpha - 4, \ldots$ with $C = P = -\tau$,
   (ii) $J_n = \alpha - 1, \alpha - 3, \ldots$ with $C = -P = \tau$.

The residues of the two sequences are related at $t = 0$. This is a possible type of conspiracy but it has not yet played an important role in phenomenology.

Class III: $M = 1$, $\tau P = \pm 1$, $\tau = (-)^n C$
This class corresponds to a sequence of trajectories which occur in degenerate pairs at $t = 0$ (parity doublets). The π, π_c conspiracy is of this type.

The phenomenological importance of Lorentz pole classifications of Regge pole families is not entirely clear. Since observed particles do not seem to occur with a sequence of angular momentum values at the same mass, the Regge pole concept is apparently more basic. Nevertheless, at $t = 0$ the Lorentz pole classifications may provide additional physical information. For example, it has been argued that the rapidly varying behavior of the pion residue in the $np \to pn$ reaction is a result of the $M = 1$ quantum number assignment. If the pion mass were zero, the pion residue would have to vanish at $t = 0$ because $M = 1$ representations with integral J do not couple to $\bar{N}N$ at $J = 0$. For the small physical pion mass, it is plausible then that the pion residue vanishes in the neighborhood of $t = 0$.

The conspiracy conditions for meson Regge poles have attracted considerable theoretical attention. Their phenomenological consequences have not been fully explored. A reasonable expectation is that conspiracies will play an increasingly important role in the description of inelastic reactions such as $\pi N \to VN$, $\pi N \to V\Delta$, $\bar{N}N \to \bar{N}\Delta$, and so forth.

Chapter 10

Finite Energy Sum Rules

10.1 DERIVATION OF FESR

A novel application of dispersion theory has recently been used to determine high energy Regge parameters from integrals over low energy scattering data. This approach has the considerable advantage of dealing directly with amplitudes, whereas high energy scattering data give bilinear products of amplitudes that are frequently hard to disentangle. The derivation in this section will be directed specifically to πN elastic and charge exchange amplitudes at small fixed t; corresponding relations can readily be generalized to other processes or to fixed u.

For the purpose of writing fixed t dispersion relations we choose $\nu = (s - u)/4M$ and t as independent variables. The conventional decomposition of the πN scattering matrix into invariant amplitudes is

$$T = -A(\nu, t) + i\gamma \cdot \frac{(q_1 + q_2)}{2} B(\nu, t)$$

The analyticity of $A(\nu, t)$ and $B(\nu, t)$ are assumed to be given by the Mandelstam representation, as illustrated in Figure 10.1. At fixed t, the branch cuts are

$$(-\infty, -\nu_0) \to u \geqslant (M + \mu)^2$$

$$(\nu_0, \infty) \to s \geqslant (M + \mu)^2$$

with $\nu_0 = \mu + t/4M$. The B amplitude has poles at

$$\nu = -\nu_B \to s = M^2$$

$$\nu = \nu_B \to u = M^2$$

where $\nu_B = (2\mu^2 - t)/4M$. The isospin even and odd amplitudes

$$A^{(\pm)} = \tfrac{1}{2}[A^{\pi^- p} \pm A^{\pi^+ p}]$$

$$B^{(\pm)} = \tfrac{1}{2}[B^{\pi^- p} \pm B^{\pi^+ p}]$$

receive contributions from t-channel exchanges with quantum numbers:

Amplitude	Quantum numbers	Example exchanges
$A^{(+)}, B^{(+)}$	$I = 0, C = +, P = +, \tau = +$	P, P'
$A^{(-)}, B^{(-)}$	$I = 1, C = -, P = -, \tau = -$	ρ

The connection between the t-channel kinematic singularity-free helicity amplitudes (cf. Section 3.2) and the invariant amplitudes

$$\tilde{f}_{++}(t, \nu) = (4M^2 - t)\left[A + \frac{\nu B}{(1 - t/4M^2)}\right]$$

$$\tilde{f}_{+-}(t, \nu) = B$$

motivates the customary use of the amplitudes $A' \equiv A + \nu B/(1 - t/4M^2)$ and B in these dispersion theoretic analyses.

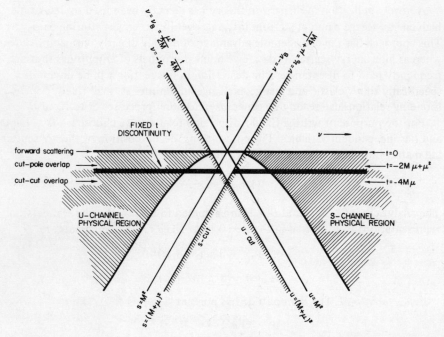

Figure 10.1. Mandelstam diagram for πN elastic scattering showing branch cuts and poles for fixed t dispersion relation.

For the FESR derivation we consider a scattering amplitude $a(\nu, t)$ with odd s–u crossing property

$$a(\nu + i\eta, t) = -a(-\nu - i\eta, t)$$

where $\eta \to 0+$. Four possibilities for $a(\nu, t)$ in πN scattering are the amplitudes $\nu A'^{(+)}$, $B^{(+)}$, $A'^{(-)}$, and $\nu B^{(-)}$. In order to write an unsubtracted dispersion relation, it is usually necessary to first subtract some part of the asymptotic behavior from the physical amplitude. For this purpose we define

$$\hat{a}(\nu, t) \equiv a(\nu, t) - a_{\text{Asym}}(\nu, t)$$

We assume that the asymptotic behavior can be expressed in terms of Regge pole exchange amplitudes. The form of a_{Asym} will be taken as

$$a_{\text{Asym}}(\nu, t) = -\nu \sum_i \frac{\gamma_i(t)}{\sin(\pi \theta_i/2)} \exp\left[-i\frac{\pi}{2}\theta_i\right](\nu^2 - \nu_0^2)^{\theta_i/2}$$

where θ_i is related to the trajectories $\alpha_i(t)$ by

$$\theta_i = \alpha_i(t) \qquad \text{for} \quad \nu A'^{(+)}$$

$$\theta_i = \alpha_i(t) - 2 \qquad \text{for} \quad B^{(+)}$$

$$\theta_i = \alpha_i(t) - 1 \qquad \text{for} \quad A'^{(-)} \text{ and } \nu B^{(-)}$$

The $\gamma_i(t)$ are the usual residue functions. For $\nu \gg \nu_0$, a_{Asym} reduces to the Regge pole expansions of Chapters 3, 4, and 5 with the choice $s_0 = 2M$.

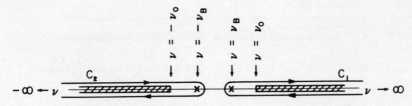

Figure 10.2. Contour $C = C_1 + C_2$ in the complex ν plane used in deriving finite energy sum rules for πN elastic amplitudes.

At a fixed value of t, we can write a Cauchy relation in the complex ν plane, $\int_C d\nu \, \tilde{a}(\nu, t) = 0$, where $C = C_1 + C_2$ is the contour encircling the cuts and poles, as shown in Figure 10.2. By the above construction of $\tilde{a}(\nu, t)$, the integral around the circular contour at $|\nu| = \infty$ makes no contribution. From the odd crossing property, the integrals over C_1 and C_2 are equal. Then since

$$\text{Im}\,\tilde{a}(\nu, t) = \frac{[\tilde{a}(\nu + i\eta, t) - \tilde{a}(\nu - i\eta, t)]}{2i} \qquad \text{for} \quad \nu \geqslant \nu_0$$

$$\text{Im}\,a(\nu, t) = 0 \qquad \text{for} \quad \nu < \nu_0$$

the Cauchy relation becomes

$$-\pi \, \text{Res}\,[a(\nu, t)]_{\nu = \nu_B} + \int_{\nu_0}^{\nu_1} d\nu \, \text{Im}\,\tilde{a}(\nu, t) = 0$$

The integral has been cut off at an upper limit ν_1 corresponding to the value of ν for which $a(\nu, t)$ is well represented by $a^{\text{Asym}}(\nu, t)$, [i.e., $\bar{a}(\nu_1, t) \approx 0$]. The integral over a^{Asym} can be explicitly evaluated, and we obtain the relation

$$-\pi \operatorname{Res}\left[a(\nu, t)\right]_{\nu=\nu_B} + \int_{\nu_0}^{\nu_1} d\nu \operatorname{Im} a(\nu, t) = \sum_i \gamma_i \frac{(\nu_1^2 - \nu_0^2)^{(\theta_i+2)/2}}{\theta_i + 2}$$

This is the so-called "finite energy sum rule" (FESR), which relates an integral over the low energy amplitude to the integrated asymptotic amplitude evaluated at $\nu = \nu_1$. The residues at $\nu = \nu_B$ for the πN amplitudes are tabulated as follows:

$a(\nu, t)$	$\operatorname{Res}\left[a(\nu, t)\right]_{\nu=\nu_0}$
$\nu A'^{(+)}$	$-(G^2/2M)\nu_B/(1 - t/4M^2)$
$B^{(+)}$	$-(G^2/2M)$
$A'^{(-)}$	$-(G^2/2M)/(1 - t/4M^2)$
$\nu B^{(-)}$	$-(G^2/2M)\nu_B$

where $G^2/4\pi = 14.6$ is the renormalized pion–nucleon coupling constant.

10.2 CONTINUOUS MOMENT SUM RULES (CMSR)

The FESR can be generalized to include information from the real part of $a(\nu, t)$ in the integral. To this end we consider the amplitude

$$b(\nu, t) \equiv \bar{a}(\nu, t) \exp\left\{i\frac{\pi}{2}(\epsilon + 1)\right\}(\nu^2 - \nu_0^2)^{(-\epsilon-1)/2}$$

Here ϵ is an arbitrary parameter ($\epsilon \leqslant 1$). The ν discontinuity of $b(\nu, t)$ also vanishes for $-\nu_0 \leqslant \nu \leqslant \nu_0$ except at the poles $\nu = \pm \nu_B$ and we can again write a Cauchy formula $\int_C d\nu \, b(\nu, t) = 0$. Carrying through the same procedure for $b(\nu, t)$ as outlined in the derivation of the FESR for $a(\nu, t)$, we arrive at the equation

$$-\pi |\nu_0^2 - \nu_B^2|^{(-\epsilon-1)/2} \xi \operatorname{Res}[a]_{\nu=\nu_B} + \int_{\nu_0}^{\nu_1} d\nu \operatorname{Im}\left\{a \exp\left[i\frac{\pi}{2}(\epsilon + 1)\right]\right\}(\nu^2 - \nu_0^2)^{(-\epsilon-1)/2}$$

$$= \sum_i \frac{\gamma_i(\nu_1^2 - \nu_0^2)^{(\theta_i-\epsilon+1)/2}}{(\theta_i - \epsilon + 1)} \frac{\sin\left(\pi(\theta_i - \epsilon - 1)/2\right)}{\sin\left(\pi\theta_i/2\right)}$$

with $\xi = 1$ for $\nu_0{}^2 > \nu_B{}^2$ and $\xi = \cos[\pi(\epsilon + 1)/2]$ for $\nu_0{}^2 < \nu_B{}^2$. This relation is usually called a "continuous moment sum rule" (CMSR) since the parameter ϵ can take on a continuous range of values. $\epsilon = -1$ corresponds to the FESR; odd integral values of ϵ give moments of the FESR. For nonintegral ϵ the evaluation of the integrand at small t

$$\mathrm{Im}\left\{a\exp\left[i\frac{\pi}{2}(\epsilon + 1)\right]\right\} = (\mathrm{Im}\,a)\cos\frac{\pi}{2}(\epsilon + 1) + (\mathrm{Re}\,a)\sin\frac{\pi}{2}(\epsilon + 1)$$

requires a knowledge of both real and imaginary parts of the scattering amplitude for $\nu_0 \leqslant \nu \leqslant \nu_1$.

10.3 πN SCATTERING APPLICATIONS

Analyses at $t = 0$

The FESR were initially used for the $A'^{(-)}$ and $\nu A'^{(+)}$ amplitudes at $t = 0$ to check the consistency of Regge parameters determined from direct fits to high energy data. For these applications the FESR integrands were evaluated from the optical theorem:

$$\mathrm{Im}\,A'^{(\pm)}(\nu, t = 0) = \frac{1}{2P_{\mathrm{Lab}}}[\sigma_t^{\pi^- p}(\nu) \pm \sigma_t^{\pi^+ p}(\nu)]$$

Since accurate total cross section data exist through the low and intermediate energy regions, the matching point ν_1 could be chosen in the asymptotic energy region $\nu_1 \sim 5$ BeV. The FESR integrals were found to match quite smoothly to the usual P, P', and ρ Regge integrated amplitudes evaluated at ν_1.

Information on Re $A'^{(\pm)}(\nu, t = 0)$ for $\nu < \nu_1$ was subsequently also included in these analyses, and solutions for the Regge trajectories and residues were obtained from simultaneous fits to CMSR and high energy scattering data. When a sufficiently broad range of ϵ values are used (e.g., $1 < \epsilon < -5$), the CMSR are sensitive to both magnitudes and phases of the Regge pole contributions, and thus contributions of different trajectories can be disentangled. The essential conclusions from these $t = 0$ analyses are as follows:

(1) the ρ Regge pole alone with $\alpha_\rho(0) = 0.58$ accounts for the $A'^{(-)}$ CMSR and scattering data at $t = 0$;

(2) three vacuum Regge poles are required to explain the $A'^{(+)}$ data. Typical solutions for the trajectory intercepts of these poles are $\alpha_P(0) = 1.0, \alpha_{P'}(0) = 0.5$, and $\alpha_{P''}(0) = -0.5$ (poorly determined).

The intercepts for P' and P'' are strongly correlated. The P'' amplitude is important only for the CMSR; the high energy amplitudes are essentially given by the P and P' contributions.

Analyses for Range of t

The principal advantage of FESR and CMSR studies is the separation of the contributions of different Regge poles to the A' and B amplitudes over a range

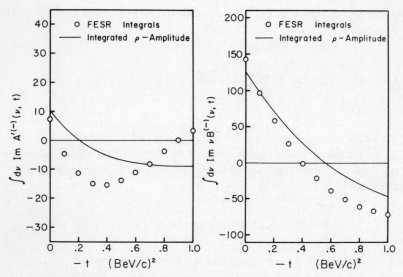

Figure 10.3. Comparison of FESR integrals (over πN phase shifts and nucleon pole) with integrated ρ Regge amplitudes evaluated at $\nu_1 \sim 2$ BeV/c.

of t. The integrals over amplitudes for $\nu < \nu_1$ are evaluated from πN phase shifts. Additional dynamical approximations are necessary for these analyses.

(i) Only contributions from Regge exchanges are included in the CMSR for $\nu > \nu_1$. Since πN phase shift results extend at present only to $\nu_1 \sim 2$ BeV, the CMSR are approximate to the extent that direct channel resonance contributions for $\nu > \nu_1$ are neglected.

(ii) For $t \neq 0$, extrapolations of the phase shift forms of the amplitudes are used in the unphysical region, $\mu \leqslant \nu \leqslant [(M^2 - t/4)(\mu^2 - t/4)]^{1/2}/M$ (cf. Figure 10.1).

Results of evaluating FESR integrals up to $\nu_1 \simeq 2$ BeV/c for $A'^{(-)}$ and $\nu B^{(-)}$ are shown by the circles in Figure 10.3 (the nucleon pole residues are included in these results). For comparison the ρ Regge amplitudes (integrated and evaluated at ν_1) from a representative high energy fit are shown by the curves in the figure. If the FESR were satisfied in this approximation, the circles and curves would coincide. The overall agreement is fair. In particular the low energy integral of the FESR "predicts" the (i) approximate relative magnitudes of the Regge ρ

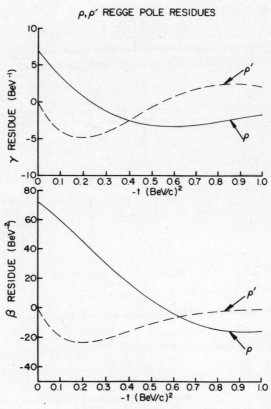

Figure 10.4. Residues for ρ and ρ' Regge poles obtained from a simultaneous fit to CMSR and $d\sigma/dt(\pi^- p \rightarrow \pi^0 n)$. The γ_i denote residues for the A' amplitude and the β_i denote B amplitude residues. From V. Barger and R. J. N. Phillips, *Phys. Rev. Letters* **21**, 865 (1968).

amplitudes $|A'^{(-)}/B^{(-)}| \ll 1$, (ii) the zero of $B^{(-)}$ at $t \simeq -0.6$ where $\alpha_\rho \rightarrow 0$, and (iii) the crossover zero of $A'^{(-)}$ at $t \simeq -0.2$.

A systematic analysis of the CMSR for $A'^{(-)}$ and $\nu B^{(-)}$ indicates the presence of a small ρ' contribution with $\alpha_{\rho'}(t) \simeq 0.8t$ in addition to the dominant ρ with $\alpha_\rho(t) = 0.55 + t$. The solutions for the ρ and ρ' residues are illustrated in Figure 10.4. The notation γ_i is used for the A' residues and β_i for the B residues. The prediction for the $\pi^- p \to \pi^0 n$ polarization from this ρ, ρ' solution is of the same size and sign as observed experimentally.

Similar FESR and CMSR calculations have been made for the trajectories:

(a) P, P', P'' in elastic πN amplitudes;

(b) P, P', ω, ρ, A_2 in elastic KN and $\bar{K}N$ amplitudes;

(c) π, π_c in $\gamma p \to \pi^0 p$.

The solutions for these Regge amplitudes are still somewhat dependent on the approximations. Nevertheless the overall usefulness of the FESR and CMSR as a tool in the study of Regge exchange amplitudes has been convincingly demonstrated.

Chapter 11

Asymptotic Projections

11.1 FUTURE OUTLOOK

Over the range of energies studied at present, phenomenological models based on Regge pole exchanges have been reasonably successful in quantitatively describing scattering data. Within the next decade, the highest accelerator kinetic energy is expected to increase thirtyfold: USSR (70 BeV, 1968); USA (200 BeV, 1973); Europe (300 BeV, ?); CERN (1000 BeV pp colliding beams, 1972). In this ultrahigh energy range the asymptotic boundary conditions given by Regge pole dominance

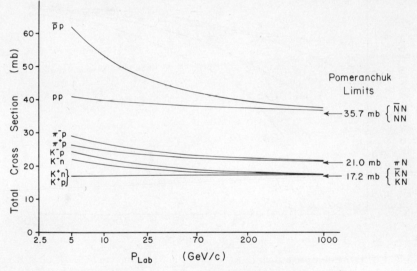

Figure 11.1. Asymptotic projections of total cross sections from the (P, P', A, ω, ρ) Regge exchange model: from V. Barger *et al., Nucl. Phys.* **B5**, 411 (1968).

can be subject to rather direct experimental tests, since only the contribution of the leading trajectory to a reaction will be appreciable. It is of course possible that Regge pole dominance at higher energies may be drastically modified by the increasing importance of cuts in the complex angular momentum plane. In order to delineate predictions of current Regge models that can be tested on the higher energy accelerators, it is of interest to extrapolate present parameterizations to higher energies. In this chapter we present projections for total cross sections, forward elastic scattering, and backward πN elastic scattering to the 50–1000-BeV range.

11.2 TOTAL CROSS SECTION PROJECTIONS

In Section 5.2 we discussed a Regge pole model with (P, P', A, ω, ρ) exchanges that satisfactorily described the total cross section data in the 5–30 BeV/c momentum range (cf. Figure 2.14). Total cross section projections from this model are shown in Figure 11.1 for laboratory momenta of 50 to 1000 BeV/c. By 200 BeV/c

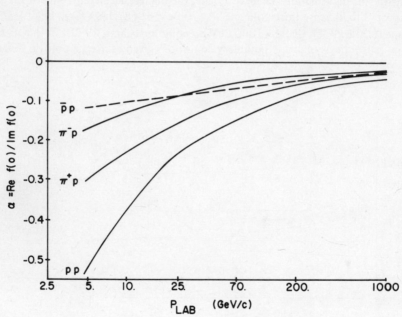

Figure 11.2. Asymptotic projections of $\alpha = \{\mathrm{Re}\, f(0)/\mathrm{Im}\, f(0)\}$ from the (P, P', A, ω, ρ) Regge exchange model: from V. Barger *et al.*, *Nucl. Phys.* **B5**, 411 (1968).

the total cross sections have leveled off and essentially reached their respective Pomeranchuk limits. If a Pomeranchuk trajectory [with $\alpha_P(0) = 1$] exists, then total cross sections should remain fairly constant over the 200–400 BeV/c range. Furthermore the SU(3) symmetry breaking in the unitary singlet Pomeranchuk coupling to $\pi\pi$ and $\bar{K}K$ would be directly measurable at these momenta.

The projections of $(\mathrm{Re}\, f/\mathrm{Im}\, f)_{t=0}$ to higher momenta from the same model are shown in Figure 11.2. Above 200 BeV/c all real parts are less than 10% of the corresponding imaginary parts.

Elastic Scattering Shrinkage

One of the most interesting projections from current Regge parameterizations concerns the effective shrinkage to be expected in the billion electron volt energy range. To investigate this question we can use an effective single pole trajectory approximation

$$\frac{d\sigma}{dt} = F(t)\left(\frac{E}{E_0}\right)^{2\alpha(t)-2}$$

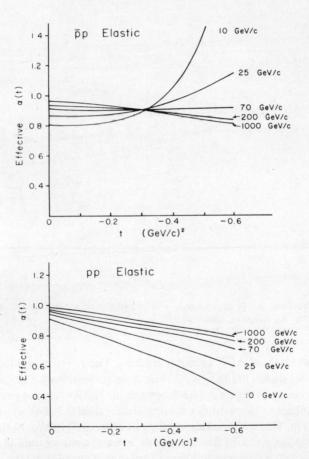

Figure 11.3. Effective one-pole representations of shrinkage patterns expected in *pp* and *p̄p* elastic scattering on the basis of Regge parameters that fit present data: from V. Barger *et al.*, *Nucl. Phys.* **B5**, 411 (1968).

to represent the multi-Regge pole situation. Using the parameters from a representative Regge fit to the existing elastic scattering data, we can calculate $d\sigma/dt$ and determine the effective trajectory at an energy E by the equation

$$2\alpha(t) - 2 = \frac{\ln\{[d\sigma(E_+, t)/dt]/[d\sigma(E_-, t)/dt]\}}{\ln[E_+/E_-]}$$

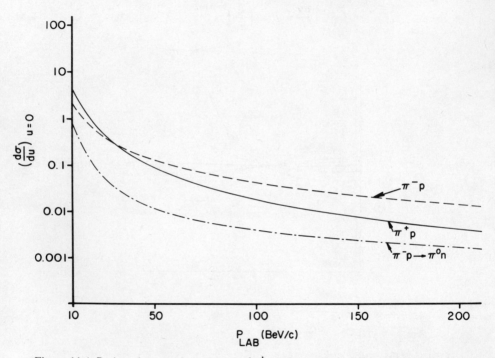

Figure 11.4. Projected energy dependences of π^+p and π^-p elastic differential cross sections at $u = 0$ from N_α, Δ_δ Regge exchange model.

where $E_+ = E + \Delta E$ and ΔE is a small increment. The effective $\alpha(t)$ for $\bar{p}p$ and pp reactions are shown in Figure 11.3. For these projections the Regge parameters from the fits shown in Figure 5.4 have been used. The $\bar{p}p$ forward peak displays large antishrinkage at momentum transfers greater than 0.3 $(\text{BeV}/c)^2$ at energies of 10–50 BeV/c. This antishrinkage disappears around 70 BeV/c. In the pp forward peak the shrinkage gradually decreases with increasing energy until the Pomeranchuk limit is reached. The Pomeranchuk trajectory in this model is $\alpha_P(t) = 1 + (1/3)t$. By 200 BeV/c the shrinkage patterns of $\bar{p}p$ and pp look almost identical and the shrinkage has essentially reached the level expected from the Pomeranchuk slope. Consequently, if the pole model remains valid, the measurement of the shrinkage at 200 BeV/c should determine the slope of the Pomeranchuk trajectory.

πN Backward Elastic Scattering

The predictions of the N_α, Δ_δ exchange model discussed in Section 7.4 for $\pi^\pm p$ backward scattering are projected to higher energies in Figures 11.4 and 11.5. Since the Δ_δ trajectory intercept $\alpha_\Delta(0) \simeq 0.2$ is higher than the N_α intercept

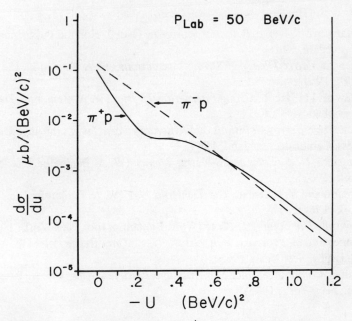

Figure 11.5. Projected angular distributions for $\pi^+ p$ and $\pi^- p$ backward elastic scattering at 50 BeV/c laboratory momentum.

$\alpha_N(0) \simeq -0.38$, the $\pi^- p$ differential cross section at $u = 0$ eventually exceeds the $\pi^+ p$ differential cross section. The present Regge parameters indicate that this crossing should occur around 35 BeV/c. In the angular distributions at 50 BeV/c shown in Figure 11.5 the N_α dip at $u \simeq -0.15$ in $\pi^+ p$ is less prominent than at lower energies, because the relative size of the Δ_δ contribution to the $\pi^+ p$ amplitude has increased. It will be of great interest to see if the gross features of this Reggeized baryon exchange model remain valid in the ultrahigh energy region.

Bibliography

B.1 THEORY AND PHENOMENOLOGY

Books

V. de Alfaro and T. Regge, *Potential Scattering* (North Holland Publishing Co., Amsterdam, 1965).

G. F. Chew, *S-Matrix Theory of Strong Interactions* (W. A. Benjamin, Inc., New York, 1961).

G. F. Chew and M. Jacob, *Strong Interaction Physics* (W. A. Benjamin, Inc., New York, 1964).

R. J. Eden, *High-Energy Collisions of Elementary Particles* (Cambridge University Press, Cambridge, England, 1967).

S. C. Frautschi, *Regge Poles and S-Matrix Theory* (W. A. Benjamin, Inc., New York, 1963).

M. Gell-Mann and Y. Ne'eman, *The Eightfold Way* (W. A. Benjamin, Inc., New York, 1964).

R. G. Newton, *The Complex j-Plane* (W. A. Benjamin, Inc., New York, 1966).

R. L. Omnes and M. Froissart, *Mandelstam Theory and Regge Poles* (W. A. Benjamin, New York, 1963).

E. J. Squires, *Complex Angular Momenta and Particle Physics* (W. A. Benjamin, Inc., New York, 1963).

Review Articles

V. Barger, "Regge poles and SU(3): Particle Classification and High Energy Scattering," *Rev. Mod. Phys.* **40**, 129 (1968).

L. Bertocchi, "Theoretical Aspects of High Energy Phenomenology," in *Proceedings of the Heidelberg International Conference on Elementary Particles* (North Holland, Amsterdam, 1968), H. Filthuth, ed., p. 197.

H. M. Chan, "High-Energy Reactions and Regge Poles," CERN Report 67-16 (1967).

G. Goldhaber, "Quantum Numbers of Boson Resonances," CERN Report 67-24, Vol. 3.

J. D. Jackson, "Peripheral Production and Decay Correlations of Resonances," *Rev. Mod. Phys.* **37**, 484 (1965).

W. Kummer, "Introduction to Regge Poles," *Fortschr. Phys.* **14**, 429 (1966).

E. Leader, "Present Phenomenological Status of the Regge-Pole Model," *Rev. Mod. Phys.* **38**, 476 (1966).

R. L. Omnes, "Regge Poles," *Ann. Rev. Nucl. Sci.* **16**, 263 (1966).

R. J. N. Phillips, "Regge Poles in High-Energy Scattering," in *Proceedings 1966 International School of Physics "Ettore Majorana" at Erice* (Academic Press, New York, 1966). A. Zichichi, ed., p. 268.

L. Van Hove, "Hadron Collisions at Very High Energies," in *Proceedings of the XIIIth International Conference on High-Energy Physics, Berkeley, California* (University of California Press, Berkeley, 1967), p. 253.

B. E. Y. Svensson, "High Energy Phenomenology and Regge Poles," CERN Report 67-24, Vol. 3.

Charge and Hypercharge Exchange Reactions

F. Arbab, N. F. Bali, and J. Dash, "Ambiguities in the Phenomenological Determination of Regge-Pole Parameters," *Phys. Rev.* **158**, 1515 (1967).

F. Arbab and C. B. Chiu, "Association between the Dip in the $\pi^- p \to \pi^0 n$ High-Energy Angular Distribution and the Zero of the ρ Trajectory," *Phys. Rev.* **147**, 1045 (1966).

R. C. Arnold, "Double-Octet Regge-Pole Model with Exchange Degeneracy for Charge and Hypercharge Reactions," *Phys. Rev.* **153**, 1506 (1967).

V. Barger and D. Cline, "SU(3) Sum Rules for Meson–Nucleon Charge Exchange Reactions," *Phys. Rev.* **156**, 1522 (1967).

B. Desai, "πN Charge-Exchange Scattering and the ρ Trajectory," *Phys. Rev.* **142**, 1255 (1966).

O. Guisan, "Present Status for the Cross Sections and the Polarization of the Reactions $\pi^- p \to \pi^0 n, \pi^- p \to \eta n$ at High Energies and Their Connections with Regge Poles," SUNY Report (1968).

G. Höhler, J. Baacke, and G. Eisenbeiss, The Parameters of the Regge-Pole Model for πN Charge Exchange Scattering," *Phys. Letters* **22**, 203 (1966).

G. Höhler, J. Baacke, H. Schaile, and P. Sonderegger, "Analysis of πN Charge Exchange from 4 to 18 GeV/c," *Phys. Letters* **20**, 79 (1965).

G. Höhler, J. Baacke, and R. Strauss, "High-Energy Behavior of the πN Forward Charge-Exchange Scattering Amplitudes," *Phys. Letters* **21**, 223 (1966).

R. K. Logan, "Single Regge-Pole Analysis of $\pi^- p$ Charge-Exchange Scattering," *Phys. Rev. Letters* **14**, 414 (1965).

V. N. Mel'nikov and K. A. Ter-Martirosyan," The Experimental Data on Charge Transfer of K Mesons on Nucleons at High Energies and the Theory of Complex Angular Momenta," *Yadernaya Fizika* **4**, 1072 (1966), English translation: *Soviet J. Nuclear Phys.* **4**, 770 (1967).

R. J. N. Phillips, "Kinematic Corrections to Regge-Pole Analysis of $\pi^- p \to \eta n$," *Nuclear Phys.* **B1**, 572 (1967).

R. J. N. Phillips and W. Rarita, "Single Regge-Pole Analysis of $\pi^- p \to \eta^0 n$," *Phys. Rev. Letters* **15**, 807 (1965).

R. J. N. Phillips and W. Rarita, "Regge Trajectories from $\pi^- p \to \eta^0 n$ data," *Phys. Letters* **19**, 598 (1965).

R. J. N. Phillips and W. Rarita, "Predictions for $\pi^- p \to \eta^0 n$ from Regge Poles and SU(3)," *Phys. Rev.* **140**, B200 (1965).

D. D. Reeder and K. V. L. Sarma, "Prediction of Polarization in $K^- p \to \bar{K}^0 n$ at High Energies," *Nuovo Cimento* **51**, A169 (1967).

D. D. Reeder and K. V. L. Sarma, "Regge Pole Description of Associated Production Reactions," *Nuovo Cimento* **53A**, 808 (1968).

D. D. Reeder and K. V. L. Sarma, "Regge Pole Analysis of Charge Exchange and Hypercharge Exchange Reactions in Pseudoscalar Meson–Baryon Scattering," *Phys. Rev.* **172**, 1566 (1968).

Conspiracy

M. Anderholtz *et al.*, "Experimental Evidence from $\pi^+ p$ Reactions at 8 GeV/c against the Hypothesis of Pion Regge Conspiracy Plus Factorization," *Phys. Letters* **27B**, 174 (1968).

F. Arbab and J. W. Dash, "Regge-Pole Analysis of $pn \to np$ and $p\bar{p} \to n\bar{n}$ Scattering," *Phys. Rev.* **163**, 1603 (1967).

J. S. Ball, W. R. Frazer, and M. Jacob, "Regge Pole Model for Photoproduction of Pions and K Mesons," *Phys. Rev. Letters* **20**, 518 (1968).

J. S. Ball and M. Jacob, "Photoproduction and Regge Behavior," *Nuovo Cimento* **54**, 620 (1968).

A. Bietti, P. Di Vecchia, F. Drago, and M. L. Paciello, "Parity Doublet Conspiracy of the Pion from Finite Energy Sum Rules in π^+ Photoproduction," *Phys. Letters* **26B**, 457 (1968).

A. Borgese and M. Colocci, "Double Conspiracy in π^+ Photoproduction," *Nuovo Cimento* **54A**, 245 (1968).

R. Brower and J. W. Dash, "Pion Photoproduction, *NN* Scattering, and Photoproduction Sum Rules," UCRL Report 18199 (1968).

F. Cooper, "Photoproduction of Charge Pions in the Forward Direction and Regge Poles," *Phys. Rev. Letters* **20**, 643 (1968).

K. Dietz and W. Korth, "Photoproduction of Positively Charged Pions at High Energies," *Phys. Letters* **26B**, 394 (1968).

B. Diu and M. Le Bellac, "Kinematical Constraints on Regge Pole Residues," *Nuovo Cimento* **53A**, 158 (1968).

L. Durand, III, "Regge Pole Models for Pion-Exchange Reactions," *Phys. Rev. Letters* **19**, 1345 (1967).

S. Frautschi and L. Jones, "Small Angle Photoproduction and Conspiracy," *Phys. Rev.* **163**, 1820 (1967).

S. Frautschi and L. Jones, "Reggeization of Pion Exchange in Production Processes," *Phys. Rev.* **164**, 1918 (1967).

M. B. Halpern, "Conspiracy and Superconvergence in Pion Photoproduction," *Phys. Rev.* **160**, 1441 (1967).

H. Högaason and Ph. Salin, "General Classification of Conspiracy Relations," *Nucl. Phys.* **B2**, 615 (1967).

M. Le Bellac, "Pion Conspiracy in $\pi N \rightarrow \rho\Delta$," *Phys. Letters* **25B**, 524 (1967).

E. Leader, "Conspiracy and Evasion: a Property of Regge Poles," *Phys. Rev.* **166**, 1599 (1968).

R. J. N. Phillips, *Nuclear Phys.* **B2**, 394 (1967).

R. F. Sawyer and H. K. Shepard, "Forward and Near Foward Limits in Regge Pole Theory," *Phys. Letters* **27B**, 164 (1968).

R. F. Sawyer, "Forward Peaks from the Exchange of Odd Parity Trajectories," *Phys. Rev. Letters* **19**, 137 (1967).

L. Sertorio and M. Toller, *Phys. Rev. Letters* **19**, 1146 (1967).

R. Sugar and R. Blankenbecler, "Dynamical Model of a Conspiring Pion," *Phys. Rev. Letters* **20**, 1014 (1968).

D. V. Volkov and V. N. Gribov, "Regge Poles in Nucleon–Nucleon and Nucleon–Antinucleon Scattering Amplitude," *Zh. Eksper. Teor. Fiz.* **44**, 1068 (1963), English translation: *Soviet Phys. JETP* **17**, 720 (1963).

Crossover Phenomenon

V. Barger and L. Durand, III, "Crossover and Polarization Phenomena in High Energy Scattering: Cuts, Conspiracies, and Secondary Regge Poles," *Phys. Rev. Letters* **19**, 1295 (1967).

A. P. Contogouris, J. Than Thanh Van, and H. J. Lubatti, "Dips in the ω-Exchange Contribution to $\pi N \rightarrow \rho N$," *Phys. Rev. Letters* **19**, 1352 (1967).

W. Rarita, R. J. Ridell, Jr., C. B. Chiu, and R. J. N. Phillips, "Regge Pole Model for πp, pp, and $\bar{p}p$ Scattering," *Phys. Rev.* **165**, 1615 (1968).

Daughter Trajectories

L. Durand, III, "Regge Poles in the Scattering of Particles of Unequal Mass Remark on a Paper by Freedman and Wang," *Phys. Rev.* **154**, 1537 (1967).

L. Durand, III, "Subsidiary Regge Trajectories with Singular Residues; Nucleon–Nucleon Scattering," *Phys. Rev. Letters* **18**, 58 (1967).

D. Z. Freedman and J.-M. Wang, "Regge Poles in Unequal Mass Scattering," *Phys. Rev. Letters* **17**, 569 (1966).

D. Z. Freedman, C. E. Jones, and J.-M. Wang, "Daughter Trajectories and Un-equal-Mass Scattering," *Phys. Rev.* **155**, 1645 (1967).

D. Z. Freedman and J.-M. Wang, "Regge Poles and Unequal-Mass Scattering Processes," *Phys. Rev.* **153**, 1596 (1967).

R. J. Oakes, "Regge Poles and the Scattering of Unequal Mass Particles," *Phys. Letters* **24B**, 154 (1967).

A. R. Swift, "A Daughter Regge Trajectory in a Field Theory Model," *J. of Math. Phys.* **8**, 2420 (1967).

A. R. Swift, "A Relativistic Model of Daughter Regge Trajectories," *Phys. Rev. Letters* **18**, 813 (1967).

Diffraction-Like Models

H. D. I. Abarbanel, S. D. Drell, and   F. J. Gilman, "Structure of High Energy, Large Momentum Transfer Collision Processes," *Phys. Rev. Letters* **20**, 280 (1968).

N. Byers and C. N. Yang, πp Charge Exchange Scattering and a Coherent Droplet Model of High Energy Exchange Processes," *Phys. Rev.* **142**, 976 (1966).

N. Byers and G. H. Thomas, "Photoproduction of π^+, π^0, and K^+ Near $t = 0$," *Phys. Rev. Letters* **20**, 129 (1968).

T. T. Chou and C. N. Yang, "Possible Existence of Kinks in High Energy Elastic pp Scattering Cross Section," *Phys. Rev. Letters* **20**, 1213 (1968).

L. Durand, III, and R. Lipes, "Diffraction Model for High Energy pp Scattering," *Phys. Rev. Letters* **20**, 637 (1968).

T. T. Wu and C. N. Yang, "Some Speculations Concerning High Energy Large Momentum Transfer Processes," *Phys. Rev.* **137**, B708 (1965).

Factorization of Regge Residues

F. Arbab and J. D. Jackson, "Factorization, Kinematic Singularities, and Conspiracies," UCRL Report-18261 (1968).

G. C. Fox and E. Leader, "Factorization of Helicity Amplitudes at High Energies," *Phys. Rev. Letters* **18**, 628 (1967).

M. Gell-Mann, "Factorization of Couplings to Regge Poles," *Phys. Rev. Letters* **8**, 263 (1962).

V. N. Gribov and I. Ya. Pomeranchuk, "Complex Angular Momentum and the Relation between the Cross-Sections of Various Processes at High Energies," *Phys. Rev. Letters* **8**, 343 (1962).

V. N. Gribov and I. Ya. Pomeranchuk, "Spin Structure of the Meson–Nucleon and Nucleon–Nucleon Scattering Amplitude at High Energies," *Phys. Rev. Letters* **8**, 412 (1962).

T. Kawai, "A Generalized Factorization Theorem and the Asymptotic Behavior of the Scattering Amplitude, *Nuovo Cimento* **50A**, 176 (1967).

E. Leader and R. C. Slansky, "General Analysis of *NN* Scattering; Critical Test for Regge-Pole Theory," *Phys. Rev.* **148**, 1491 (1966). [Erratum, *ibid.*, **156**, 1742 (1967)].

Fermion Regge Exchanges

V. Barger and D. Cline, "Regge Recurrences and $\pi^- p$ Elastic Scattering at 180°," *Phys. Rev. Letters* **16**, 931 (1966).

V. Barger and D. Cline, "Fermion Regge-Pole Model and the Structure of Pion-Nucleon Elastic Scattering in the Backward Hemisphere," *Phys. Rev.* **155**, 1792 (1967).

V. Barger and D. Cline, "$\overline{N}N$ Annihilation into Two Pseudoscalar Mesons at High Energy," *Phys. Letters* **25B**, 415 (1967).

V. Barger and D. Cline, "Backward πN Charge Exchange Scattering and Pole Extrapolations of Regge Exchange Amplitudes," *Phys. Rev. Letters* **19**, 1504 (1967).

V. Barger and D. Cline, "Evidence for Linear Extrapolations of Baryon Exchange Trajectories through Particle Mass Spectra," *Phys. Rev. Letters* **21**, 392 (1968).

V. Barger and D. Cline, "Prediction of the Mean Backward $\pi^- p \to \pi^0 n$ Differential Cross Section Down to 2.0 BeV/c, *Phys. Letters* **27B**, 312 (1968).

C. B. Chiu and J. D. Stack, "Regge-Pole Model for High-Energy Backward $\pi^{\pm} p$ Scattering," *Phys. Rev.* **153**, 1575 (1967).

B. R. Desai, "Exchange of Even- and Odd-Parity Baryon–Meson Resonances and Backward Elastic Scattering," *Phys. Rev. Letters* **17**, 498 (1966).

V. N. Gribov, "Fermion Regge Poles and the Asymptotic Behavior of Meson-Nucleon Large-Angle Scattering," *Ah. Eksper. Teor. Fiz.* **43**, 1529 (1962); English translation: *Soviet Phys. JETP* **16**, 1080 (1963).

H. Högaason, "Models for Backward Associated Production in $\pi^- p \to \Lambda K^0$," CERN Preprint TH. 777.

H. Högaason, "πN Resonances and Backward Scattering," in *Proceedings of the CERN Topical Conference on Hadron Collisions at High Energy*, CERN Report 68-7, p. 460.

S. W. MacDowell, *Phys. Rev.* **166**, 774 (1959).

V. Singh, "Regge Poles in πN Scattering and in $\pi\pi \to N\overline{N}$," *Phys. Rev.* **129**, 1889 (1963).

J. D. Stack, "Polarization as a Test for Regge Behaviour in the backward $\pi^{\pm} p$ Elastic Scattering," *Phys. Rev. Letters* **16**, 286 (1966).

Finite Energy Sum Rules

V. Barger and R. J. N. Phillips, "Vacuum Exchange Amplitudes From a Family of Sum Rules," *Phys. Letters* **26B**, 730 (1968).

V. Barger and R. J. N. Phillips, "Evidence for a Flat Pomeranchuk Trajectory and Location of a Secondary Rho Regge Pole," Rutherford Laboratory Report (July, 1968).

G. V. Dass and C. Michael, "Factorization, ω Crossover, Polarization, and Finite Energy Sum Rules for Kaon–Nucleon Scattering," *Phys. Rev. Letters* **20**, 1066 (1968).

A. della Selva, L. Masperi, and R. Odorice, Non-Vanishing Asymptotic Total πN Cross Sections from Continuous Moment Sum Rules," *Nuovo Cimento* **55A**, 602 (1968).

P. Di Vecchia, F. Drago, C. F. Fontan, R. Odorico, and M. L. Paciello, "Determination of the Pion and Conspirator Residues and Trajectories, in π^+ Photoproduction from Continuous Moment Sum Rules," Trieste Report (May, 1968).

R. Dolen, D. Horn, and C. Schmid, "Prediction of Regge Parameters of ρ Poles from Low Energy πN data," *Phys. Rev. Letters* **19**, 402 (1967).

R. Dolen, D. Horn, and C. Schmid, "Finite Energy Sum Rules and Their Applications to πN Charge Exchange," *Phys. Rev.* **166**, 1768 (1968).

H. Harari, "Pomeranchuk Trajectory and Its Relation to Low Energy Scattering Amplitudes," *Phys. Rev. Letters* **20**, 1395 (1968).

K. Igi and S. Matsuda, "New Sum Rules and Singularities in the Complex j-Plane," *Phys. Rev. Letters* **18**, 625 (1967).

K. Igi and S. Matsuda, "Ghost Eliminating Zeros in the Regge Pole Model," *Phys. Rev. Letters* **19**, 928 (1967).

A. A. Logunov, L. D. Soloviev, and A. N. Tavkhelidze, "Dispersion Sum Rules and High Energy Scattering," *Phys. Letters* **24B**, 181 (1967).

Y. Liu and S. Okubo, "Tests of New πN Superconvergent Dispersion Relations," *Phys. Rev. Letters* **19**, 190 (1967).

M. G. Olsson, "On the Decoupling of a Second Rho in Forward πN Scattering," *Phys. Letters,* **26B**, 310 (1967).

M. G. Olsson, "Vacuum Exchanges," University of Wisconsin Report (1968).

J. H. Schwarz, "Superconvergence Relations from Regge-Pole Theory," *Phys. Rev.* **159**, 1268 (1967).

Fixed Poles and Regge Cuts

H. D. I. Abarbanel, F. E. Low, I. J. Muzinich, S. Nussinov, and J. E. Schwarz, "High-Energy Limit of Photon Scattering on Hadrons," *Phys. Rev.* **160**, 1329 (1967).

H. D. Abarbanel and S. Nussinov, "Implications of Regge Behaviour for Processes Involving Photons," *Phys. Rev.* **158**, 1462 (1967).

D. Branson, S. Nussinov, S. B. Treiman, and W. I. Weisberger, "Contributions of Regge Cuts to Foward Nucleon–Nucleon Scattering," *Phys. Letters* **25B**, 141 (1967).

J. B. Bronzan, I. S. Gerstein, B. W. Lee, and F. E. Low, "Current Algebra and Non-Regge Behaviour of Weak Amplitudes," *Phys. Rev. Letters* **18**, 32 (1967).

J. B. Bronzan, I. S. Gerstein, B. W. Lee, and F. E. Low, "Current Algebra and Non-Regge Behaviour of Weak Amplitudes," *Phys. Rev.* **157**, 1448 (1967).

C. B. Chiu and J. Finkelstein, "Suggestive Features in πN Charge-Exchange Polarization Associated with Regge Cuts," *Nuovo Cimento* **48A**, 820 (1967).

V. M. de Lany, D. J. Gross, I. J. Muzinich, and V. L. Teplitz, "Polarization Test for Cuts in Angular Momentum," *Phys. Rev. Letters* **18**, 149 (1967).

J.-L. Gervais and F. J. Yndurain, "Regge Cuts Imply Vanishing Total Cross Sections or Essentially Constant Diffraction Peaks," *Phys. Rev. Letters* **20**, 27 (1968).

V. N. Gribov, "On the possible Experimental Investigations of Regge Branch Points," *Yadernaya Fizika* **5**, 197 (1967), English translation: *Soviet J. Nucl. Phys.* **5**, 138 (1967).

V. N. Gribov, I. Ya. Pomeranchuk, and K. A. Ter-Martirosyan, "Moving Branch Points in j-Plane and Regge Pole Unitarity Condition," *Phys. Rev.* **139**, B184 (1965).

C. E. Jones and V. L. Teplitz, "Branch Points, Fixed Poles, and Falling Trajectories in the complex j-Plane, *Phys. Rev.* **159**, 1271 (1967).

S. Mandelstam, "Cuts in the Angular-Momentum Plane, I," *Nuovo Cimento* **30**, 1127 (1963); II, *Nuovo Cimento* **30**, 1148 (1963).

S. Mandelstam and Ling-Lie Wang, "Gribov–Pomeranchuk Poles in Scattering Amplitudes," *Phys. Rev.* **160**, 1490 (1967).

A. H. Mueller and T. L. Trueman, "Spin Dependence of High-Energy Scattering Amplitudes, I and II," *Phys. Rev.* **160**, 1296 and 1306 (1967).

R. Oehme, "Fixed Poles in the Complex Angular Momentum Plane," *Phys. Rev. Letters* **18**, 1222 (1967).

P. Osborne and J. C. Polkinghorne, "Double Regge Poles and Regge Cuts," *Nuovo Cimento* **47A**, 526 (1967).

R. J. N. Phillips, "Two Reggeon Branch Points and Double Charge Exchange," *Phys. Letters* **24B**, 432 (1967).

R. J. N. Phillips, "Tests for Regge Cuts in NN Scattering," *Phys. Letters* **25B**, 517 (1967).

D. L. Pursey and L. Sertorio, "Regge Cuts and πp Total Cross-Sections," *Phys. Rev.* **155**, 1591 (1967).

H. J. Rothe, "Study of Branch Points in the Angular-Momentum Plane," *Phys. Rev.* **159**, 1471 (1967).

H. K. Shepard, "Pomeranchuk Exchange Contribution to Forward Photon Processes," *Phys. Rev.* **159**, 1362 (1967).

Y. Srivastava, "Condensation of Regge Cuts, Vanishing Total Cross-Sections, and Twisting Trajectories," *Phys. Rev. Letters* **19**, 47 (1967).

Interference Model

J. Baacke and M. Yvert, "Regge Poles and Resonances in $\pi^- p$ Charge Exchange Scattering between 2.5 and 6 GeV/c, *Nuovo Cimento* **51A**, 761 (1967).

V. Barger and D. Cline, "Regge Recurrences and $\pi^- p$ Elastic Scattering at 180°," *Phys. Rev. Letters* **16**, 913 (1966).

V. Barger and M. Olsson, "Interference of Regge ρ-Exchange with Direct Channel Fermion Resonances," *Phys. Rev.* **151**, 1123 (1967).

V. Barger and L. Durand, III, "The Interference Model and Finite Energy Sum Rules," *Phys. Letters* **26B**, 588 (1968).

C. B. Chiu and A. V. Stirling, "Validity of the Interference Model for πN Scattering?," *Phys. Letters* **26B**, 236 (1968).

R. Dolen, D. Horn, and C. Schmid, "Finite Energy Sum Rules and Their Application to πN Charge Exchange," *Phys. Rev.* **166**, 1768 (1968).

L. Durand, III, "Regge Pole Exchange and Direct Channel Resonances in Models for High Energy Scattering Amplitudes," *Phys. Rev.* **166**, 1680 (1968).

Kinematic Singularities and Threshold Conditions

G. Cohen-Tannoudji, A. Morel, and H. Navelet, "Kinematical Singularities, Crossing Matrix, and Kinematical Constraints for Two-Body Helicity Amplitudes," *Ann. Phys.* **46**, 239 (1968).

B. Diu and M. LeBellac, "Kinematical Constraints on Regge-Pole Residues," *Nuovo Cimento* **53A**, 158 (1968).

M. Gell-Mann, M. Goldberger, F. Low, E. Marx, and F. Zachariasen, "Elementary Particles of Conventional Field Theory as Regge Poles," III, *Phys. Rev.* **133**, B145 (1964).

Y. Hara, "Analycity Properties of Helicity Amplitudes and Construction of Kinematical Singularity-Free Amplitudes for Any Spin," *Phys. Rev.* **135**, B507 (1964).

J. D. Jackson and G. E. Hite, "Kinematic Singularities and Threshold Relations for Helicity Amplitudes," *Phys. Rev.* **169**, 1248 (1968).

L. L. Wang, "General Method of Constructing Helicity Amplitudes Free from Kinematical Singularities or Zeros," *Phys. Rev.* **142**, 1187 (1966).

L. L. Wang, "Regge-Pole Formulas for Differential Cross-Sections of Quasi Two-Body πN and NN Interactions," *Phys. Rev.* **153**, 1664 (1967).

Lorentz Poles

N. F. Bali, J. S. Ball, G. F. Chew, and A. Pignotti, "Analytic S-Matrix Approach to Zero-Momentum Transfer Symmetry," *Phys. Rev.* **161**, 1459 (1967).

G. Domokos and G. L. Tindle, "On the Algebraic Classification of Regge Poles," Berkeley Preprint (1968).

G. Domokos, "Four-Dimensional Symmetry," *Phys. Rev.* **159**, 1387 (1967).

D. Z. Freedman and J.-M. Wang, "O(4) Symmerty and Regge-Pole Theory," *Phys. Rev.* **160**, 1560 (1967).

D. Z. Freedman and J.-M. Wang, "O(4) Symmetry and Regge Pole Theory," *Phys. Rev. Letters* **18**, 863 (1967).

E. H. Roffman, "Complex Inhomogeneous Lorentz Group and Complex Angular Momentum," *Phys. Rev. Letters* **16**, 210 (1966).

M. H. Rubin, "An Expansion of the Two-Particle Scattering Amplitude in Terms of the Matrix Elements of the Lorentz Group," *Phys. Rev.* **162**, 1551 (1967).

R. F. Sawyer, "O(4) and Forward Production Processes at High Energies," *Phys. Rev. Letters* **18**, 1212 (1967).

J. C. Taylor, "Factorization of Regge and Toller Poles," *Nucl. Phys.* **B3**, 504 (1967).

M. Toller, "Three-Dimensional Lorentz Group and Harmonic Analysis of the Scattering Amplitudes," *Nuovo Cimento* **37**, 631 (1965).

M. Toller, "On the Group Theoretical Approach to Complex Angular Momentum and Signature," CERN Preprint TH 770 (May, 1967).

M. Toller, "An Expansion of the Scattering Amplitude at Vanishing Four-Momentum Transfer Using Representations of the Lorentz Group," *Nuovo Cimento* **53A**, 671 (1968).

Multiperipheral Regge Models

N. F. Bali, G. F. Chew, and A. Pignotti, "Kinematics of Production Processes and the Multi-Regge-Pole Hypothesis," *Phys. Rev.* **163**, 1572 (1967).

E. L. Berger, E. Gellert, G. A. Smith, E. Cotton and P. E. Schlein, "Double Regge Pole Model Analysis of $pp \to \Delta^{++} p \pi^-$ at 6.6 GeV/c," *Phys. Rev. Letters* **20**, 964 (1968).

E. L. Berger, "Reggeized $\pi\rho$ Mass Enhancement in the A_1 Region," *Phys. Rev.* **166**, 1525 (1968).

G. F. Chew and A. Pignotti, "Dolen–Horn–Schmid Duality and the Deck Effect," *Phys. Rev. Letters* **20**, 1078 (1968).

Chan Hong-Mo, K. Kajantie, and G. Ranft, "A Regge Model for High-Energy
    Collisions Producing Three Final Particles," *Nuovo Cimento* **49A**, 157
    (1967).
Chan Hong-Mo, K. Kajantie, G. Ranft, W. Beusch, and E. Flaminio, "Double
    Regge Analysis of High-Energy Experiments Producing Three Final Par-
    ticles," *Nuovo Cimento* **51A**, 696 (1967).
Chan Hong-Mo, J. Loskiewicz, and W. W. M. Allison, "A Reggeized Multi-Peri-
    pheral Model for Inelastic Processes at High Energy," CERN Report
    TH 866 (1968).
J. Finkelstein and K. Kajantie, "Total Cross-Section for n-Particle Production in
    a Multi-Regge Model," CERN Report TH 857 (1967).
K. Kajantie, "On the High Energy Behaviour of the n-Particle Production Cross-
    Section in a Multi-Regge Model," *Nuovo Cimento* **53A**, 424 (1968).
F. Zachariasen and G. Zweig, "Bounded Momentum Transfer Restrictions on
    High-Energy Interactions," *Phys. Rev.* **160**, 1322 (1967).
F. Zachariasen and G. Zweig, "High-Energy Interactions and Multi-Regge-Pole
    Hypothesis," *Phys. Rev.* **160**, 1326 (1967).

Particle Classification

A. Ahmadzadeh, "SU(3) Symmetry, Exchange Degeneracy, and Lorentz Pole
    Classification of Conspirator Families," *Phys. Rev. Letters* **20**, 1125 (1968).
A. Ahmadzadeh, "Exchange Degeneracy Classification of Regge Trajectories and
    the Total Cross-Sections," *Phys. Rev. Letters* **16**, 953 (1966).
R. C. Arnold, "Meson Symmetries," *Phys. Rev. Letters* **14**, 657 (1965).
V. Barger and D. Cline, "Regge Recurrences and $\pi^- p$ Elastic Scattering at $180°$,"
    Phys. Rev. Letters **16**, 931 (1966).
V. Barger and D. Cline, "Fermion Regge Pole Model and the Structure of Pion–
    Nucleon Elastic Scattering in the Backward Hemisphere," *Phys. Rev.*
    155, 1792 (1967).
V. Barger and D. Cline, "Degenerate Regge Trajectories and Parity Doublets of
    Baryon Resonances," *Phys. Letters* **26B**, 83 (1967).
V. Barger and D. Cline, "Evidence for N^* Regge Trajectory Clans with Approxi-
    mate Parity Degeneracy," *Phys. Rev. Letters* **20**, 298 (1968).
P. Carruthers and M. M. Nieto, "Dynamical Model for Negative Parity Regge
    Trajectories in the πN System," Cornell University Preprint (January,
    1967).
G. F. Chew and S. C. Frautschi, "Principle of Equivalence for All Strongly Inter-
    acting Particles within the S-Matrix Framework," *Phys. Rev. Letters* **7**, 394
    (1961).

D. Cline, "Isotopic-Spin One-Boson Regge Trajectories," *Nuovo Cimento* **45A**, 750 (1966).

P. D. B. Collins, R. C. Johnson, and E. J. Squires, "Heavy Bosons, Regge Trajectories, and Dynamical Theories," *Phys. Letters* **26B**, 223 (1968).

D. H. Lyth, "Parity Doubling, Asymmetric Fermion Trajectories, and Low Energy πN Dynamics," *Phys. Rev. Letters* **20**, 641 (1968).

A. Pignotti, "Hitherto Overlooked SU(3) Octet of Regge Poles Implied by Bootstrap Dynamics," *Phys. Rev.* **134**, B630 (1964).

R. M. Spector, "Example of a Regge Daughter Trajectory for $I = 1$, $Y = 0$ Boson Resonances," *Phys. Letters* **25B**, 551 (1967).

D. G. Sutherland, "Some Remarks on Higher Mesons," *Nucl. Phys.* **B2**, 157 (1967).

Photo-Induced Reactions

J. P. Ader, M. Capdeville, and Ph. Salin, "A Regge-Pole Model Fit of Pion and K-Meson Photoproduction," *Nucl. Phys.* **B3**, 407 (1967).

F. Buccella and M. Colocci, "High-Energy Photoproduction of Vector Mesons and Regge Poles," *Phys. Letters* **24B**, 61 (1967).

B. Diu and M. Le Bellac, "Photoproduction of Charged Pions in a Regge Pole Model," *Phys. Letters* **24B**, 416 (1967).

P. di Vecchia and F. Drago, "Neutral Non-Strange 0^--Meson Photoproduction and Regge Poles," *Phys. Letters* **24B**, 405 (1967).

W. Drechsler, X^0-Photoproduction in Regge-Pole Model," *Nuovo Cimento* **45A**, 263 (1966).

W. Drechsler, "Regge-Pole Contribution to X^0 Photoproduction," *Phys. Letters* **23**, 272 (1966).

S. Drell and J. D. Sullivan, "Pion Photoproduction at 0°," *Phys. Rev. Letters* **19**, 268 (1967).

P. G. O. Freund, "Photoproduction of Vector Mesons as Virtual Vector Meson–Proton Scattering," *Nuovo Cimento* **48A**, 541 (1967).

M. P. Locher and H. Rollnik, "Reggeized Vector–Meson Exchange for π^0 Photoproduction," *Phys. Letters* **22**, 696 (1966).

G. Zweig, "The Reaction $\gamma N \to \pi N$ at High Energies," *Nuovo Cimento* **32**, 689 (1964).

Polarization and Spin Dependence

G. Altarelli, A. Borgese, F. Buccella, and M. Colocci, "Regge Recurrences and πp Charge-Exchange Polarization at High-Energy," *Nuovo Cimento* **48A**, 245 (1967).

C. B. Chiu, R. J. N. Phillips, and W. Rarita, "πN Polarization and Regge Poles," *Phys. Rev.* **153**, 1485 (1967).

B. R. Desai, D. T. Gregorich, and R. Ramachandran, "πN Charge-Exchange Polarization and the Baryon Trajectories in the Direct Channel," *Phys. Rev. Letters* **18**, 565 (1967).

Y. Hara, "Spin Independence of Total Cross-Sections," *Phys. Letters* **23**, 696 (1966).

Y. Hara, "Total Cross-Sections at High Energies," *Progr. Theor. Phys.* **37**, 941 (1967).

Keh Ying Lin, "Regge-Pole Theory and Spin-Independence of the Total Cross-Sections," *Phys. Rev.* **159**, 1362 (1967).

R. K. Logan, J. Beaupre, and L. Sertorio, "$\pi^- p$ Charge Exchange Polarization and the Possibility of a second ρ-Meson," *Phys. Rev. Letters* **18**, 259 (1967).

R. K. Logan and L. Sertorio, "Regge-Pole Analysis of πp Charge Exchange Polarization," *Phys. Rev. Letters* **17**, 834 (1966).

R. K. Logan and L. Sertorio, "A Regge-Pole Model of $\pi^- p \rightarrow \eta n$ Polarization, *Nuovo Cimento* (to be published).

R. J. N. Phillips, "Resonance Tails and High Energy πN Charge Exchange," *Nuovo Cimento* **45A**, 245 (1966).

W. Rarita, R. J. Riddell, Jr., C. B. Chiu, and R. J. N. Phillips, "Regge-Pole Model for πp, pp, and $\bar{p}p$ Scattering," *Phys. Rev.* **165**, 1615 (1968).

D. D. Reeder and K. V. L. Sarma, "Prediction of Polarization in $K^- p \rightarrow \bar{K}^0 n$ at High Energies," *Nuovo Cimento* **51A**, 169 (1967).

L. Serterio and M. Toller, "Conspiring Regge Trajectories and the Polarization in High Energy, Charge Exchange, Pion Nucleon Scattering," *Phys. Rev. Letters* **19**, 1146 (1967).

H. Steiner, "Spin-Dependent Effects in πN and NN Interactions," UCRL Report 17903 (1967).

Regge Pole and Single Particle Exchanges

L. Durand, III, "Connection between Regge Pole and Single Particle Exchange Models for High-Energy Reactions," *Phys. Rev.* **161**, 1610 (1967).

L. Van Hove, "Regge Pole and Single Particle Exchange Mechanism in High Energy Collisions," *Phys. Letters* **24B**, 183 (1967).

R. L. Sugar and J. C. Sullivan, "Daughter Regge Trajectories in the Van Hove Model," *Phys. Rev.* **166**, 1515 (1968).

Resonance Production Reactions

R. C. Arnold, "Application of $SU(6)_W$ in a Model for Vector Meson Production at High Energies," *Phys Rev.* **162**, 1334 (1967).

M. Barmawi, "Regge-Pole Analysis of $\pi^+ n \to \omega p$," *Phys. Rev. Letters* **16**, 595 (1966).

M. Barmawi, "The Regge-Pole Contribution to Vector Meson Production," *Phys. Rev.* **142**, 1088 (1966).

H. Caprasse and H. Stremnitzer, "A Regge Pole Analysis of $\pi^+ p \to \pi^0 N^{*++}$," *Nuovo Cimento* **44A**, 1245 (1966).

J. D. Jackson and G. E. Hite, "Kinematic Singularities and Threshold Relations for Helicity Amplitudes," *Phys. Rev.* **169**, 1248 (1968).

L. Jones, "Implication of Unequal Mass Kinematics for the Regge-Pole Model of Vector Meson Production," *Phys. Rev.* **163**, 1523 (1967).

L. Jones, "Information about Regge-Pole Couplings from Vector Meson Production," *Phys. Rev.* **163**, 1530 (1967).

A. B. Kaidalov, "Factorization of Amplitudes and Pair Production of Resonances at High Energy," *Zh. Eksper. Teor. Fiz. Pis'ma* **4**, 484 (1966), English translation: *JETP Letters,* **4**, 325 (1966).

R. Dashen and S. Frautschi, "Chew–Low Model for Regge-Pole Couplings," *Phys. Rev.* **152**, 1450 (1966).

M. Krammer and U. Maor, "Regge-Pole Parameters for the Reaction $\pi^+ p \to \pi^0 \Delta^{++}$ (1238)," *Nuovo Cimento* **50A**, 963 (1967).

M. L. Paciello and A. Pugliese, "A Regge-Pole Analysis of ρ^- Decay Angular Distributions and Production in $\pi^- p \to \rho^- p$," *Phys. Letters* **24B**, 431 (1967).

D. P. Roy, "N^* Production in High Energy πp and Kp Collisions by Regge-Pole Model," *Nuovo Cimento* **40A**, 513 (1965).

R. Thews, "Regge Poles in Resonance Production," *Phys. Rev.* **155**, 1624 (1967).

L. L. Wang, "Prediction of a Minimum in the High Energy $\pi N \to \omega N$ Differential Cross-Section," *Phys. Rev. Letters* **16**, 756 (1966).

SU(3) and Universality

A. Ahmadzadeh and C. H. Chan, "Sum Rules for High-Energy Scattering Phenomena," *Phys. Letters* **22**, 692 (1966).

V. Barger and L. Durand, III, "Experimental Evaluation of Quark and Regge-Pole Models for High-Energy Scattering," *Phys. Rev.* **156**, 1525 (1967).

V. Barger and M. H. Rubin, "New Sum Rule for Meson–Baryon Total Cross-Sections at High Energies," *Phys. Rev.* **140**, B1365 (1965).

V. Barger and D. Cline, "SU(3) Sum Rules for Meson–Nucleon Charge Exchange Reactions," *Phys. Rev.* **156**, 1522 (1967).

V. Barger and D. Cline, "Implications of Isospin Dependence of $\bar{N}N$ Annihilation Cross-Sections," *Phys. Letters* **26B**, 591 (1968).

V. Barger and M. Olsson, "SU(3) Symmetry Tests for Regge Residues," *Phys. Rev. Letters* **18**, 294 (1967).

V. Barger, M. Olsson, and D. D. Reeder, "Asymptotic Projections of Scattering Models," *Nucl. Phys.* **B5**, 411 (1968).

F. S. Chen-Cheung, "Relation Among the πN and KN Charge-Exchange Cross-Sections from the SU(3) Regge-Pole Theory," *Phys. Rev.* **156**, 1520 (1967).

P. G. O. Freund, "Relation between πp, pp, and $\bar{p}p$ Scattering at High Energies," *Phys. Rev. Letters* **15**, 929 (1965).

C. A. Levinson, N. S. Wall, and H. J. Lipkin, "Quark Models, Universality, Symmetry, and High Energy Scattering," *Phys. Rev. Letters* **17**, 1122 (1966).

R. F. Sawyer, "Johnson–Treiman Relations from Vector–Meson Exchange," *Phys. Rev. Letters* **14**, 471 (1965).

Total Cross Sections and Forward Elastic Scattering

A. Ahmadzadeh, "Exchange Degeneracy Classification of Regge Trajectories and the Total Cross Sections," *Phys. Rev. Letters* **16**, 952 (1966).

V. Barger and M. Olsson, "Analysis of Total Cross-Section Differences at High-Energies," *Phys. Rev. Letters* **15**, 930 (1965).

V. Barger and M. Olsson, "Real Part of the pn Scattering Amplitudes from an SU(3) Regge Pole Model," *Phys. Rev. Letters* **16**, 545 (1966).

V. Barger and M. Olsson, "Forward Elastic Scattering at High Energy in an SU(3) Regge-Pole Model," *Phys. Rev.* **146**, 1080 (1966).

V. Barger and M. Olsson, "Regge-Pole Model and Total Cross Sections in the Intermediate Laboratory Momentum Range 2–6 GeV/c," *Phys. Rev.* **148**, 1428 (1966).

V. Barger, M. Olsson, and D. Reeder, "Asymptotic Projections of Scattering Models," *Nucl. Phys.* **B5**, 411 (1968).

V. Barger, "Total Cross Sections and Elastic Scattering near the Forward Direction," *Proceedings of the CERN Topical Conference on Hadron Collisions at High Energy,* CERN Report 68-7, p. 3.

V. Barger and R. J. N. Phillips, "Interpretation of Recurring Minima in Elastic Scattering at Large Momentum Transfers," *Phys. Rev. Letters* **20**, 564 (1968).

A. Białas, E. Bialas, O. Czyzewski, and A. Kotanski, "Regge Recurrences and πp Elastic Scattering at High-Momentum Transfers," *Nuovo Cimento* **48A**, 1111 (1967).

N. E. Booth, "Dips in Differential Cross Sections," University of Chicago Report EFI-68-28.

N. Cabibbo, L. Horwitz, and Y. Ne'eman, "The Algebra of Scalar and Vector Vertex Strengths in Regge Residues," *Phys. Letters* **22**, 336 (1966).

N. Cabibbo, J. J. J. Kokkedee, L. Horwitz, and Y. Ne'eman, "Possible Vanishing of Strong Interaction Cross-Sections at Infinite Energies," *Nuovo Cimento* **45A**, 275 (1966).

T. O. Binford and B. P. Desai, "High-Energy Elastic Scattering at Low Momentum Transfers," *Phys. Rev.* **138**, B1167 (1965).

C. B. Chiu, S.-Y. Chu, and L.-L. Wang, "Regge-Pole Model for πN and NN Secondary Maxima and the No-Compensation Mechanism," *Phys. Rev.* **161**, 1563 (1967).

G. Cohen-Tannoudji, A. Morel, and H. Navelet, "A Phenomenological Analysis of High-Energy Data in πN and KN Systems: Shadow Scattering and Regge Singularities," *Nuovo Cimento* **48A**, 1075 (1967).

B. Desai and P. Freund, "2^+ Mesons and High Energy Scattering," *Phys. Rev. Letters* **16**, 622 (1966).

S. Meshkov and G. B. Yodh, "SU(3), Meson–Baryon Scattering, and Asymptotic Limits," *Phys. Rev. Letters* **19**, 603 (1967).

S. Frautschi, "Regge Trajectories and Minima in Differential Cross-Sections," *Phys. Rev. Letters* **17**, 722 (1966).

R. J. N. Phillips and W. Rarita, "Regge Poles and the Phase of the Foward-Scattering Amplitudes," *Phys. Rev. Letters* **14**, 502 (1965).

R. J. N. Phillips and W. Rarita, "Regge-Pole Models for High-Energy πN, KN, and $\bar{K}N$ Scattering," *Phys. Rev.* **139**, B1336 (1965).

W. Rarita, R. J. Riddell, Jr., C. B. Chiu, and R. J. N. Phillips, "Regge-Pole Model for πp, pp, and $\bar{p}p$ Scattering," *Phys. Rev.* **165**, 1615 (1968).

B.2 EXPERIMENTAL REFERENCES

Experimental Data Used in Figures

Chapter 1

1.2–1.6 A. H. Rosenfeld *et al.*, "Data on Particles and Resonant States," *Rev. Mod. Phys.* **40**, 77 (1968).

Chapter 2

2.5 S. W. Barnes *et al.*, *Phys. Rev.* **117**, 238 (1960). For a more complete listing of πN scattering data see N. M. Focacci and G. Giacomelli, "Pion–Proton Elastic Scattering," CERN (European Organization for Nuclear Research) report NP 66-18 (1966); *Supplement of Progress of Theoretical Physics* **41** and **42** (1967), Chapter 1.

2.6   See N. M. Focacci and G. Giacomelli, CERN report NP 66-18 (1966).

2.7 $(\pi^{\pm}p)$ W. F. Baker *et al.*, *Phys. Letters* **25B**, 361 (1967).

        $(K^{\pm}p)$ J. Banaigs *et al.*, *Phys. Letters* **24B**, 317 (1967); D. Cline, C.
        Moore, and D. Reeder, *Phys. Rev. Letters* **19**, 675 (1967).

2.8 $(\pi^+p \to \Sigma^+K^+)$ R. Kofler, D. Hartung, and D. D. Reeder, *Phys. Rev.*
        163, 1479 (1967).

        $(\pi^-p \to \Sigma^-K^+)$ O. I. Dahl *et al.*, *Phys. Rev.* **163**, 1430 (1967).

        $(K^-p \to \bar{K}^0n$ and $K^-p \to K^+ \, \Xi^-)$ J. Badier *et al.*, Saclay Report (1966).

2.9   G. W. London *et al.*, *Phys. Rev.* **143**, 1034 (1966).

2.10   C. Baltay *et al.*, *Phys. Rev.* **140**, B1027 (1965).

2.12   For references to experimental data see N. M. Focacci and G. Giacomelli,
        "Pion–Proton Scattering," CERN report NP 66-18 (1966); Y. Sumi,
        Supplement of Progress of Theoretical Physics (Japan) **41** and **42**, 8
        (1967).

2.13   For references to experimental data see Y. Sumi, *Supplement of Progress of Theoretical Physics* (Japan) **41** and **42**, 13 (1967); see also R.
        Cool *et al.*, *Phys. Rev. Letters* **17**, 102 (1966) and J. D. Davies *et al.*,
        Phys. Rev. Letters **18**, 62 (1967).

2.14   K. J. Foley *et al.*, *Phys. Rev. Letters* **19**, 193, 330, 857 (1967); W.
        Galbraith *et al.*, *Phys. Rev.* **138**, B913 (1965); G. Belletini *et al.*, *Phys.
        Letters* **19**, 341 (1965).

2.16 $(pp \to pp)$ A. R. Clyde, UCRL Rept. 16275 (1966) (unpublished).

        $(\bar{p}p \to \bar{p}p)$ O. Czyzewski *et al.*, *Phys. Letters* **15**, 188 (1965); B. Escoubes
        et al., ibid **5**, 132 (1963); B. Barish *et al.*, *Phys. Rev. Letters* **17**, 720
        (1966).

        $(\bar{p}p \to \bar{n}n)$ O. Czyzewski *et al.*, *Phys. Letters* **20**, 554 (1966).

        $(np \to pn)$ H. Palevsky *et al.*, *Phys. Rev. Letters* **9**, 509 (1962).

        $(\pi^{\pm}p \to \pi^{\pm}p)$ C. T. Coffin *et al.*, *Phys. Rev. Letters* **15**, 838 (1965),
        17, 458 (1966).

        $(\pi^-p \to \pi^0n)$ P. Sonderegger *et al.*, *Phys. Letters* **20**, 75 (1966); M. A.
        Wahlig *et al.*, *Phys. Rev. Letters* **13**, 103 (1964).

        $(K^-p \to K^-p)$ J. Gordon *et al.*, *Phys. Letters* **21**, 117 (1966); J. Mott
        et al., *Phys. Letters* **23**, 171 (1966).

        $(K^+p \to K^+p)$ W. De Baere *et al.*, *Nuovo Cimento* **35**, 885 (1966).

        $(K^-p \to \bar{K}^0n)$ A. Brody and L. Lyons, *Nuovo Cimento* **45**, 1027
        (1966); P. Asbury *et al.*, *Phys. Letters* **23**, 396 (1966).

2.17 $(\pi^-p \to \pi^0n)$ M. Wahlig *et al.*, *Phys. Rev. Letters* **13**, 103 (1964); P.
        Sonderegger *et al.*, *Phys. Letters* **20**, 75 (1966).

        $(\pi^-p \to \eta n)$ O. Guisan *et al.*, *Phys. Letters* **18**, 200 (1965); M. Wahlig,
        Phys. Rev. Letters **17**, 222 (1966).

        $(K^-p \to \bar{K}^0n)$ P. Asbury *et al.*, *Phys. Letters* **23**, 396 (1966).

$(K^+n \to K^0p)$ I. Butterworth *et al., Phys. Rev. Letters* **15**, 734 (1965); D. Cline, D. Reeder, and J. Penn, Wisconsin Report (1968).

2.18   M. Kreisler *et al., Phys. Rev. Letters* **16**, 1217 (1966); J. Cox *et al., Phys. Rev. Letters* **21**, 641 (1968); A. R. Clyde, UCRL Rep. 16275 (1966) (unpublished).

2.19   J. L. Friedes *et al., Phys. Rev. Letters* **15**, 38 (1965); see R. R. Wilson, *Ann. Phys.* (New York) **32**, 201 (1965) for a discussion and experimental references.

2.20   M. Kreisler *et al., Phys. Rev. Letters* **16**, 1217 (1966); J. Cox *et al., Phys. Rev. Letters* **21**, 641 (1968).

2.21   (*np*)   M. Kreisler *et al., Phys. Rev. Letters* **16**, 1217 (1966).
($\bar{p}p$)   W. Katz, B. Forma, and T. Ferbel, *Phys. Rev. Letters* **19**, 265 (1967).

2.22   C. M. Ankenbrandt *et al.*, UCRL Rept. 17763, *Phys. Rev.*, to be published.

2.23   From data compilation and fit by D. R. O. Morrison, *Phys. Letters* **22**, 528 (1966).

2.24   C. M. Ankenbrandt *et al., Nuovo Cimento* **35**, 1052 (1965); UCRL 17763, *Phys. Rev.* (to be published); E. W. Anderson *et al., Phys. Rev. Letters* **16**, 855 (1966); I. M. Blair *et al., Phys. Letters* **17**, 789 (1966). See also G. Cocconi *et al., Phys. Rev. Letters* **7**, 450 (1961).

2.25   O. I. Dahl *et al., Phys. Rev.* **163**, 1430 (1967).

Chapter 4
4.1   A. V. Stirling *et al., Phys. Rev. Letters* **14**, 763 (1965); O. Guisan (private communication).

4.2   O. Guisan *et al., Phys. Letters* **18**, 200 (1965); O. Guisan (private communication).

4.3   K. J. Foley *et al., Phys. Rev. Letters* **19**, 193 (1967); W. Galbraith *et al.*, in *Proceedings of the Athens Conference on Resonant Particles, Ohio University, Athens, Ohio,* B. A. Munir, ed. (F. V. Research Institute, Athens, Ohio, 1965).

4.4   For a list of experimental references see V. Barger and D. Cline, *Phys. Rev.* **156**, 1522 (1967); the 5.5 BeV/c $K^+n \to K^0p$ data are from D. Cline, D. Reeder, and J. Penn, University of Wisconsin Report (1968).

4.5   For a list of experimental references see V. Barger and M. Olsson, *Phys. Rev. Letters* **18**, 294 (1967).

4.7, 4.8   R. Kofler, R. Hartung, and D. Reeder, *Phys. Rev.* **163**, 1479 (1967).

4.9 $(K^-p \to \Sigma\pi)$ J. Loos, U. Kruse, and E. Goldwasser, *Phys. Rev.* (to be published).
$(\pi^+p \to \Sigma^+K^+)$ A. Cooper *et al., Phys. Rev. Letters* **26**, 472 (1968).

$(\pi^-p \to \Lambda K$ and $\Sigma^\circ K)$ O. I. Dahl *et al., Phys. Rev.* **163**, 1430 (1967).

$(K^-p \to \Lambda\pi)$ D. Hodge, thesis, University of Wisconsin (1968) (unpublished).

4.10 $(\pi^+p \to \pi^0\Delta^{++})$ Aachen–Berlin–CERN collaboration reported in CERN report 68-7, p. 105.

$(K^+p \to K^0\Delta^{++})$ Y. Goldschmidt Clermont *et al., Nuovo Cimento* **36**, 539 (1966).

Chapter 5

5.1   W. Galbraith *et al., Phys. Rev.* **138**, B913 (1956); G. Belletini *et al., Phys. Letters* **19**, 341 (1965).

5.2   K. J. Foley *et al., Phys. Rev. Letters* **19**, 193, 330, 857 (1967).

5.3   C. T. Coffin *et al., Phys. Rev. Letters* **15**, 838; **17**, 458 (1966); K. J. Foley *et al., Phys. Rev. Letters* **11**, 425 (1967); J. Orear *et al., Phys. Rev.* **152**, 1162 (1966).

5.4   (*pp* data)   K. J. Foley *et al., Phys. Rev. Letters* **10**, 376 (1963); **11**, 425, 503 (1963); **15**, 45 (1965); A. R. Clyde, UCRL 16275 (1966) (unpublished).
      ($\bar{p}p$ data)   B. Barish *et al., Phys. Rev. Letters* **17**, 720 (1966); O. Czyzewski *et al., Phys. Letters* **15**, 188 (1965); B. Escoubes *et al., Phys. Letters* **15**, 45 (1965); W. Katz *et al., Phys. Rev. Letters* **14**, 265 (1967).

5.6   (3.5 BeV/c data)   C. T. Coffin *et al., Phys. Rev. Letters* **15**, 838; **17**, 458 (1966).
      (5.9 BeV/c data)   A. Ashmore *et al., Phys. Rev. Letters* **21**, 387 (1968).

5.7   (*pp* data)   A. R. Clyde, UCRL 16275 (1966) (unpublished).
      ($\bar{p}p$ data)   A. Ashmore *et al., Phys. Rev. Letters* **21**, 387 (1968).

5.8, 5.9 M. Borghini *et al., Phys. Letters* **21**, 114 (1966); **24B**, 77 (1967).

5.10   For references to the experimental data, see A. Contogouris, J. Than Thank Van, and H. J. Lubatti, *Phys. Rev. Letters* **19**, 1352 (1967).

5.11   K. J. Foley *et al., Phys. Rev. Letters* **11**, 425 (1963); L. Hand *et al., Rev. Mod. Phys.* **35**, 335 (1963).

Chapter 6

6.2–6.4 C. Lovelace, "Nucleon Resonances and Low Energy Scattering," *Proceedings of the Heidelberg Conference on Elementary Particles,* H. Filthuth, ed. (John Wiley and Sons, New York, 1968); A. H. Rosenfeld *et al., Rev. Mod. Phys.* **40**, 77 (1968).

6.5   M. N. Foccaci *et al., Phys. Rev. Letters* **17**, 890 (1966).

6.6, 6.7 A. H. Rosenfeld *et al., Rev. Mod. Phys.* **40**, 77 (1968).

Chapter 7

7.1, 7.2 J. Orear *et al., Phys. Rev. Letters* **21**, 389 (1968).

7.3 $(\pi^{\pm}p)$ W. F. Baker *et al., Phys. Letters* **25B**, 361 (1967).
$(K^{+}p)$ J. Banaigs *et al., Phys. Letters* **24B**, 317 (1967); D. Cline *et al., Phys. Rev. Letters* **19**, 675 (1967).

7.4 O. I. Dahl *et al., Phys. Rev.* **163**, 1430 (1967); M. Pepin *et al., Phys. Letters* **26B**, 35 (1967).

7.5 "Aachen, Berlin, Birmingham, Bonn, Hamburg, London, Munchen Collaboration," *Phys. Rev.* **138**, B897 (1965).

7.6 M. Derrick, "Backward Peaks," CERN report 68-7, Vol. I (1968).

7.8, 7.9 J. Orear *et al., Phys. Rev. Letters* **21**, 389 (1968).

7.14 V. Barger, *Rev. Mod. Phys.* **40**, 129 (1968); M. Derrick, "Backward Peaks," CERN report 68-7, Vol. I (1968).

Chapter 8

8.1, 8.2 T. Devlin *et al., Phys. Rev. Letters* **14**, 1031 (1965); A. Diddens *et al., ibid.* **10**, 262 (1963); A. Stirling *et al.,* data quoted by B. Amblard *et al., Phys. Letters* **10**, 138 (1964); A. Citron *et al., Phys. Rev.* **144**, 1101 (1966).

8.3 L. Guerriero, *Proc. Roy. Soc.* (London) **A289**, 471 (1966); C. Chiu, UCRL Rept. 16209 (1966) (unpublished); P. Brogeaud *et al., Phys. Letters* **10**, 134 (1964). P. Falk-Vairant *et al.,* the data are quoted in G. Hohler *et al., ibid.* **21**, 223 (1966); M. A. Azimov *et al., JETP Pis'ma Vedaktsiyu* **3**, 336 (1966), English translation: *JEPT Letters* **3**, 216 (1966).

8.4 O. Guisan *et al.* (private communication).

8.5 G. Buschhorn *et al., Phys. Rev. Letters* **20**, 230 (1968).

8.6, 8.7 A. S. Carroll *et al., Phys. Rev. Letters* **20**, 607 (1968); W. F. Baker *et al., Phys. Letters* **23**, 605 (1966); T. Dobrowolski *et al., Phys. Letters* **24B**, 203 (1967); W. F. Baker *et al., Phys. Letters* **25B**, 361 (1967); C. T. Coffin *et al., Phys. Rev.* **159**, 1169 (1967); S. W. Kormanyos *et al., Phys. Rev. Letters* **16**, 709 (1966); H. Brody *et al., Phys. Rev. Letters* **16**, 828 (1966).

8.8 J. Banaigs *et al.,* Paper submitted to the XIVth International Conference on High Energy Physics, Vienna, 1968.

8.10, 8.11 A. S. Carroll *et al., Phys. Rev. Letters* **20**, 607 (1968); S. Kormanyos *et al., Phys. Rev. Letters* **16**, 709 (1966).

8.12 J. Berryhill and D. Cline, *Phys. Rev. Letters* **21**, 766 (1968).

8.13 U. Amaldi, Jr., *Nuovo Cimento* **34**, 825 (1964); T. Elioff *et al., Phys. Rev.* **128**, 869 (1962); R. F. George *et al., Phys. Rev. Letters* **15**, 214 (1965).

8.14   W. Galbraith *et al.*, *Phys. Rev.* **138**, B913 (1965); D. V. Bugg *et al.*,
          Phys. Rev. **146**, 980 (1966); R. J. Abrams *et al.*, *Phys. Rev. Letters* **19**,
          259 (1967); R. L. Cool *et al.*, *Phys. Rev. Letters* **16**, 1228 (1966); R.
          J. Abrams *et al.*, *Phys. Rev. Letters* **19**, 678 (1967); R. J. Abrams *et al.*,
          Phys. Rev. Letters **18**, 1209 (1967).

Chapter 9
9.1   A. M. Boyarski *et al.*, *Phys. Rev. Letters* **20**, 300 (1968).
9.2   ($\bar{p}p \to \bar{n}n$)   P. Astbury *et al.*, *Phys. Letters* **22**, 537 (1966); **23**, 160
          (1966).
          ($np \to pn$)   H. Palevsky *et al.*, *Phys. Rev. Letters* **9**, 509 (1962); G.
          Manning *et al.*, *Nuovo Cimento* **41**, 167 (1966).

Index